CALLBACK

Foreword by Donald D. Engen, Vice Admiral, USN (RET.)

Illustrations by Bob Stevens

CALLBACK

NASA's Aviation Safety Reporting System

Rex Hardy

Smithsonian Institution Press
Washington, D.C.

90 91 92   4   3   2   1

Library of Congress Cataloging-in-Publication Data

Hardy, Rex.
    Callback / Rex Hardy.
        p.   cm.
    ISBN 0-87474-463-6
    1. Aviation safety reporting system—History.   I. Title.
TL553.5.H384 1990
629.132'52—dc20   89-600326

∞ The paper used in this publication meets the minimum requirements of the
American National Standard for Permanence of Paper for Printed Library
Materials
Z39.48—1984.

For permission to reproduce individual illustrations appearing in this book,
please correspond directly with the author. The Smithsonian Institution Press
does not retain reproduction rights for these illustrations individually or
maintain a file of addresses for photo or illustration sources.

Contents

Foreword

Rex Hardy has chronicled the evolution and summarized the important lessons of one of the most productive and successful aviation safety programs ever achieved. This is the story of the Aviation Safety Reporting System (ASRS), the program that is run by NASA for, and funded solely by, the FAA. The story is told by one who helped develop the delicately balanced reporting system that walks the edge between accident prevention and enforcement. The book is more than a chronicle; it is laced with aviation safety lessons important to all who fly. In this respect, this *CALLBACK* book is an interesting textbook that the serious pilot will not want to put down.

I first became acquainted with Rex Hardy when, as a member of the NTSB, I visited the ASRS offices near NASA's Ames Research Center in California. I was struck by the dedication and knowledge of a small crew of Battelle Memorial Institute analysts and pilots banded together and under contract to NASA to do something important for aviation safety. Subsequently, as administrator of the FAA, I continued to supply strong financial support for the good that this small dedicated group of professionals was doing. I have never been let down in my expectations. Today, ASRS continues to provide valuable and timely accident prevention.

Our aviation heritage is built on the experience of flying, both good experience and bad. Pilots can learn as much from one form as the other, but one finds the most attentive lessons in the bad experiences. In fact, the FAR have been crafted from such experiences, as well. Each regulation has been written with purpose and is based on something that happened or almost happened, mostly bad. This does not say that aviation is haphazard. It does say a great deal for aviation pioneers, who led the way, and for those through whose wisdom the ASRS was developed.

In this book, Rex Hardy provides the historical perspective of the development of the ASRS, including the building of the team that created this effective accident prevention tool. He provides the reader with interesting aviation stories of what almost happened. Each one is a valuable lesson in itself. From these, the serious pilot and the interested passenger will be able to catalogue in his or her mind valuable lessons. In this way, judgment is built. Some say this includes that sixth sense of recognition of the first signs of an accident about to happen. Such recognition is particularly important to that person who is always the first to arrive at the scene of the aviation accident—the pilot.

Vice Admiral Donald D. Engen, USN (RET.)
President, Aircraft Owners and Pilots Association,
Air Safety Foundation

Preflight

This book is about flying and flying people, but it is not, in general, filled with excitement and tales of high adventure. It is not a work of fiction, nor a history, nor an autobiography (although traces of each of these may appear on occasion). It is not about the heroic achievements of intrepid and famous aviators; instead it chronicles the problems encountered by many all-too-human anonymous airmen. In the doing, it may provide some insight into causes of common—and some uncommon—hazards to safe flight. Here you will find true accounts of errors of omission and commission in the conduct of flying operations, as reported to NASA's ASRS by the errant perpetrators (and, sometimes, victims).

Thrilling stories of drama and courage, of flying accomplishment and skill in war and in peace, may be found in the works of the great aviation writers: Charles Lindbergh, Antoine de Saint-Exupéry, Ernest Gann, Neville Shute, Elliot White Springs, and others. In this book, adventures and misadventures of professional pilots, of amateurs of greater or lesser skill and experience, and of those on the ground who play their parts with radarscope and microphone instead of stick and rudder, are described in the participants' own words.

The book also recounts the background, workings, and reasons for the establishment of ASRS, an underpublicized organization that collects and studies these accounts, distilling and circulating useful wisdom from them. It also describes the unique group of dedicated people who make the system tick.

As you read the narratives, please remember that each has been submitted voluntarily and that, although literary quality may vary, each has been written for a constructive reason. Sometimes more than one purpose may be discerned; a chapter in the book discusses reporting motives and their frequent interrelationship. The stories of safety-related incidents, reprinted from *CALLBACK,* are accompanied by my own observations and opinions, based on more than fifty years of varied flying experience and wide acquaintance with the wonderful world of aviation and its inhabitants.

The book is really about flying safety. There have been a lot of publications wailing about the unsafe skies, and a good many scholarly works covering various aspects of the subject in less than sparkling prose. Here, as in *CALLBACK* itself, I have tried to provide worthwhile material in readable style. Aviation today *is* safe; it can be kept safe by constant awareness. I hope *CALLBACK* has, in a small way, fostered that awareness in its readers.

CALLBACK, as you will learn in the chapters ahead, is a monthly bulletin published by ASRS. It was originated by me, and edited for 100 issues, as one of my duties as an ASRS staff member. Since I was given a relatively free hand in this enterprise, it inevitably reflected elements of my personality and philosophy. Inevitably, too, because its intended audience is composed of members of the aviation community and its contents rely extensively on narratives contributed by pilots and air traffic controllers, *CALLBACK* is written in the special vernacular of aviation, which includes a great many acronyms and much jargon and flying slang. To translate all this into everyday language would seem patronizing and unnecessary to most readers; I hope those nonflying people who may encounter this book will be tolerant and will be able to find their way among all the IFRS, VMCS, GPWSS and Mode Cs, which, after all, are usually clear from the context.

The basic material for the bulletin comes largely from the reports submitted to ASRS, and I gratefully acknowledge these contributions from the thousands of reporters whose accounts I have read; without them, obviously, there would have been no *CALLBACK* bulletin and no *CALLBACK* book. Many others have earned my gratitude for their contributions to this book. The notion of a book based on *CALLBACK,* suggested by readers from time to time, was first seriously promoted by Robert Beatty Parke, then publisher of *Flying* magazine, who had become familiar with *CALLBACK* while writing a *Flying* article about ASRS. His encouragement was invaluable to me, and continued long after his retirement from the magazine. Bob Parke's patient prodding and wise advice kept me from putting aside the book project, and his efforts to generate interest and to find a suitable publisher made the venture possible. Thanks are due to Felix Lowe, director of the Smithsonian Institution Press, for his understanding and willingness to tackle this unorthodox undertaking! Vicky Macintyre, Ruth Spiegel, and Craig Reynolds, my editors at the Press, have shown those same attributes; their wise counsel, cooperation, and good nature have smoothed many rough spots and brought needed clarity to the final result.

My superiors at ASRS, Project Manager Edgar Cheaney and, later, his successor Loren Rosenthal, and NASA ASRS Program Chief William Reynard, gave their enthusiastic support and the necessary approvals to proceed. Charles Billings, NASA research scientist, who established the ASRS project and saw it through its formative years, and his colleague, John Lauber, now a member of the NTSB, but then a NASA aviation human factors expert, gave welcome encouragement to the *CALLBACK* idea in its early days.

Heartfelt thanks go, too, to the other members of the ASRS staff for their cooperation, most notably to Jean Davies, project business manager and wise counsel to the group. Mrs. Davies helped cheerfully in many ways and offered constant encouragement. Her death while the book was in preparation has been a sad blow to us all and a great personal loss. Project secretary Donna Fife has been a stalwart backup. Nancy Mandella's energy and good sense have been invaluable in organizing and keeping up to date the *CALLBACK* mailing list and attending to correspondence, requests, and subscription matters.

It would be presumptuous to refer to Rowena Morrison, my very able successor in the *CALLBACK* editorial chair, as a protégé. I do however, acknowledge a special debt of gratitude to Dr. Morrison, who has kindly read the complete manuscript, offering welcome approbation and useful suggestions. It is gratifying, too, that *CALLBACK*, under the Morrison guidance, has carried on the intent and spirit of my own efforts, while showing improvement in many ways, and that I have been permitted to maintain a connection to this labor of love by contributing a monthly column.

I thank my respected colleagues, the Old Eagles, who have a chapter to themselves, for their loyalty and companionship from the beginning. Cherished friends and congenial office mates Captains (ret.) William Monan (Pan Am) and Harry Orlady (United) have cheered me on all the way and have contributed material to the book as well as strong moral support. Thanks, too, to ALPA for permission to quote from their monthly publication. Jerome Lederer, dean of aviation-safety professionals, has been a much appreciated *CALLBACK* adherent and occasional contributor. John Enders, president of the Flight Safety Foundation, and his organization have also provided valued support.

I feel especially fortunate in my two well-known collaborators: Bob Stevens's perceptive and witty pictures capture the flavor of the book and add immensely to it; and I owe much to my fellow naval aviator, Donald Engen, for his gracious foreword. Admiral Engen has been a powerful booster of ASRS and of *CALLBACK* since his tenure as an NTSB member, later as FAA administrator, and now as president of the AOPA Air Safety Foundation. An author with such a distinguished advocate is lucky indeed.

Members of NASA's ASRS Advisory Committee and its long-time chairman John Winant, and the NBAA, which he headed until his retirement, have been active backers, as have AOPA, ALPA, Allied Pilots Association, and the Civil Air Patrol. Many other organizations and individuals, including the faithful readers of *CALLBACK,* have earned my thanks.

As has, of course, Jan Hardy, who has been in my corner all the way.

Monterey, California

Glossary

*The asterisk denotes reporters' comments as quoted in the bulletin.

Most readers of this book are assumed to be conversant with aviation vocabulary. For the benefit of those not familiar with this special language and as a refresher for those who may be a little rusty, here is a list of the special forms used in the book and their meanings.

AB. *Alert Bulletin* issued by ASRS.

ADVTECH. New generation advanced technology aircraft.

AGL. Altitude above ground.

ALPA. Air Line Pilots Association.

AOPA. Aircraft Owners and Pilots Association.

APU. Auxiliary power unit.

ARTS. Feature of ATC computer/radar.

ASRP. FAA's Aviation Safety Reporting Program.

ASRS. Aviation Safety Reporting System, operated by NASA under ASRP.

ATA. Airport traffic area.

ATC. Air Traffic Control.

ATIS. Airport Terminal Information System.

BCL. Battelle's Columbus Laboratories, the division of Battelle Memorial Institute that, under contract to NASA, performs the day-to-day work of running ASRS.

CAA. Civil Aeronautics Authority, forerunner of FAA. Also name of aviation's governing body in United Kingdom.

CAB. Civil Aeronautics Board.

CASRP. Confidential Aviation Safety Reporting Program. Canadian Counterpart of ASRS.

CENTER. Air route traffic control center (ARTCC). Unit of ATC controlling en route traffic.

CDU. Control Display Unit (in ADVTECH aircraft).

CFIT, CFTT. Controlled flight into terrain, controlled flight toward terrain.

CHIRP. Confidential Human Factors Incident Reporting. British counterpart of ASRS.

CPT, CPTP. Pre–World War II government-sponsored Civil Pilot Training Program.

CYA. Cover your anatomy, a euphemism.

DME. Aircraft distance measuring equipment.

DOD. Department of Defense.

EEC. Electronic engine control "in" or "for" ADVTECH aircraft.

ETA. Estimated time of arrival.

FAA. Federal Aviation Administration.

FAR. Federal Aviation Regulations.

F/E. Flight engineer. Usually second officer, or S/O.

FL. Flight level. Aircraft's altitude referenced to standard barometric pressure (29.92), with last two digits dropped; used above 18,000 feet (FL180) for traffic control; below FL180, height above sea level is referenced to local barometric setting and is expressed directly in hundreds or thousands of feet. *See* MSL.

FMC, FMS. Flight management computer, flight management system. Features of ADVTECH aircraft.

F/O. First officer, copilot.

FPM. Feet per minute, used to express climb or descent rate.

FSS. Flight service station.

GA. General aviation. All flying activity with the exception of air carrier and military.

GPWS. Ground proximity warning system.

G/S. Glide slope, component of an ILS.

GUMPS. Gas (quantity), undercarriage (down), mixture (fuel), propellor (pitch), stabilizer (setting). Mnemonic reminder of landing checklist items.

HSI. Horizontal situation indicator, aircraft instrument.

IFR. Instrument Flight Rules; apply when flight cannot be made in visual conditions.

ILS. Instrument landing system.

IMC. Instrument meterological conditions, requiring flight under IFR.

LFR. Low-frequency range, a radio navigation aid no longer in use.

LOC. Localizer, component of an ILS.

LTSS. Less than standard separation of aircraft. ATC term.

MODE C. An altitude-reporting feature of aircraft transponder.

MSL. Mean sea level. Reference used for altitude determination.

NACA. National Advisory Committee for Aeronautics, forerunner of NASA.

NASA. National Aeronautics and Space Administration.

NBAA. National Business Aircraft Association.

NMAC. Near midair collision.

NTSB. National Transportation Safety Board.

O.M. Outer marker, component of an ILS.

P.A. Aircraft public address system.

P.C. Potential conflict in air traffic.

PCA. Positive control area. An area or altitude band in which all air traffic must be under ATC jurisdiction; above FL180.

PIC. Pilot in command.

PMS. Performance management system, feature of ADVTECH aircraft.

QAP. Quality assurance program. Feature of ATC.

RVR. Runway visual range. Measure of runway visibility.

SID. Standard instrument departure.

S/O. Second officer, flight engineer.

SOP. Standard operating procedures.

SPIFR. Single pilot flight under IFR.

SQUAWK. Transponder code assigned by ATC for flight identification.

TCA. Terminal control area.

T.O. Takeoff.

TRACON. Terminal radar control, ATC facility incorporating approach and/or departure control functions.

UNICOM. Radio frequency used for non-ATC communication.

VASI. Visual approach slope indicator.

VFR. Visual flight rules.

VMC. Visual meteorological conditions.

VOR. Visual omnidirectional range, a NAVAID.

WX. Abbreviation for "weather."

ZULU. Greenwich mean time (used in ATC and weather communications).

1

A Rose by Any
Other Name....

CRASH!! At nine minutes past eleven o'clock on Sunday morning, December 1, 1974, TWA Flight 514, inbound to Washington's Dulles Airport through cloudy and turbulent skies, descended below the minimum safe altitude for the area and collided with a Virginia mountain top.

According to NASA's official history of the Aviation Safety Reporting System—from which I feel free to quote, since I was the author—

> The ensuing hue and cry probably would have subsided in time, as usual with such occurrences, had not a disturbing yet provocative circumstance emerged during the National Transportation Safety Board's (NTSB) investigation of the accident. Only six weeks before the TWA crash a United Airlines crew had very narrowly escaped the same fate when the same approach and the same location were used. The ambiguous nature of the charted approach procedure and the differences in its interpretation between pilots and controllers were then brought to the attention of the airline.

If this event had occurred a year earlier it is probable that it would have remained only a worrisome memory to the participants. In January of 1974, however, United had instituted a new internal reporting procedure termed its "Flight Safety Awareness Program," under which crew members were encouraged to report to the company any incident they felt involved a safety problem to the company. The United pilots in the Dulles incident followed this course of action; other United pilots were made aware of the trap, and the FAA was notified of the circumstances. Regrettably, there was no generally accepted avenue for spreading the word.

For many years, aviation authorities believed that the fear of legal liability and of regulatory or disciplinary action had prevented the dissemination of safety incident information. In 1966 Bobbie R. Allen, director of the Bureau of Safety of the U.S. CAB, speaking at a safety seminar in Madrid, referred to the vast body of such information as a "sleeping giant." Mr. Allen continued,

> In the event that the fear of exposure cannot be overcome by other means, it might be profitable if we explored a system of incident reporting which would assure a substantial flow of vital information to the computer for processing, and at the same time, would provide some method designed to effectively eliminate the personal aspect of the individual occurrences so that the information derived would be helpful to all and harmful to none.

Mr. Allen was articulating a long-recognized objective, but one that had frustrated all efforts at accomplishment. Frequent references to the need for information and dissemination had occurred for years and would recur. At another safety conference a participant mentioned a "cherished dream of air-safety professionals everywhere . . . that the world's airlines can achieve an effective incident-reporting and human-factors analytic system. If we can achieve such a system we will have taken a major step toward the precise identification of the root causes of our most perplexing problems."

Quoting again from the NASA history,

> TWA's flight to Dulles, with its culminating tragedy, was subjected to the full glare of media publicity. United's narrow avoidance received little public recognition. TWA 514 may be seen as the actual catalyst that precipitated the Aviation Safety Reporting System (ASRS); in fact the United incident, attracting scant notice, may have been more influential because it prompted vigorous expression by the National Transportation Safety Board (NTSB).

In its report on the TWA accident, the Board stated that it was "encouraged that such safety awareness programs [as United's] have been initiated. . . . In retrospect, the Board finds it most unfortunate that an incident of this nature was not, at the time of its occurrence, subject to uninhibited reporting . . . which might have resulted in broad and timely dissemination of the safety message issued by the carrier to its own flightcrews. . . . Subsequent to the accident, the Federal Aviation Administration (FAA) has . . . established an incident reporting system which is intended to identify unsafe operating conditions so that they can be corrected before an accident occurs.

The notion of incident reporting was not new; however, all attempts to institute a formal program of information collection and dissemination had been stymied in the past by a pervading apprehension. "Fear of legal consequences"—the term appears often in the literature of aviation safety—had remained an effective block to the various proposals and suggestions that, over the years, had been offered in the effort to provide circulation throughout the industry of unsafe incidents, practices, and situations.

And there had indeed been many such proposals and suggestions—both domestic and international—including a short-lived one by FAA advertised as "nonpunitive" and intended to gather data concerning near midair conflicts. Reaction to this program was apathy because the pilots lacked confidence in the promised immunity. In time all attempts at information gathering evaporated—until the status quo was rudely altered by the crash of TWA 514.

"Confidentiality" and "anonymity" were announced features of all the early information-exchange programs but, despite some local and temporary successes, all were defeated by widespread worry over liability, incrimination, disciplinary action, and publicity. By the time of the TWA accident, public concern had reached a level demanding government action. Prompted by the report of a special advisory group composed of retired airline pilots ("The Six Old Men"), and by various other recommendations, not to mention the NTSB comments, the FAA in May 1975 announced the inauguration of a voluntary, confidential, nonpunitive incident-reporting scheme—the Aviation Safety Reporting Program—"to encourage the reporting and identification of deficiencies and discrepancies in the system before they cause accidents or incidents."

Although anonymity and limited immunity were offered to reporters to the ASRP, it soon became obvious that the FAA's good intentions would not carry the day. With the same reasoning as in the past, the aviation community failed to report to any significant degree. Rightly or wrongly, the FAA, both maker of the law (the Federal Aviation Regulations) and its enforcer, was not generally viewed as a properly neutral referee.

Refusing to throw in the towel, however, the agency acknowledged past criticism and suggestions and turned to a neutral third party—NASA—to collect, process, and analyze the voluntarily submitted reports that it hoped would flow in from a supportive aviation community. By agreement between the two government organizations, NASA now would act in the capacity of an "honest broker"—a middleman between the FAA and the aviation community—as operator of the newly established Aviation Safety Reporting System, funded by the FAA under the umbrella of the three-month-old ASRP.

A number of considerations combined to make this a felicitous decision and one that promised, at last, to provide the long-awaited avenue for reporting and disseminating safety information arising from incidents. NASA and its staff members had inherited from its predecessor, the respected National Advisory Committee for Aeronautics, a reputation as aviation's good guys. The agency lacked any regulatory function and wielded no enforcement authority, and thus the prospective reporting community accepted it as an impartial operator of the new system.

Recognizing that accident investigation had been effective in determining what had happened but had not seriously addressed the equally important question of why, and had failed to take into account the fact that a large proportion of aircraft accidents were the result of human error, a group of NASA scientists had long been engaged in the study of human factors involved in aircraft mishaps.

The NASA/FAA Memorandum of Agreement, signed in August 1975, described the rationale of the agreement from the standpoint of the two agencies:

> The FAA has determined that the effectiveness of the ASRP would be greatly enhanced if the receipt, processing, and analysis of the raw information received were . . . accomplished by NASA rather than the FAA. This would further ensure the anonymity of the reporter and consequently increase the flow of information so necessary for the effective evaluation of the safety and efficiency of the aviation system. NASA has determined that undertaking this task would be consistent with its aviation research and development responsibilities and would significantly increase its ability to fulfill those responsibilities.

The memorandum described the proposed ASRS functions as "(1) receipt, deidentification and initial processing; (2) analysis and interpretation; (3) dissemination of reports and other data." In addition to such procedures, it included two provisions of great subsequent significance. One was a waiver of disciplinary action to be offered to reporters (the so-called immunity feature discussed in a later chapter of this book)—in fact, articulation of the nonincrimination principle that had for so long been the bone of contention in incident-reporting attempts.

Second, NASA agreed to form an ASRS subcommittee to "advise NASA on the design and conduct of the ASRS and to provide an additional means of communication with the aviation community." Committee membership was to be appointed from "elements involved in the operational aspects of the national aviation system including FAA and DOD." There were also to be representatives from airline, corporate, and general aviation pilot groups, air traffic control, and airline, manufacturer, and airport operator associations.

The NASA group charged with formulating plans for the new organization made an early decision to use outside contracted aid—another decision that was to have important consequences. Questioned by a prospective bidder ("Why is NASA going out of house to do this work?"), NASA replied, "The best interests of the Government would be served by contracting out for the services." A major factor in this determination was the obvious requirement for operationally experienced staff. NASA was given six months to prepare a proposal request, evaluate the bids, and award a contract for the operation of the system.

In April 1976 the contract was awarded to Battelle Memorial Institute's Columbus Laboratories, a large prestigious research institution (BCL has twice been awarded a renewed contract, after new competitions). Less than one month later the firm had established an operations office in Mountain View, California— just outside the Moffett Field Naval Air Station headquarters of NASA's Ames Research Center—and had assembled a small administrative and clerical staff to commence, in cooperation with the NASA group, the development of the system.

Press announcements of the new ASRS initially received enthusiastic response from all segments of the aviation community. Encouraged by their associations, airline pilots began to submit reports on the newly developed reporting form, as did general aviation pilots (although GA participation accounted for only a small proportion of the intake and has never approached that of the airline group). The Air Force and Navy agreed to forward their own pilots' safety reports when interface with civil aircraft was involved (principally, of course, with respect to near-midair collisions), and air traffic controllers were urged by their union likewise to report incidents in which there appeared to be a safety issue.

Within a short time, reports were flowing in to the NASA Moffett Field post office box at a rate of 100 to 150 each week—a rate that was to remain constant, with an occasional spike stimulated by some highly publicized flying occurrence—until the controllers' strike in the summer of 1981, when it decreased drastically. Within a few years the report rate began to rise again until, in the 1987–88 period, a rate of 1,600 reports per month became the norm.

Direction of the new ASRS fell to Charles Billings, an experienced flight surgeon who, with aviation psychologist John Lauber, had conducted much of NASA's earlier human-factors research and was one of the architects of the final system (Dr. Lauber was subsequently appointed to membership on the NTSB and has continued, with his fellow members, to be a strong ASRS supporter). "Charlie" Billings, until he was assigned higher NASA responsibilities, was assisted by aviation lawyer William Reynard, who then became ASRS chief; the Battelle contingent was led, after a brief initial setting-up period, by research scientist/engineer Edgar Cheaney, transferred from BCL's Ohio headquarters after taking a leading part in the preparation of the original project proposal. The fact that Billings, Lauber, Reynard, and Cheaney were all active pilots added materially to their understanding of the program's purpose, potential, and problems. Empathy and shared enthusiasm combined to build a close working relationship between government agency and contractor personnel, and ensured exemplary morale in the critical early days of the project.

From the beginning, earnest attention was given to the security issues arising from the confidentiality guarantee to prospective reporters. The new ASRS offices were equipped with secure locks and telephone systems, an entry bell, and sophisticated alarm systems for entrances and file safes. Each staff member's private office had a locking door that had to be closed during telephone callbacks to reporters and whenever visitors were on board. All visitors had to be registered, badged, and escorted while on the premises. Each morning incoming reports were conveyed in a locked pouch by a bonded courier who brought them from the post office to ASRS. After time- and date-stamping, they had to be stored in locked files when not in the custody of a staff member. An advisory group subcommittee was responsible for surveillance over security compliance and made periodic unannounced inspections to ensure that staff members observed the required precautions.

This cloak-and-dagger procedure still exists for the protection of those reporters who, inadvertently, may have violated some provision of the FAR, although the regulations themselves include a provision that FAA may not seek, and ASRS may not provide, any information that could identify an individual reporter or be used in an enforcement proceeding. FAA's ASRS Advisory Circular (AC 00-46C is the current edition) gives details of the immunity provisions of the program and assures users that all identities will be protected. It is the policy that not only must confidentiality be respected but also it must be seen to be inviolate.

With procedures and quarters established, an advance cadre on deck, and reports flowing in, it became imperative to acquire a processing staff. With NASA's approval, the decision was made to seek locally domiciled professional pilots and air traffic controllers rather than import Battelle research personnel and try to inculcate flight operations lore, and to train them in the systems and procedures required by the enterprise. Accordingly, an airline captain and an air traffic controller, both retired after long careers, were recruited to form the nucleus of the unique group that was to become the ASRS operating force (the "Old Eagles," who have the next chapter to themselves).

After brief training, these early arrivals proved adept at their jobs. Their extensive experience enabled them to bring keen insight to the analysis and diagnosis of the incoming incident reports and they soon mastered the task of preparing the reports for computer entry. (One of Battelle's qualifications for the contract award was an extensive and highly regarded computer capability at its Ohio headquarters.) Additional pilot and controller analysts soon joined the charter group, were trained, and tackled the backlog of reports that had accumulated, while other retirees with flying and academic credentials were brought in to conduct the research specified in the original plans and to make a start on the also-intended dissemination of information. I was among these; on the strength of forty years of widely diversified military and civil flying and a modest quantity of published writing, I became the output supervisor (and soon thereafter deputy to Project Manager Cheaney—although I retained the output function).

Output (discussed later in this book) was to include the *Alert Bulletin,* to be issued when a report called attention to a hazardous—or perceived by the reporter to be hazardous—situation or procedure; periodic reports of the program's progress; research papers on topical subjects, based on the received reports ("input"); and responses to "special requests" for information from media, FAA and NTSB, and other outside sources—although these were usually fielded by the manager directly.

All the reports required a final check to detect processing errors and to ensure complete anonymity before being passed to the data entry staff; this quality-control function, too, fell to me. I estimate that, over the years, I read more than 60,000 of these true confessions of error and accounts of other safety-related occurrences until, overwhelmed by the ever-growing influx, I devised a plan for the analysts to check each other's work. The final check duty not only was full of interest, but it provided the raw material for a projected new form of output assigned to me, which was to become the most widely known ASRS product—and which was to bring me immense satisfaction and pleasure throughout my final working years.

According to the NASA ASRS history:

> The Advisory Committee, meeting for a June [1978] evaluation, reviewed the results of a survey undertaken . . . at the behest of the Committee. This served to emphasize the points made so often in the past: A large proportion of the flying population lacked knowledge of the ASRS, and in particular of the immunity feature; in addition, suspicion of FAA's credibility was widespread. [A published doctoral thesis stated that, in the beginning, various groups made] announcements of the program. Since that time, the Air Line Pilots Association, the National Business Aircraft Association, and the Professional Air Traffic Controllers Organization have been the only industry groups which have done more than provide token encouragement for use of ASRS reports. . . .
>
> Several steps were taken to fill the awareness and credibility gaps that had been noted. A means of regular communication with potential users of the ASRS had been recommended repeatedly; the project's Output Supervisor was assigned the task of preparing a monthly bulletin, although it was far from clear to anyone just what form the bulletin was to take—or to whom it was to be distributed. It was hoped that this step would provide, as suggested by Committee member Captain James LeBel of Western

Airlines, "Continuous imaginative publicity on ASRS, . . . increase the timeliness and the readability of flight safety information to the aviation community."

In the words of present ASRS Chief Bill Reynard, "ASRS is aviation's best-kept secret." Few ideas had emerged to rectify this. Another far-from-clear item was what to call the bulletin. Although pleased with my assignment (as publisher, editor, writer, circulation manager, and entire staff of this venture, according to manager Ed Cheaney's briefing), I was not enthralled with the various titles suggested; I felt that a well-chosen name would be essential in gaining initial acceptance for our publication.

As a working pilot, I had been exposed for many years to a formidable barrage of well-intentioned literature dealing with safety (as Mark Twain remarked about the weather, everybody talks about it, but nobody does anything about it), but much of it consisted of well-intentioned but dull exhortations, scholarly dissertations, pedantic lectures, or detailed accident reports. During World War II, the Navy's Grampaw Pettibone, with his anecdotes, scoldings, and advice to pilots, seemed in retrospect to have been more successful in influencing its intended audience than had any more formal efforts. I determined that MY publication (I early assumed an unwarranted—but, in view of my solo responsibility, perhaps excusable—proprietary stance) would be short, readable, and would neither hide behind pretentious authoritarianism nor insult its constituency with a patronizing attitude.

For starters, ASRS *Monthly Report* just wouldn't do, nor would NASA's *AVIATION SAFETY REPORTING SYSTEM BULLETIN,* if we expected the troops in the field—the pilots and controllers—to pay any heed. To attract the attention of the desired audience, which I believed I understood and toward which I felt considerable empathy, something brief and catchy was required; unfortunately, nothing unhackneyed seemed to be suggested. Pondering the problem while toiling over a stack of processed reports awaiting final checking, and noting the occasional circled entry "CBC" on one of the coding forms attached to each report, I thought of the project's operating procedures manual and its provisions for communicating directly with ASRS reporters by telephone, when needed, to clarify a report. Eureka! *CALLBACK* was born. Issue No. 1, in July 1979, explains in its lead article,

CALLBACK? That's a code term used at ASRS when a contact is initiated with someone who has sent in a report. The idea is to establish a dialogue in the interest of aviation safety. This *CALLBACK* will come to you each month with the same objective. If you'd like to be on *CALLBACK*'s mailing list, just send us a card. Safety is a serious subject, but we hope you will find this bulletin interesting, instructive, and even—sometimes—entertaining. We intend to bring you a summary of report processing activity and safety suggestions received, news of trends we have noted, briefs of unusual occurrences, suggested Alert Bulletins. We hope you will keep the dialogue going by letting us know if you have questions about us or about what ASRS is doing in the field of aviation safety; we especially hope you will continue to submit reports of safety-related incidents.

Under the heading, "Who, What, Where, When, Why, How?" we (I became the editorial "we" and continued the convention until my valedictory in issue No. 100) described ourselves as

professional pilots retired after careers on the airlines, the military services, in flight testing, and in corporate aviation. We have flown far more than 100,000 hours, in most kinds of aircraft, under all sorts of conditions. We're air traffic controllers with combined experience exceeding 100 years in the busiest towers and centers. We're also flight surgeons and aviation lawyers and research experts and data processing people and administrators. And most of us have long backgrounds in private flying. We can lend an understanding ear to your problems and it is our business to ensure that your experiences are added to the growing body of knowledge that is making flying safer for everyone.

After a brief discussion of the program processing details, I concluded,

We study, analyze, and diagnose the reports you send from your cockpits, your radar rooms, your airports, and then code them for entry into our database. Sometimes we *CALLBACK* to request more information. When we do that, pilots talk to pilots, controllers to controllers; we speak your language.

At the bottom of the front page was an identifying note reading, "An Informal Monthly Bulletin from the Office of the NASA Aviation Safety Reporting System," with our Moffett Field post office box number. At the top, the name *CALLBACK* appeared, in large squared-off letters in style familiar to generations of airmen from its use in airplane wing and tail license symbols. NASA artists provided a project logo based on a foreshortened airport runway with the letters ASRS in place of the usual directional numbers. The new publication was to be printed—naturally—on blue paper.

In that first issue, in addition to the explanatory information, I included a discussion of FAA's newly clarified ASRS immunity provisions, a few excerpts from reporters' comments about the project, a short list of recent *Alert Bulletins* and a couple of humorous flying anecdotes. In one corner appeared the "Box Score" of reports received to date (17,649) and for the previous month (430), divided into those from controllers, from pilots, and from others. "Others" comprised dispatchers, mechanics, flight attendants, airport managers or attendants, and, not infrequently, passengers or simply concerned observers. The box score continued as a regular monthly feature until the controllers' strike in July 1981 caused a major drop in that segment, when it became quarterly. Ultimately, because of little apparent interest, it was dropped altogether and replaced by an annual summary of ASRS activity. By comparison, if the box score had appeared in *CALLBACK* No. 100 (October 1987), my last as editor, it would have shown a total of 79,826 reports received, with 1,535 in the current month.

After typing the copy for the first *CALLBACK*, I assembled the various articles into two dummy pages with scissors and transparent tape, reducing it on the office copier to fit an ordinary $8\frac{1}{2}$-by-11-inch page, and submitted it to Cheaney for approval, which was granted quickly. Dr. Billings, as the overall ASRS commander-in-chief, likewise approved. In doing so, he ran some professional risk; other NASA officials, after reading early issues, expressed concern about the informal tone of what was unquestionably a government publication.

Happily—and unexpectedly—letters of approbation soon began to arrive from readers, and the members of the Advisory Committee expressed their own approval in strong terms. *CALLBACK* had apparently hit the spot, justifying Billings's confidence and, though some bureaucratic misgiving persisted, silenced the critics. Throughout my $8\frac{1}{2}$-year editorial tenure and its 100 *CALLBACK*s, the two NASA Chiefs, Ed Cheaney, and Loren Rosenthal, his successor as project manager, backed my efforts with consistent and greatly appreciated support (Cheaney's retirement preceded my own by a few months; it is the project's good fortune that his knowledge and experience will remain available as he becomes a part-time member of the research staff). I, too, will still be around. Rowena Morrison, my successor as editor, has asked me to continue my association by contributing a monthly *CALLBACK* column.

In an effort both to economize and to provide a reasonably

professional appearance for our publication, the amiable poly-
math Charlie Billings suggested that a NASA word processor
could produce a more professional appearance than my type-
written manuscript, and would be less expensive than having
the bulletin set in type by a printer. Accordingly, on a warm
June afternoon in 1979, the versatile Billings processed away on
a computer screen as I dictated line by line from my typescript. I
carried the very neat result, with our masthead design, to a
small print shop only two miles away, viewed a proof the next
day, and a few days later conveyed the three boxes containing the
three thousand copies of our original order back to the ASRS
office.

We had previously compiled a list of recipients for our jour-
nalistic debut from directories and suggestions, typing the
names on small index cards and then onto master sheets that
could be used in the office copy machine to produce labels. The
labels were in turn affixed to NASA envelopes and dropped in the
corner mailbox by the office receptionist. These cottage-industry
production methods prevailed until, as the circulation multi-
plied exponentially, it was decided that proper typesetting would
improve the publication's appearance and add little to the unit
cost. It was also found that the growing mailing list could be
entered in the Battelle computer, which could itself turn out
labels arranged by zip code.

By this time we realized that we could no longer justify the
first-class envelope mailing, so the page length of the bulletin
was increased to accommodate a mailing strip to which the labels could be attached and CALLBACK became bulk mail. Hence-
forth, with the aid of two temporary helpers three days per
month, the regularly updated computerized address labels were
applied and the zip-coded bundles were trundled off to the post
office by our regular courier. The three original boxes grew to a
number much too large for the trunk of my car and were delivered by the ever-helpful printer's truck.

As CALLBACK attracted attention, the original three thousand "subscribers" expanded from individual requests and from
several bulk consumers. The NBAA asked for a monthly consign-
ment of three thousand to be included in the organization's regular mailing to its members. The Association of Flight Instruc-
tors asked for a supply, as did the Civil Air Patrol, and a number
of airline operations bases and most FAA Air Traffic Control centers and towers joined in. In June 1983, at the request of the
Federal Air Surgeon, all 8,500 FAA-designated Aviation Medical

Examiners were added to the list. By the end of 1988, 50,000 *CALLBACK*s were being printed and distributed each month.

Like ASRS itself, the little bulletin has become an accepted component of the national aviation system and continues to do its part in enhancing safety awareness. I think the title, unusual and brief, has had considerable effect on this acceptance, contradicting the well-known opinion of the great Shakespeare, whose words have so often appeared in *CALLBACK:*

> What's in a name? That which we call a rose
> By any other name would smell as sweet.

2

Nest of Old Eagles

Six hours out of Capetown we crossed over the jagged cliffs of the Antarctic Ice Barrier and flew down the flat, wind-swept plateau of the Polar ice cap.

Up front in the 747SP cockpit, we had long since lapsed into silence. For a thousand miles we had been running over the ice and snow; stretched out beneath us was the vast expanse and grandeur of an ice continent. Mountain-like glaciers, majestic in their icy massiveness, sweeping slopes of snow split with deep, serrated-edged crevasses, steep hills that abruptly fell off into yawning canyons far below—we were flying over a thousand Grand Canyons sheathed in frozen white.

The scenic beauty was incredible. Yet, it was a disturbing scene; what lay below had the shape of earth but was not earth. Our eyes scanned restlessly, seeking to fasten upon a tree, any form of vegetation, any living thing that might represent the normal realities of the earth. Nothing moved. Nothing lived. From the emptiness, from the vast stillness of the frozen hills, came a sense of the desolate wastelands of Antarctica.

There was loneliness, too, in the cockpit . . . we had moved 2500 miles from the nearest land . . . All night long we had held to our southerly course . . .

When our 747's twin navigational displays read out 70 miles "to go," we called the Polar Station. The charts labelled it as the "Amundsen-Scott Station," a dual name tag remembrance of the first two explorers to reach the geographic south pole.

The Polar Station's VHF response was immediate. "Clipper 50? This is South Pole Station." The surprise, the questioning tone was obvious. An American accent.

We answered. "Roger, we'll be over your station in . . ." a downward glance at the inertial navigation readouts, ". . . in eight minutes. We are at Flight Level three five zero."

"Roger, Clipper 50. But . . . ," a long pause, "what are you *doing down here?*"

The cockpit exploded into roaring laughter, probably in exaggerated over-reaction to our silent, introspective hours over the ice. We told him what we were "doing down there." We were operating the third leg of PAN AM's 50th Anniversary flight, hence our "Clipper 50" aircraft call sign. We were on a round-the-world schedule but instead of the usual globe-circling routing via the Equator, we were flying via the North and South Poles. "Pole vaulting," some South African journalist had dubbed it.

A line pilot had suggested the pole-to-pole routing. . . . "Recently, I was browsing through the Guiness Book of Records and noticed that. . . ." Why not run such a flight and make commercial history?

Capt. W. P. Monan's description of the flight and the polar scenery, and the late-night, bad weather ILS approach and landing at Aukland after fourteen hours and five minutes of flying, continues:

A groundcrew man came up to us. "How was it?" he asked, curiously. We had seen an ice age, still intact. Our 747 had been a time machine; for a few hours we had seen life on Earth a million years ago.

I gave the groundman the time-honored airman's response. "Routine," I said, "just a routine flight." We walked away from the airplane. I was aware that none of us looked back as we entered the Terminal Building.

The next month I retired from the airline. I did not make the usual "last command" flight, with the birthday cake and congratulatory wires and the stewardesses' kisses on the cheek and the well-wishers waving at the gate.

Flying Clipper 50 over the South Pole seemed like a good way to end a flying career.

In Chapter 1 I noted that Battelle, the ASRS contractor, had decided (with NASA's approval) to engage a staff composed of recently retired professional pilots and air traffic controllers. Recruiting commenced, fortuitously, shortly after the dramatic final flight of Capt. William Paul Monan, Pan American World Airways (ret.), who was among the group of "Old Eagles" assembled in accordance with this policy. Bill Monan has served as a consultant on the ASRS research staff since the project's early days.

Battelle's advance contingent had acquired quarters in a building across the Bayshore Freeway from Moffett Field Naval Air Station (which is shared by NASA's Ames Research Center), in Mountain View, California. Bill Monan and I, also a retired pilot/new ASRS recruit, shared a cubbyhole across the hall from the project suite while the new offices were being remodeled and soon discovered many common interests.

It is tempting to speculate on the career directions (and directional changes) influenced by events completely unplanned and unexpected. Before entering Pensacola en route to gaining my naval aviator's wings, I had entertained an ambition to teach history. While a college student, Bill Monan was a participant, as were many of our ASRS Old Eagle colleagues, in the Civil Pilot Training Program (CPTP)—the government's scheme to increase the nation's supply of pilots prior to World War II. Presto! Academia's loss of a pair of budding scholars was, I like to think, aviation's gain.

Completing all the CPT courses, Monan joined expanding Pan American Airways and was soon flying large seaplanes throughout the Caribbean and Latin America. The flying boats and amphibians gave way to DC-3's and 4's, to transatlantic flights in Constellations, to the first generation jet transports, and finally to the jumbo Boeing 747. During his distinguished Pan Am service as one of the line's master ocean captains, Monan was domiciled in Miami, New York, Rio de Janeiro, Los Angeles, and San Francisco, retiring there as chief pilot for Pacific-Alaska operations.

The author of a number of NASA-published ASRS research studies of flight crew issues, his work has dealt extensively with communications problems and includes papers on call sign misunderstandings; clearance acknowledgements ("The Hearback Problem"); go-arounds; visual approaches; and pilot/ATC information transfer. One of the Monan studies, "Distraction in the Cockpit," led to FAA's "Sterile Cockpit" regulation. Several of the papers, condensed as "*CALLBACK*'s, Capsule Commentaries," appear in the appendix to this book.

Bill Monan's influence has had a profound impact on the ASRS project and on its staff members. His professional reputation and experience, combined with erudition, dignified demeanor, and civility, impress visitors and staff members alike. These qualities have been especially apparent at staff meetings when, after the digressions and irrelevancies common to such gatherings, Bill's temperately expressed good sense often has restored perspective and brought the discussion back on track.

Another Pan American 747 flight is described in the April 1978 issue of the *Air Line Pilot*. The story does credit both to the captain and to his wife, who wrote it.

The Last Trip

I'm taking a trip. I'm going more than halfway around the world, from San Francisco to Iran and back to the Hawaiian Islands, where the working part will end. My seat is in First Class, my husband is the pilot, and when we get home to California, he will retire. He didn't think I'd want to go.

"It's a long trip," he said, "a hard trip."

I know it's long and hard and he won't smile for days when he gets home. A First Class seat, a special gift from Pan Am, is hard to turn down, and so is a special trip. His last trip. Nine countries in 11 days; 13 takeoffs and 13 landings. . . .

The flight continues—over the Himalyas, to Delhi, Teheran, Bangkok . . . , then—

In the first glow of day, while other passengers are sleeping, the Captain leans over my seat, points out the window towards Mandalay and says in a low voice, "It's my last sunrise."

He leaves quickly while tears slide down my cheeks, and I wonder if maybe they are close to sliding down his too.

Hong Kong, Taiwan, Okinawa, Guam. The thirteenth takeoff, the thirteenth landing to go. Along the way, presents to the captain from officials at each airport, flowers for his wife. . . . Then, Honolulu:

This is where it will end for us. The trip will be over and here we will stay. A few days, a few weeks, with no one to tell us what to do or where to go. Just warm, hard sand and soft salt water. Maybe we will pretend for a little while that it hasn't happened . . .

But the trip was not quite over. It didn't end in Honolulu; the holiday had to await another time.

All schedules are upset. The Captain is informed that he must
continue on to Los Angeles the next morning. . . . I see how glad
he is that it isn't over yet. . . . Another delay, another departure,
and somehow this seems the right thing to do. . . . Tomorrow, the
14th takeoff and the final landing.

Jean Somers

Maybe the final landing as an airline pilot—but Capt. Robert
Somers (who has since made many more in his own Cessna) soon
landed in the ASRS nest of Old Eagles. Bob Somers, like Bill
Monan, joined Pan American with CPT credentials following a
spell building Beechcraft airplanes and as a TWA instrument instructor. Like Monan, Somers flew the Clipper flying boats and,
later, the full range of Pan Am aircraft, culminating as a 747
skipper in Pan Am's round-the-world service.

Somers joined a retired United Airlines captain, William Samuels (who soon departed to pursue his own travel and photog-
raphy interests), to become the first of the ASRS pilot analysts.
Albert Maus, a retired air traffic controller, was already on station and there had been a few other early comers, with most of us
following within a short period. *CALLBACK* No. 48, in June
1983, had this to say on the subject:

Behind the Locked Door

ASRS guarantees to reporters confidentiality and anonymity; rigid
security measures ensure that no identifying information is retained. We have even gone to the extreme of maintaining reticence
about our own individual identities. We now blow our own cover in
the belief that it will add to your confidence to know that when
you report to ASRS, and when you talk with a staff member on
callback, you are dealing with people who have been there themselves and who speak your language. Our staff is a unique group
embodying long experience in all types of flying, in air traffic
control, and in research.

Overall direction of the program is the responsibility of William
Reynard, NASA ASRS Program Chief. An attorney, with a strong
background in aviation, safety, and in the armed forces, Bill Reynard is a Commercial multi-engine and instrument-rated Pilot.
Day-to-day operation of the program is performed under contract
to NASA by Battelle Memorial Institute, a leading research organization. The Battelle-organized operational staff is composed of em-
ployee and consultant experts directed by Ed Cheaney, an engineer and twenty-five year Battelle veteran, who has led many
transportation- and safety-related projects during his career. He
too is an active General Aviation pilot. Under the direction of Reynard and Cheaney, and supported by a dedicated and competent

administrative and clerical group, are the professional analysis and research staffs who deal with the data received. Brief sketches lift our veil.

The *CALLBACK* article summarized briefly the staff members at the time. Both Maus and Samuels had departed, but Donald George, who had joined ASRS almost at the beginning, was there and remains at this writing as senior analyst. When World War II interrupted college, Don became an Army Air Corps cadet; after commissioning, he flew Martin B26 bombers in the European theater, and subsequently C47's for the Transport Command (and later in the USAF Reserve). Following the war he became a CAA (later FAA) air traffic control specialist, serving in a number of en route, tower, and approach facilities and retiring as a supervisor in Washington Tower.

Don is a graduate of FAA management courses, has served on many ATC advisory committees, and on the Flight Safety Foundation Task Force to evaluate the post-strike ATC system. His quick wit and impatience with less-than-best-effort performance has earned for him the reputation of house curmudgeon (there are those who feel I sometimes run him a close second). The George insistence on high-quality work has set an example in the training of new staff and his contributions to ASRS operating procedures have been substantial.

Nearly contemporary with Don George in ASRS service is Arlo Severns, another highly experienced ATC specialist. "Smokey" Severns learned to fly in 1941, worked as an airport attendant and weather observer at Los Angeles Airport, and became one of the earliest Air Traffic Control trainees there. After service in several centers and towers and as an Oceanic controller, he was assigned to aid in the establishment of an air traffic control system for the Phillipine government, spending two years in Manila.

Returning to the United States, he spent five years as a radar controller and team supervisor in Oakland Tower; the following four he was in Okinawa as an ATC advisor to the U.S. Air Force. Smokey's final FAA years were served as evaluation officer at Bay TRACON, back in Oakland. Throughout this long and varied career he has remained active in general aviation; he has owned several airplanes and, now retired from ASRS, is building his own open-cockpit biplane. Articulate and congenial, Smokey has enlivened countless coffee breaks and pizza lunches with colorful anecdotes from a seemingly endless store. Here's one, in his own words, that amused all the Old Eagles and should bring a chuckle to readers who remember the low-frequency radio ranges, with their Morse code beams and cones of silence:

> We had a Low Frequency Range at Oakland, located almost on the airport, at the north end. During the early 1050's we had a lot of military charter flights operating out of Oakland. Our standard instrument departure called for a climb out on a heading of 240 degrees to 2500 feet, procedure turn and cross back over the Oakland LFR at 3000.
>
> One night we had some C-46 charters going out. Our weather was typical, a layer of stratus clouds, ceiling around 1200, tops 2000. This was about the time the CAA had begun installing some "Omni Ranges" [now commonly called "VOR's," of course], a more modern version of the old LFR. Some of them even had voice identifiers instead of the old Morse code. About every thirty seconds a sepulchral voice would come on the Omni frequency and say, "This is the Podunk Omni Range. This is the Podunk Omni Range."
>
> After an aircraft had departed, we had to wait until the pilot reported back over the Oakland range before we could release the next departure. We got so that we almost knew to the second how long it would take for a C-46 to report back over. On this evening, after the last one had departed, one of our controllers, Bob O'Neill, said, "I'm going to have some fun." Checking the clock carefully, he waited until he knew the C-46 was about to cross the range station. Then he selected the range frequency on his microphone and intoned, "This is the Oakland Cone of Silence. This is the Oakland Cone of Silence." The C-46 pilot came on the tower frequency with a shout. "Hey, Oakland Tower! I just heard a voice identifier on your cone of silence! How long have you had that?" And Bob said, "Oh, that's something new. They're just trying it out." The pilot said, "Well, I think it's a great idea. I wish they'd get them all over."
>
> For months afterward we'd occasionally get a query from a pilot who'd heard about the voice identifier on our cone of silence, wondering what had happened to it.

"Good morning," said the trim, white-haired, middle-aged gentleman who greeted me on my first morning at ASRS, "I'm Perry Thomas; sing out if there is anything I can do to help." Typically, as I soon learned, courteous and thoughtful. I was to learn, also, from the plaque on his office wall, that James Perry Thomas was captain, retired, United Airlines. Had we met in other circumstances I should have cast him as a bank president rather than an aviator (it was this dignified and authoritative manner that caused me to adopt the sobriquet "J.P." instead of "Perry," used by everybody else). It seems odd that Perry and I had not met before; we had much in common. We were both California natives—rare in our group (in fact, rare in any group in these times of rapidly increasing population)—and close in age. We had both learned to fly in California in the prewar years; we had many mutual friends and shared many recollections of places, people, aircraft, and experiences.

After CPT, Thomas instructed Air Corps cadets, joining United to fly DC-3's and soon, the line's wartime transpacific routes in the C-87 and DC-4. He flew all United's aircraft types and was one of the line's first jet-qualified pilots, spending several weeks in France to check out in the Caravelle before flying one back to the United States. Later he was DC-10 training captain, San Francisco flight manager, and ended his long career in the 747. Like most of us, he had been an active GA pilot and a flight instructor, and like all of us, he loved aviation. Early in his training, so he claims, he was astonished to learn that some people were actually paid for flying.

Perry Thomas had another distinction: Although several of the Old Eagles owned motor homes, the Thomas vehicle was notable for its size and accoutrements, which included, in addition to a well-equipped galley, comfortable bunks for four, a full-size bathtub and shower, easy chairs and color television, and a raised flight deck with autopilot and two-way radio (callsign: "Big Bird").

Big Bird was handy for project field trips. One fine morning we all made the hundred-mile round-trip to Oakland Center, gaining useful insight into the workings of a busy ATC facility and enjoying a rolling repast (not available to the generous and self-sacrificing owner/driver) of Bloody Marys and sandwiches. Another time, when I had unexpectedly come by four VIP invitations to view the landing of a Space Shuttle, J.P. provided this luxurious machine to convey himself, Ed Cheaney, Bob Somers, and me to Edwards Air Force Base. After an enjoyable voyage through California's valleys and mountain passes, we made camp beside the desert runway, dined on steak cooked by the versatile Thomas, slept comfortably, and were up in time to watch the impressive dawn landing from our own mobile quarters.

Perry Thomas and Bob Somers made up the pilot analyst group. Project policy required that all newly joined members of the professional staff be trained in report processing, regardless of permanent assignment, so I spent several weeks beside Perry or Bob learning the procedure, and learning a good deal about my mentors at the same time. Battelle had provided a comfortable private office for each of us, but we frequently came together around the coffee pot or the copy machine (complete collections of maps, charts, manuals, regulations, and reference materials are kept up to date and consulted and copied during report processing).

A lifetime of odd hours and early risings has conditioned all of us; the analysts, in particular, prefer to start work very early in the morning, establishing 8 A.M. and 10 A.M. coffee breaks as regular schedule features. These sessions, in which we were joined by controller-analysts Severns and George, researcher Monan and, often, by Project Manager Cheaney, encouraged us to share information and to compare notes. They also provided the occasions for many a war story and reminiscence.

The hangar flying continued during our regular brown-bag lunches, with the troops eating on their laps in my office, and reached spectacular heights on Wednesdays, when our traditional pizza repast took place. Bob Somers volunteered one day to fetch pizza for anybody interested; all hands, including clerical and administrative, joined in at the feast, standing around the manager's large conference table and eating without benefit of utensils. The innovation was so popular that Bob did it again the following week, inviting a few NASA people, and thereafter it became regular routine, usually attended by Dr. Billings, Bill Reynard, and John Lauber (now a member of NTSB, but then a NASA human factors researcher), and often by visitors and outside guests. In time ASRS Wednesday pizza became so popular that Washington FAA officials, Advisory Committee members, out-of-town airline pilots, and just friends were to be found standing by the tall windows overlooking the Moffett runways enjoying this undignified but congenial picnic. The spectacular daily takeoff and climb of a NASA U2 often added visual—and aural—counterpoint to lunch.

Pan American Capt. John Raabe was one of those friends. On his retirement he seemed a logical choice to join the nest; report volume was increasing and analyst staff increases were in order. Jack (or "Robbie") was a natural, known to us all and with similar credentials. A CPT graduate (of course), he had at first instructed Air Corps students, signing on with Pan Am when new hires were still checked out in the big seaplanes.

It would be foolish to attribute rank to members of a group so well matched as this unique collection of world class aviators; every pilot on the staff, for instance, held a DC-3 rating—a matter of awe to younger ASRS troops, who tended to equate the grand old "goonie" with the Wright Flyer. Nevertheless, a pecking order of sorts was recognized by four of us—Monan, Somers, Raabe, Hardy—who enjoyed the inestimable privilege of flying the oceans in the romantic flying boats, complete with the accompanying celestial navigation lore.

So Robbie joined us, bringing a résumé that included, after the big boats, qualification in all the Pan Am aircraft; service as a line, training, and check captain; participation in company and industry research and safety programs; instructor and flight engineer ratings. At retirement he was flying 747 round-the-world trips.

Harry Orlady missed the flying boats, but he hasn't missed much else. Son of a World War I pilot, Harry O joined United Airlines fresh from college (and CPT, naturally!) at an age sufficiently young to assure him of UAL seniority number two at retirement (the number one pilot, hired at the same time, had a later birth date) and to make his first flights for the airline on the Boeing 247, matching Perry Thomas in this old timers' distinction. His fourth decade on the line was spent flying Jumbos between Chicago and Honolulu. Harry was one of the Old Eagles, along with Perry Thomas, whose egos were ruffled when they read in an early CALLBACK a reference to "wide-body Captains"; in future I was forced to substitute the more cumbersome "Captains of wide-body aircraft." "Old controllers" likewise had to be replaced with a more flattering euphemism.

Harry O did not become an official member of the ASRS staff until his airline retirement in 1982 but, in fact, was instrumental in the inauguration of the program. He had been the principal developer of the United Airlines Flight Safety Awareness Program, which pioneered the concept of nonpunitive incident reporting. Working with Billings and Lauber of NASA, he was involved in the beginnings of ASRS, which took many of its principles from the UAL scheme. In 1974 Harry was presented the United Airlines Distinguished Service Award "for dedication to the field of flight safety as displayed by his professional excellence in the development of . . . the Program."

There was no star system at ASRS, but Captain Orlady was certainly the most visible presence. His official dossier covers eight pages of achievements, honors, and awards; among them, fellow of the Aerospace Medical Association, and member of the Human Factors Society and of the Association of Aviation Psychologists. He has participated in committees, conferences, and symposia, both international and domestic; has often lectured on flight safety and human factors; and is the author of more than sixty technical papers. During his career as a United captain, he flew Douglas DC-3, DC-4, DC-6, DC-7, and DC-8 airplanes, as well as the Boeing 720 and 747, and served as an officer in his Air Line Pilots Association council.

As an ASRS consultant, and the staff's principal research scientist, Captain Orlady has published NASA studies on fatigue in the cockpit, a subject on which he is an acknowledged authority, and on pilot/copilot exchange of duties (condensed for *CALLBACK*, see the appendix), and has been the leader in the project's investigation of problems relating to the new high-technology automated cockpits. Distinguished in the fields of flying and scholarship alike, Harry O was also an enthusiastic coffee break and lunch raconteur, a loyal and amiable companion, and a highly respected colleague.

During the first years, report-processing procedures were refined by the ASRS founding fathers and the Old Eagle analysts developed considerable skill in analyzing and coding for database entry the incident reports that continued to flow in. The average time for each report was about $1\frac{1}{2}$ hours. As intake increased, it became necessary to enlarge the staff, not to mention the quarters to house it. Funding increases allowed the recruiting of additional analysts, and we were fortunate in being able to attract a flock of new Old Eagles fully qualified to occupy the nest. In this group, most of whom subsequently dropped out as budget squeezing emerged, were Capt. Russ Cottle, a United Airlines flight operations vice-president, and TWA Captain William Dixon. Bill Dixon had been a wartime pilot in Europe and, during his TWA career, flew the first commercial airliner allowed into the People's Republic of China. This flight was made in a Boeing 747 accompanying President Richard Nixon's historic mission. Other newcomers included Controller James McMeans, an active GA pilot, who had completed a long career in both military and FAA air traffic control, Ted MacEachen, a former controller turned American Airlines captain, and Captain William McDowell, a USAF B-17 and B-29 pilot before joining UAL.

The funding cutback effects were visible for a time and had the result of renewing a report backlog that had not existed since early days. Battelle headquarters in Ohio dispatched operations and computer expert Loren Rosenthal to streamline processing and research procedures; he accomplished this task with considerable efficiency. The most visible effects of this effort were that report-processing time has been cut to about twenty minutes, and Rosenthal has succeeded Ed Cheaney as project manager.

The incident report rate of four hundred per month, that had remained at that level so long, began a steady rise in the mid-1980s, paralleling the rise in air traffic and boosted by increasing awareness of ASRS. A second generation of not-so-old eagles then came aboard to cope with the added load. Leading this procession were Capts. Robert Petersen and Bill Richards, from UAL, and Capt. Lloyd McBeth, from American Airlines. Jeanne McElhatton, a general aviation pilot and instructor of long experience joined in, and the ATC ranks were augmented by Rawley (Bob) Wright and Ward Stevenson, both retired from Oakland Center, and Vince Mellone, who had been chief of Bay TRACON.

The place seems more crowded now, although additional space has become available. The old manager's office/pizza parlor, with its windows overlooking Moffett and with its Navy aircraft and U2 comings and goings, has been partitioned into several offices and has been replaced by a windowless conference room, but the pizza still comes in on Wednesdays, as do occasional visitors. Happily, among these, now and then, are the familiar faces of Bob Somers, Perry Thomas, and Smokey Severns, pioneers whose early efforts added so much to the project's success and whose company helped to make it such a jolly place. Don George and Jack Raabe are still regulars. Bill Monan, Harry O, and I have cut our schedules considerably and, as venerable consultants, pop in for a few days each month—always including a Wednesday or two. Ed Cheaney, likewise, continues as a part-time research consultant.

The nest now has a population of different eagles, but some of the old ones are still in evidence to provide continuity. The important thing is that the major ASRS contribution to flying safety proceeds as before, now more thoroughly systematized and organized, but with its mission still conducted by a band of enormously experienced, strongly motivated, empathetic, mutually supportive, and highly dedicated airmen.

3

Immunity, Philanthropy, Therapy

Pilots and air traffic controllers are notoriously averse to paper-work. Notwithstanding this prejudice, each month about sixteen hundred of them, plus a scattering of flight attendants, dis-patchers, mechanics, passengers, and assorted others involved one way or another with the flight of aircraft, voluntarily submit to NASA's ASRS accounts of unsafe occurrences and situations (or occurrences and situations perceived by them as unsafe—which is not necessarily the same thing). No imperative in law or other-wise mandates this unburdening. The operative motives affecting reporters to the program are worth examining.

Commencing with *CALLBACK* No. 1, in July 1979, the bul-letin's brief two pages of text have concluded with a tag line—an exhortation in bold type soliciting reports. Here are some of them:

Share Your Hard-earned Lessons—Report to ASRS
Show a Constructive Attitude—Report to ASRS

26

Human Error?—Tell ASRS about It
Reporting to ASRS Is Valuable to Others—And to You Too
Report to ASRS—We're Listening
Reporting to ASRS Is Better than Taking the Fifth
Confession Is Good for the Soul—Tell ASRS Your Troubles
Don't Be Ashamed—Confess to ASRS
Don't Say "@#&*!"—Report to ASRS

Stimulus to report, though not mentioned in *CALLBACK*'s stated raison d'etre, was emphatically a factor in the decision to inaugurate a monthly publication. The first of the one-liners read, "Report to ASRS! Our Output Depends on Your Input." Despite our urging, the question arises—and is put frequently— why should a pilot or controller (or anyone else for that matter) take the trouble to fill out NASA Form ARC 277, check the many question boxes, write a coherent narrative, and mail the form in?

An infinite number of reasons, often overlapping, may be deduced as incentives for voluntarily telling a government agency about your aerial misadventures but, viewed analytically, they can be sorted into three well-defined groups. These may be thought of simplistically as immunity, philanthropy, and therapy. No tabulation of submission categories has been attempted, nor is such a count possible ("Why did you report?" is not asked on the form), and many of the reports falling into one of the prime divisions contain hints of the others, but it is undoubtedly the first of the three that is most compelling; the inference is strong that this accounts for nearly half the intake.

"Immunity" is not a precisely accurate label. "Waiver of disciplinary action" more closely fits the bill. Here is the gospel according to FAA:

> The filing of a report with NASA concerning an incident or occurrence involving a violation of the Act or the Federal Aviation Regulations is considered by the FAA to be indicative of a constructive attitude. Such an attitude will tend to prevent future violations. Accordingly, although a finding of a violation may be made, neither a civil penalty nor certificate suspension will be imposed if:
> (1) The violation was inadvertent and not deliberate.

That paragraph, headed "Enforcement Policy," comes from the FAA Advisory Circular (currently AC 00-46C) describing the ASRP and NASA's participation in the program as administrator of the ASRS.

So much for immunity. The feature is well-known to most air traffic controllers and pilots, not to mention airline flight operations departments and FAA enforcement authorities. If you, a controller, have figured in a loss-of-separation occurrence and an "operational error" has been declared; if you, a pilot, have deviated from prescribed procedure; and if you have filed an ASRS report within ten days of the event, you will, even though judged to have been at fault, escape the fine or enforced period "on the bench" to which you might otherwise have been subjected. It must be mentioned in passing that, in addition to the ten-day reporting requirement, there are a few other qualifications to the waiver privilege.

Excluded from consideration are incidents involving NTSB-reportable accidents, those in which there appears to have been criminal activity, and those that disclose "a lack of qualification or competency." Such reports are seldom received. The rules also specify that the culprit must have had a clean record for the preceding five years. This does not inhibit reporting as often as one chooses; it merely affirms that if a waiver of punishment has been granted, another violation within five years may carry a penalty. A footnote to the rules mentions that these provisions do not apply to air traffic controllers (since most are employed directly by FAA), but that provisions concerning them are addressed in internal FAA directives. In practice, the effectiveness of the waiver provisions are similar for pilots and for controllers (and, though not generally recognized, for others certificated by FAA such as mechanics).

The limiting caveats listed have little practical effect on reporting rate. A pilot running a load of hashish across the border, a victim of a genuine crash, a pilot flying without a valid license or unqualified for his task—these are not likely to reveal all voluntarily in a public document. The confidentiality—anonymity once the report has been processed—normally accorded ASRS reports does not extend to these excluded classes. Reports of criminal activity are virtually nonexistent (rumor says there have been a handful, but the only eyes to have seen them are those of the NASA attorney/program monitor who screens all incoming reports). Similarly, reports (rare) of true accidents (gear-up landings, scraped pods or wing tips, bent props, blown-tire-induced off-runway excursions do not count) are screened out. Criminal activity reports would be forwarded to the Department of Justice, accident reports to the NTSB. Relatively few participants in the National Aviation System suffer the stigma of records besmirched by prior violations.

Remaining then, is the large eligible reporting population:

those who have become involved in, or who observe, a hazardous occurrence or situation. You overshoot an assigned altitude on a departure clearance—for any of a multitude of causes—and you are very likely to hear about it officially. Your best course is to submit an ASRS report forthwith. And if you want to ensure that you qualify under the ten-day blanket, you would be wise to obtain proof of mailing from the post office. Now you have turned in a CYA report. Many of these reports make clear their necessity: The misdemeanor has been noted. The pilot is directed to telephone the tower after landing; the controller is relieved from his position. On the other hand, many are submitted for insurance; often the reporter is not certain whether, in fact, he committed a violation. More often, he is not sure the violation, of which he is well aware, has been detected—or, if detected, recorded.

Here is a narrative describing a minor deviation from an assigned flight level. Apparently the altitude bust was not observed, or was ignored because no potential conflict existed. Typically, the pilot had permitted himself to become distracted at a critical time in his climb and reported at once to ASRS—just in case. Frequently, because he is—justifiably—at equal risk, the copilot will also report. He needs to cover his "anatomy," too, because he has fallen down on his responsibility to monitor.

> Climbing to FL200. The aircraft was on autopilot, with rate of climb controlled by the pitch knob. Just prior to level-off I was distracted by the cockpit door opening behind me. At 19,900 feet I attempted to level off with the autopilot pitch trim; however this was not effective enough to stop the ascent. I immediately disconnected the autopilot and manually pushed the aircraft back to 20,000. Inertia carried the aircraft to 20,300, which triggered the altitude alert aural warning. Recovery to 20,000 was immediate with no apparent disruption to ATC. . . . ATC made NO transmission concerning this overshoot.

ASRS's analyst, like his colleagues, an old-timer, skeptically points out that the trim knob requires a very gentle touch for a smooth and positive level-off, and requires lead time to work. Perhaps having been in the same pickle himself during his long career, he also wonders why such interest in the flight attendant's entry through the door; he speculates that the errant captain was hungry and that his breakfast had just appeared; also that he suspected a possible violation action.

Noncompliance with altitude assignments represents, as we examine in more detail later, a large segment of ASRS report intake. Often these deviations are trivial, and nothing further is heard about them. On the other hand, they are sometimes very significant and can lead to potential conflicts with other traffic; these, especially, bring inquiry and—unless they have been reported under the waiver provisions of the ASRS rules—retribution. There exists among air carrier pilots, understandably perhaps, an impression that the hand of the FAA is poised above their pocketbooks; the slightest infraction can lead to fine or suspension, either of which will have—at least temporarily—a chilling effect on the pilots' (rumored) extravagant lifestyles. Sensitivity to possible retribution is not as prevalent among general aviation pilots, whose misdemeanors are more commonly caused by ignorance or inexperience than by inadvertence or carelessness.

> I rented a small aircraft at the airport for the purpose of flying to the coast to practice maneuvers, stalls, etc. Flying over the town after takeoff I had the whim to find my old baseball field that I had played on for so many years as a youth. In doing so I inadvertently went below the minimum altitude (1000') in an area considered to be congested. Upon finding the field after approximately five minutes, I made a pass over at about three to four hundred feet. After passing I climbed out to 2500' en route to the coast, which turned out to be fogged in, so I then returned to the airport. After landing I was made well aware of my mistake by the Airport Manager. . . . Apparently several complaints were phoned in of a low-flying plane in the area. . . . This is a totally ignorant mistake on my part. . . . I've learned a valuable lesson and am very sorry. . . . I wanted to make aviation my career. This is a very humiliating experience and never again will I "not think" before acting. . . . Such an unnecessary, idiotic mistake!

ASRS receives no follow-on information on violation outcomes. The private pilot who told that story evidently expected a dire sequel but will probably survive to fly again, chastened, wiser, and safer. His report is interesting in other ways as it illustrates the combined reporting motives so often observed. Aside from CYA (which may not have been effective, since the violation could have been interpreted as deliberate or otherwise outside the immunity envelope), the transgressor is using the system for its cathartic benefit. Confession is said to be good for the soul, and therapy undoubtedly provides a strong impetus to report.

Before leaving, for the moment, the immunity discussion, mention must be made of the 100 percent pure CYA, in which a violator attempts to beat the rap while withholding the expected quid pro quo. When you report a transgression (or any incident, for that matter) you receive in return the identification slip portion of the reporting form, date- and time-stamped to establish the details of ASRS receipt, as evidence that you have shown that "constructive attitude" and are deserving of leniency. But you are expected to play fair. ASRS is interested in, and in fact exists (notwithstanding your personal concern with protecting your backside), primarily to gather and to study the human frailties underlying unsafe practices. It is your personal desire to avoid punishment; it is your obligation to tell us the causes and circumstances of your deviant performance. *CALLBACK* No. 55 (January 1984) carried a story under the heading "Something for Nothing" that gave examples of a report type (fortunately rare) that, in withholding details, is a con. "Play fair, Troops," *CALLBACK* said. Here are some complete reports indicative of a selfish, rather than constructive, attitude:

> I let an aircraft enter Center's airspace without coordinating with Center.

> See captain's report.

> I was the data controller when the incident took place.

> Controller said he would have to report us. I was the copilot on the flight.

> Two aircraft got within five miles of each other.

Stories like these may bring you your ticket to immunity; they leave the ASRS research cupboard bare. We try to fill in the blanks in such accounts by means of telephone callbacks, but that doesn't always work. Occasionally, incident reports somewhat better than those above, but disappointing in a different way, arrive at ASRS: A flightcrew member, clearly for CYA purposes and presumably in caucus with the other (or others), fills out one form listing each person's name on the single ID strip. Bad news! Each person desiring immunity consideration must submit his own form. A variant of this ploy is the submission by two or more crew members of duplicate reports—identical except for the names at the top. On the other hand, individual reports from each participant in an incident are highly valued. More often than not, additional insight is gained through analysis of these accounts, with reference to the different perspectives represented.

I have mentioned those reports that embody overlapping

motives, immunity-cum-therapy, in particular. CYA plus philanthropy is another prevalent combination. Here a pilot, hoping for immunity for his (alleged) unintended violation, hopes also that knowledge of his experience may serve to alert others to the sort of problem he faced.

> Climbed out to an altitude of 2500 feet. The outside air temp was 43 degrees and in the open cockpit it became uncomfortably cold. I descended to 1000 feet and it warmed up to about 55. As I approached abeam the mountain, the air became quite turbulent and it was difficult to maintain a constant altitude. The winds were reported at 30 to 40 knots. I had a ground speed of about 35, so decided to stop for fuel. When I landed, the tower said they had a phone number for me to call. When I called this number I found out it was Flight Standards. They informed me that someone thought I flew too low over a town. By submitting this report I thought it might be a warning to other pilots flying low performance airplanes in these conditions. Being on the lee side of a mountain with these kinds of winds and with limited power it may be difficult to maintain minimum altitude.

"Everything's Coming Up Roses" was the heading to a *CALLBACK* reprise of an unusual—indeed unique—narrative from a general aviation pilot that exemplifies the report class I call "philanthropy." In telling ASRS of the event, the reporter has no discernible motive other than a desire to share with others an odd but educational experience.

> Maybe minor, but possibly a potential hazard—refueled my aircraft with 35 gallons of 100 octane fuel—even watched it happen. Went inside—came back and out of habit looked in tanks and drained a sample. Imagine my surprise at seeing a pink sample! I was ready to yell and scream, when I realized my eye glasses (brown-rose colored) had changed the color. Suppose I had worn green sunglasses and looked at a clear fuel? Moral: Look at fuel samples without sunglasses.

Stories like this one often end with a moral. And they provide an opportunity for *CALLBACK* to lecture. In this case, we reminded readers that 80-octane fuel is colored red; 100 is green (or blue); jet fuel is clear. We pointed out that "things won't come up roses if you put jet fuel in a recip—and vice versa. Likewise if you feed 80 octane to an engine requiring 100." A report from a professional, again with a pertinent recommendation, carries a different warning:

Our widebody aircraft was moving onto the active runway for takeoff when the crew of another aircraft informed us that we had two spoilers on our left wing in the FULL UP position. We aborted takeoff and returned to the ramp for maintenance inspection. Two spoilers on left wing were jammed in full up position and would not return to normal position. Cycling controls, switches and systems was no help. . . . Trying to push spoilers down manually was no help. . . . There is no cockpit indication of this condition and horn will not sound. Follow-up from maintenance: Control rods from spoiler mixer were dry and lacked lubrication. . . . Recommendation: Pre-flight inspection of top of both wings to ensure spoilers are flush.

No motive beyond a desire to share—and the alert crew that spotted the anomaly deserves credit, too. One reporter who luckily came through a difficult experience ended his report, "Anyway, I learned from that. Maybe this recounting will help somebody else, too." Here is some more disinterested sharing of experience:

FAA examiners and FAA regulations do not control the use of white strobe lights on aircraft while they are in ramp or taxiway areas. Airlines and most jet aircraft pilots abide by the placard in the aircraft to turn off strobe lights after landing and turn them on in lineup check. Some small jet aircraft pilots are prone to violate this; also some flight schools are teaching students to turn on strobes while in congested areas. This is not only annoying, but is dangerous to night vision of adjacent aircraft crews in taxiways and run-up areas. The strobe effect makes prop aircraft dangerous to ground personnel or other persons moving around in vicinity of an aircraft with engine running.

Engine failure at 3500' . . . prepared for forced landing. There were four types of terrain available: Lakes; open swamps; small timber up to 20 feet tall with small butts up to five inches; and heavy, large timber up to fifty feet tall with large butt size. I chose the small timber and entered it with airspeed in excess of 70 MPH. The aircraft clipped off the small trees for a distance of 85 paces before a wheel touched the ground and then stopped in another 20 paces. Because the small trees brought the aircraft to a stop gently, none of the occupants were injured. . . . The point of this is that the safest forced landing terrain—other than a hard, smooth, long surface like a road or runway—is in small timber, brush, new growth, probably not over 20 feet tall.

CALLBACK quoted the adage, "A good landing is one you can walk away from." As you will have deduced, my categorization of philanthropy in the context of ASRS reporting includes those narratives submitted with the altruistic intent of contributing useful safety information to the aviation community. In that spirit, a controller's report enlightening pilots on the subject of new ATC procedural measures appeared in a *CALLBACK* story headed "To Err Is Human . . . To Be Observed Is Now Computerized." A "concerned and thoughtful controller," we wrote, described the new QAP instituted in the Air Route Traffic Control Centers during 1984. The reporter alerted pilots to this new ATC feature and warned of its potential for causing them trouble. *CALLBACK* pointed out that an element of QAP was "Computer Detected Error," known to controllers as "Big Brother," "Squeal-a-Deal," "Lie Detector," and "Snitch Patch"—or, commonly, just "Snitch." Snitch's real purpose is to prevent, or to attempt to prevent, the loss of prescribed distance between aircraft. It is a tool designed to improve controller performance by measuring, with great accuracy, the distance separating potentially conflicting traffic and to call immediate attention to the conflict. The reporting controller described an altitude bust that resulted in LTSS and he explained how Snitch could spoil the errant pilot's day, even though the controller was minded to ignore the affair. Clarifying, the reporter continued:

> Conflict Alert [long an ATC feature] merely indicates the possibility of less than adequate separation impending. Snitch says it has occurred. In the past, a deviation could be overlooked if nobody complained; with Snitch it is impossible to overlook the situation. Pilots should be made aware of this, since their mistakes could result in action being taken against them regardless of how the controller feels about it. In this case there was more than two miles horizontal and 400 feet vertical separation at the closest point, so there was no real danger—but who knows what could have happened? As the controller I was completely in the clear, but I think pilots should be made aware of Snitch. As a general rule, pilots and controllers have a good relationship. In situations like this it was not the controller who turned the infraction in, but Snitch. If pilots suffer penalties in situations like this (suspension, etc.), don't blame the controller. . . . It is out of the controller's hands.

Admittedly, my immunity/therapy/philanthropy classification is arbitrary. The lines of demarcation setting apart the three basic reporting motives are often blurred, but at least one of the three may be discerned in all ASRS submissions. More often than not, two, and frequently all three, appear in a report. Complaints—criticism of procedures, policies, equipment, facilities, other people—turn up regularly. The strong gripes fall, probably, into the therapy grouping (you may be able to lay off your personal guilt!), although a note of dissatisfaction may be appended to philanthropic reports and, of course, many complaints are thrown in simply as excuses to justify some careless blunder reported primarily for CYA purposes. The NMAC is a special case, to be considered later in this book. ASRS files contain a great many NMAC accounts; the total grows daily from air carrier and general aviation pilots and is augmented by the official hazard reports passed to ASRS from Air Force and Naval Aviation safety offices. The typical NMAC is diagnosed as "fail see-and-avoid" and is not conducive to blame assignment; immunity is seldom the driving force for reporting close encounters; philanthropic reasons appear at times, but the most common motive is therapeutic ("nobody minding the store; I must be more vigilant").

CALLBACK frequently quotes brief fragments from lengthy reports to make a particular point—or to fill space. Many of these (*CALLBACK* calls them "nuggets") deal with motivation, and they reveal complex human factors at work. Here are some examples:

> I can't believe I've written this much! But it's good therapy, Guys, and I'm damn glad that ASRS provides an outlet for this stuff.

> Despite what you folks do with these reports, writing them definitely has a sobering effect on me as I reflect on the possible implications of my occasional mistakes—thanks for the sounding board.

> Why did it happen? DUMB! . . . Good night, fellows, it's been a real long day and I've got a lot to think about. Experience is a wonderful teacher—if we survive our mistakes. DUMB!

> Moral: Know EXACTLY where you are—not ABOUT where you are.

> The only reason we made a mistake is habit—and maybe that we were in the middle of a personal conversation which caused me not to really think.

> There is no excuse for this sort of thing. . . . MEA CULPA!

> Moral: Be extra cautious with abnormally high or low altimeter settings.

> Suggest I pay attention to business in future.

> Don't be complacent. Cross-check the other guy at all times. One pilot should always mind the store.

No excuse. . . . succumbed to distraction.

Moral: Don't let distractions lead you down the primrose path.

I had always thought, "It can't happen to me!" WRONG!

It will be observed that lessons have been learned, not only from the incidents that triggered the reports, but through the self-evaluation of underlying causes and the discipline brought to bear on the act of filling out the reports. It will also be observed that complacency and distraction rank high among the hindrances to safe flight. The phrases so often repeated in ASRS reports, "mind the store," and "fly the airplane," summarize the accepted techniques for keeping those twin hindrances at bay.

CALLBACK No. 38 (8/82) carried an article headed "Accidents That Didn't Happen" quoting Bill Reynard. Consistent with the bulletin's anonymity policy, Bill was identified only as "NASA's ASRS Chief", and he addressed the general topic of incident reporting:

> Program participants have expressed the notion that the fact of having to organize and express the relevant facts and issues associated with a given event or situation has proved to be an extremely valuable learning experience for the reporter. . . . The event analysis and performance critique that takes place at both ends of the reporting process is clearly a significant, but unmeasurable, benefit of the ASRS program. . . . The most obvious, as well as the most undocumentable, category of ASRS achievements is the element of accidents avoided and deaths prevented; it is impossible to document a non-event. However, given the array of research, Alert Bulletins, publications and assistance offered and utilized as a result of ASRS operations, it seems reasonable to assert that the presence and product of the ASRS has prevented accidents and saved lives.

To its reporters, the ASRS serves in a triple capacity: It acts as the intermediary in obtaining leniency for sinners; it provides a discrete and confidential means for confessing those sins and thus clearing worried consciences; and it acts as a medium for distributing the philanthropically reported safety lessons.

Concluding this chapter on report motivation is a narrative from a pilot who felt no need for confession and absolution, who felt no charitable impulse to share newly gained experience, and who was certainly barking up the wrong tree in his quest for immunity:

Hot air balloon flight. Normal takeoff. After one hour of flight became becalmed and engaged light thermal activity holding aircraft over city. Spent two hours over residential area trying to find landing area until fuel ran out and made forced landing on residential street. There was no damage to the aerostat. The only reason this report is being submitted is because of the hassle of the local police department. I have no recommendations except make a little wind blow in one direction. This is hardly ever a problem in this state, but was today.

ASRS can offer only sympathy in cases like this. The waiver of disciplinary action is offered by FAA and is applicable only to FAA's own enforcement proceedings. If you're nailed by the local PD, you're on your own.

4

We Read Back. . . .

For many years media viewers, not excluding the specialized aviation press, have been proclaiming with alarm that some aberration of human behavior is responsible for 80 percent of aircraft mishaps. Accident reports lend credence to this figure by citing the human factor as a contributory cause in a large proportion of crashes, but the true proportion of accidents and incidents involving pilot (or controller) performance lapses, undoubtedly large, is impossible to determine. A related and more readily substantiated statistic is that 70 percent of the incident reports submitted to NASA's ASRS directly or indirectly mention some communication anomaly—referred to by safety professionals as flawed information transfer.

All aspects of aviation depend on an accurate exchange of information; the consequences of error in these exchanges range from minor to dire. In times past, material or environmental influences often played a role in cases of missed, misunderstood, or misinterpreted messages; today, thanks largely to spectacular

38

developments in the field of electronics, great strides have been made in eliminating difficulties attributed to weather conditions or unreliable "avionics." Sadly, less improvement is evident in the human element in the communication equation, which remains flying's area of greatest vulnerability. Carelessness in radio transmission, and at the receiving end, is responsible for many hazardous occurrences in flight (and on the ground)—and ASRS hears about them frequently. Several of the program's research studies have discussed the topic of information transfer; some of these, condensed by *CALLBACK,* appear in the appendix.

The ASRS bulletin inevitably took early editorial note of communication problems, and some aspect of the subject has turned up in most issues of *CALLBACK.* For starters, the second issue (August 1979) carried a short item headed, "Cross Above, or Below, or Something," based on an article in the *Journal of the Air Traffic Control Association* dealing with air/ground communications. The journal pointed out the dangers of partly blocked messages, nonstandard phraseology, and plain misunderstandings. The use of "not" was cited as an example. "Some controllers still use such non-standard phraseologies as, 'Cross Warwick not above 6000 feet.' Consider the implications if a spike of noise happens to come along and blot out the word 'not.'" A column in *CALLBACK* No. 3 (September 1973) carried two articles, each foreshadowing many to come in future:

CALLBACK Says Readback

From a controller: "Aircraft A cleared to descend to FL280. Aircraft B cleared to climb to FL270. Aircraft A issued a heading of 240. Pilot acknowledged with, 'Roger, two four zero.' Aircraft took it as an altitude change instead of a heading and he descended through Aircraft B's altitude. Neither aircraft took evasive action. Altitude was observed at 27,200. I questioned the pilot. He said I cleared him to FL240 and he acknowledged it. A full readback by the pilot would have prevented the incident, as his misunderstanding would have been noticed prior to descending below FL280."

Here's another one: Aircraft heading 300 degrees at FL270 was given a vector to three one zero. Captain's attention was diverted temporarily; returning to his instruments he was surprised to find the aircraft climbing. F/O had acknowledged, "Three one zero," but was climbing to it instead of turning to it.

Runway Two Zero is sometimes confused with Runway Two; Flight 925 takes a clearance intended for Flight 529. ASRS diagnosticians, coding reports for computer storage, use the term, "Similar Sounding A/N," among others, to help researchers in the later retrieval of reports such as these. "A/N" is shorter than "Alpha/Numerics" and we know what the phrase means: Letters, words, and numbers that sound like others. But, as the controller says, a full readback would eliminate incidents like these. Or, as a grizzled old bird(man) on the ASRS staff says, "'Okay' is not okay."

Marching to a Different Drummer

1. From a recent ASRS report: Air carrier pilot . . . cleared for visual approach . . . contact the tower. Switching frequencies, he was unable to get a word in because of heavy chatter between controller and several aircraft evidently in the pattern. Well—not to worry—Approach Control had given our man traffic to follow so he drilled right on in, trying from time to time to make his call. Approaching threshold, with his traffic turning off, but still with no landing clearance, he elected to take a wave-off. Announcing his intention to the tower, he finally had an answer: "You are talking to the wrong tower." Dialing in the correct numbers this time, our pilot made a second approach and landed uneventfully.

2. Pilot of small aircraft had a near collision with a light twin on final for ABC Airport. From a controller's report: "The pilot contacted FSS to open his flight plan, then changed to what he thought was the ABC local frequency for clearance through the Airport Traffic Area. He had in fact changed to XYZ's local frequency and was cleared through their ATA. The pilot realized his mistake at the time of the occurrence and changed to ABC's frequency." Admittedly the frequencies were pretty close—but somebody wasn't listening.

In May 1980 *CALLBACK* No. 11 printed an article demonstrating that communication problems are not exclusive to U.S. aviation and presenting still another statistic on the human element:

One World Note

"An intensive campaign was run aimed at the reporting of communication problems. About 1100 pilots and flight engineers were involved. Almost 40% of the reports received from flight crews are concerned with 'lack of compliance to communication standards' in connection with 'ground movement' or 'altitude change/clearance.' Pilots, as well as controllers, are reported to be negligent in this respect. Correct understanding of communication related to these flight parts is obviously important. The reports tell of the concern many pilots feel about this problem. Some problems frequently reported are:

"The omission of letters in flight numbers, which is especially dangerous when there are flights with similar digit combinations in an area at the same time.

"The omission of the words 'Flight Level,' especially in connection with the number 'two,' which could be misunderstood for 'to.'

Another reported aspect of 'to' is the likelihood of it being understood as 'through.'

"Speaking faster than necessary for the actual radio traffic.

"The tendency to deviate from standard phraseology in connection with lineup and takeoff."

If you think that sounds like just another sermon from ASRS, you're wrong. It is snitched directly from "Hazard Briefs," published by HARP . . . HARP is not what you probably think, either; it is the name used by the Aeronautical Research Institute of Sweden. HARP has described the problem in clear English; we're thankful we don't have to reciprocate in their tongue. How do you say, "altitude bust" in Swedish? But we all seem to HARP on the same old tunes, don't we? Play it again, Sam.

The old refrains have been reprised often in ASRS publications. The prolific Captain Monan dealt in detail with the callsign problem in one of his studies; the ASRS database contains hundreds of reports mentioning too-rapid speech. One reporter complained that "too many controllers are issuing clearances like tobacco auctioneers." A very experienced pilot, whose report was reprinted in *CALLBACK,* agreed. His story was followed by an example of the two/to confusion mentioned by HARP:

Linguistics(?)

*I am reminded of a story of a Southern state copilot who was given a very complicated ATC clearance at machine gun rate. When Clearance Delivery had finished, the copilot asked for a repeat. The repeat came back at even a faster rate. The copilot, in a Southern drawl, said, 'Clearance Delivery, do y'all heah how fast Ah'm talkin'?' 'Affirmative, I do; why?' The response was, 'That's just about as fast as Ah can write, too. Would y'all please repeat the clearance one moah tahm?' . . ."

We received a clearance from Departure Control (at a foreign airport) to 'Climb TWO Five Zero.' I observed the copilot repeat that clearance and dial 25,000 into the altitude window on the autopilot control system. When the controller came back on the radio I made a gentle descent TO the 5000 feet that he requested, observing the VFR traffic which was about 1500 feet above us. . . . It was strictly a matter of semantics."

Another Monan study, reprinted in the appendix in *CALLBACK's* condensed form, is entitled, "Readback Related Errors in ATC Communications: The Hearback Problem." In a footnote, Captain Monan credits *CALLBACK* with the first use of the term

*The asterisk is used throughout to denote reporters' comments as quoted in the bulletin.

"hearback"; I printed a collection of report excerpts in that same No. 11 (May 1980) quoted above describing controller-missed readbacks and using the newly coined word as the heading:

Hearback

On the subject of radio communication, we have had a lot to say about the importance of reading back clearance and instructions. "A clearance is not a clearance until it has been heard and acknowledged," "Okay" is not ok, and all that. It might also be said that an acknowledgment is not an acknowledgment until IT has been heard and understood.

A pilot, told to turn left after takeoff, turned right because "that's what they usually give us on this departure." He had acknowledged "right turn after takeoff" and his readback had not been corrected by the controller, who heard what he expected to hear. Or thought he did.

Controller report to ASRS: "Aircraft 'A' departed Runway 9 Left, IFR, assigned 1500'. I gave him 'radar contact' and told him to climb to and maintain 2000'. I was working Aircraft 'B' ten miles northeast, level at 3000, inbound to land. The pilot of 'A' acknowledged my transmission but said, 'climb and maintain 3000.' I did not catch him saying '3000' and rogered his transmission . . . When I next noticed the altitude readout of 'A' I saw that he was at 2600' in close proximity to 'B', level at 3000."

"Inbound we were cleared out of 10,000' to 6000 by Approach Control. We confirmed the altitude, wrote it down and dialed it in our Altitude Alert. On descent at 6800', we were instructed to climb and maintain 8000 immediately. We acknowledged and started to climb back through 7000 and were told to maintain 7000 at that time. Approach said we were not cleared to 6000. Copilot stated he acknowledged clearance to 6000."

". . . received clearance to climb to 8000'. I looked at First Officer and said, 'He did say 8000, didn't he?' F/O said, 'Yes, 8000 feet.' I read the clearance back to Center and believe I received an acknowledgment. As we passed 4000, Center requested our altitude and was given 4000 feet. He then said we had been cleared to 3000 and gave us and another aircraft immediate turns."

These faulty hearbacks can occur at both ends of the chain. Controller says, "Right," pilot reads back, "Left," and is uncorrected. Or pilot says, "Descending to six," controller reads back, "One six," and is uncorrected. Either way it can mean trouble. An interesting letter tells in detail about a flightcrew that believed it had been cleared for an ILS approach to the left runway; radios were set and procedures reviewed accordingly when, in fact, the clearance had been for the parallel right. ATIS had reported approaches in progress on the left, the crew was expecting that, and their acknowledgment went unchallenged. Fortunately the error was caught in time to avert a conflict, but consider the implication of a go-around using the wrong procedure.

Sometimes these things are caused by partially blocked transmissions, sometimes, as HARP said, by similar-flight-number confusion; usually somebody was complacent or distracted. Dangerous, no matter how caused! Listen with care!

Variants of the "not listening" or "hearing what you want to hear" syndromes, as reported by pilots and controllers, fall into the "hearback" category and have been noted in many issues of *CALLBACK*. The bottom line, as it were, concludes a report from an embarrassed pilot: "The pilot should listen better, but so must the controller." In March 1984 (*CALLBACK* No. 57), I devoted most of a page to the subject, using two controller reports and two from pilots to emphasize the importance of effective hearback and to highlight that it sometimes takes more than one bad hearback to snarl things up:

*Inbound air carrier was cleared to descend to 12,000'. Pilot read back 10,000. Center missed it. The aircraft checked in with me (Approach Control) out of 16,000 for 10,000. Normal altitude for this route is descending to 12,000 and I missed the 10,000. A minute or so later another aircraft departed. . . . When they were about 6 or 7 miles apart, it finally dawned on me that the inbound was level at 10,000 and the outbound was about 9500, climbing. I turned the inbound left; by the time they were on parallel courses separation was down to less than the required 3 miles. In my opinion the Center controller, the flightcrew, and I, the Approach controller, all heard what we wanted to hear. There were 6 or more aircraft on the frequency at the time, but the tape of the report by the aircraft descending to 10 was quite clear.

I was working Center sectors which comprise airspace adjacent to Approach Control airspace. Flight "XY," inbound, was cleared to cross an intersection at the Approach Control boundary at or below 15,000, to maintain 12,000. His readback was, "Roger, Airline 'YX' (numbers transposed) is cleared to cross at or below 15 for 10. I failed to notice that the pilot read back the wrong altitude, though I did notice that he used the wrong callsign (having transposed the digits). Subsequently the aircraft, at 10,000', passed within about 2 miles of an opposite-direction air carrier climbing out.

This suggests that the Approach controller must also have failed to notice that the inbound aircraft was descending to 10 (his Mode C was operational). . . . Problem is that a pilot and at least two controllers (I being one of them) failed to insist on clear, "by-the-book," communications. I suspect that the erroneous callsign may have served to subconsciously divert my attention from the rest of the readback, which contained a more significant error. Furthermore, the Approach controller must have failed to verify the clearance altitude when the aircraft checked in, or to notice when the aircraft continued its descent through the usual altitude of 12,000'.

Descent clearance was received from Center (at this time a Flight Attendant was passing a meal tray over the Flight Engineer to the Captain. Both were necessarily distracted). First Officer, flying, received clearance to descend from Flight Level 330 to FL190 and acknowledged according to standard procedure. Passing FL270, Center called and inquired about our altitude. F/O responded, "Flight Level 270," and Center advised that the clearance was to FL 290. . . . F/O advised Center that he understood the clearance was to FL190 and acknowledged same. Captain and F/E were distracted at the moment of altitude clearance. Obviously, in a three-person crew, at least two should be monitoring communications. Sometimes distractions occur for brief moments, which can scarcely be avoided. The F/O readback of the altitude clearance should have provided the necessary crosscheck—but didn't.

Departed, assigned heading 225 degrees, climb to 5000, change to Departure Control. Departure cleared flight to FL230, heading 120, which I read back. As we were turning, the heading of 120 did not sound correct, so I asked for verification. Departure asked our present heading; I said 150 degrees. He said, "Turn right to 160," and that the correct heading should have been 210. I replied that I had read back 120 and had not been challenged.

Muddled perception of altitude, heading, and airspeed assignments are common and often figure in ASRS reports. One of the earliest to be noted by *CALLBACK* was "an occurrence in which a flightcrew assumed a heading of 210 degrees instead of a speed of 210 knots. This was unsnarled without dire results; the interesting thing was the cause of the misunderstanding: The controller intending to give the speed restriction rose from his chair to coordinate with his adjacent mate, lost his balance, and hit the neighboring controller on the head with his telephone, thus initiating the confusion." A *CALLBACK* article headed "The Numbers Game" was devoted largely to incidents like this one, some with more serious outcomes. Before printing examples, I wrote, "Anything to do with flying seems to be extraordinarily dependent on numbers—altitudes, altimeter settings, flight levels, headings, courses, Mach numbers, weights, CG's, airway numbers, flight numbers, frequencies, numbers, numbers, numbers. . . . A large proportion of the ASRS report intake involves number trouble."

Throughout their careers, pilots and air traffic controllers alike are subject to frequent exhortation on the subject of phraseology and the need to observe standardized conventions and forms of expression. For various reasons, members of both groups fall into bad habits that lead to clearance misinterpretation and risk-laden incidents. Altitude "busts"—deviations from assigned altitudes—constitute the single largest anomaly reported to ASRS (and carried in *CALLBACK*) and are frequently triggered by faulty communication. Clearance deviation accounts show many permutations; a substantial number involve hearing—or imagined hearing, by pilots and controllers—of expected information.

A report of phraseology-engendered confusion was the inspiration for one of *CALLBACK*'s most appropriate quotations: "Well, if I called the wrong number, why did you answer?" (from a James Thurber cartoon). In the reported case, the aircraft commenced to climb to FL290, when the controller intended a heading change to 290 degrees. The reporting captain offered a recipe for preventing this sort of error: "1. Controllers use the words 'heading,' 'degrees,' 'flight level,' 'airspeed,' etc. when giving instructions which include numbers. 2. Closer attention by flightcrew and requesting verification if in doubt prior to taking any action." Another validation of that advice:

*Received clearance to descend to FL330. The next clearance—as we understood it—was to descend to two seven zero which, we believe, we read back as "Leaving 330 for 270." Descent was started; at FL325 Center requested our altitude, which we reported as 32,500. Center requested that we return to FL330. . . . We were then requested to slow to two seven zero. . . . Evidently the misunderstanding occurred between Flight Level clearance and speed reduction clearance; Center deleted the word "knots" after the initial speed reduction request to two seven zero.

Some controllers of long experience rely on the maxim, "Never mention an altitude unless you want the pilot to go there." Official ATC procedures are specific about how and when this may be done, but misunderstandings do take place, and the usual result is busted altitudes—and sometimes conflicts:

*We were at FL230 when ATC called out (we thought) "Converging traffic; descend to 220." During our slow descent to 220, ATC called, "I read your altitude at 22,300. Climb back to FL230." I should have been more alert to possible misunderstanding. . . . We found out the other traffic was at 220.

I issued "traffic at ten o'clock, three miles, level at 6000, to pass under you." Aircraft acknowledged, "We have him." I observed his altitude readout at 6800 and asked him if he was maintaining 7000 as instructed. He stated he read back 6000.

The outcome was, in ASRS terminology, LTSS and, as is mandatory in such occurrences, an ATC internal inquiry. *CALLBACK* reported another similar altitude bust/LTSS incident in the same column, this one perhaps, in ASRS parlance, a "PC" (Potential Collision) or even an NMAC. Chapter 5 deals with those.

*I called traffic: "You have crossing traffic at 6000, two o'clock, ten miles. Aircraft replied, "What's his altitude?" I responded, "He's at 6000." Later, a playback of the tape revealed that the pilot interpreted my traffic information as a clearance and replied, "Roger, we're out of 7000 for 6000." I did not hear or acknowledge this—for whatever reason. . . . The aircraft reported, "We just had an airplane go by our nose." I replied, "Roger, that's the traffic I called to you at 6000." Aircraft replied, "He sure was!"

CALLBACK No. 19 (January 1981) included a column emphasizing the potential hazard attendant on less than precise terminology—and less than precise listening:

One Little Word

"Pilot reported by his fix six minutes later than his ETA; he gave no estimate for the next checkpoint, so I had to ask for one. He replied, 'We'll be there in 39.' I wrote in '39' as his estimate. . . . I missed one little word—'IN'—which would have given a clue about separation. Proper position reporting, non-radar, requires a ZULU clock-time estimate be given. Many pilots do not know that, or want me to do their addition for them."

Happened to be another airplane in the neighborhood. LTSS.

"Prior to arrival at the VOR the crew was told to 'expect' 210 knots at 4 miles. Copilot, flying, missed that call due to descending and thunderstorm avoidance. Upon arrival at the VOR, the Captain said, '210 knots at 4' and began making a PA. . . . The copilot left his altitude and started down, believing it to mean 4000 feet. Shortly thereafter the controller said to descend to 7000."

"During descent the pilot was told to 'slow to 170, descent in 4 miles.' . . . We understood 'slow to 170, descend to 4,' and started descent. At 9500 the controller advised us to maintain 10,000."

"Air carrier cleared via heading 180 degrees to intercept 034 degree radial; turned northeast on radial in face of another aircraft at same altitude. I had to descend that aircraft immediately without coordination due to fact that first aircraft was no longer on my frequency (pilot later explained that he confused RADIAL 034 with HEADING 034)."

LTSS.

"Aircraft receives ATC clearance: 'Position and hold.' Readback is: 'On the hold.' Given any crew or ATC distraction, such a non-standard readback could be easily misinterpreted as: 'On the go,' a common, though non-standard, response to takeoff clearance."

You have been warned!

Many of the errors attributed to faulty communication actually involve a combination of factors. Very early in *CALLBACK*'s run (No. 4, October 1979) the phenomenon known as "clipping" occupied part of an article also discussing callsign problems. Later (in No. 31, January 1982) a complete column was devoted to the topic:

A pilot climbing through FL260 was sure he had been cleared to the requested 370, but some little question in his mind caused him to ask Center for confirmation. ". . . There returned a resounding 'Negative! Maintain 260'," which, with a mild forward push, he was able to do. He was quite certain of what he had heard, but there were other transmissions on the air and he suspected possible interference or blockage of part of the clearance he believed was for him. He tells us about it very graphically: "This occurrence proves that even though one is alert to a situation, one can still get a bloodied nose for not being triple cautious in today's environment."

He mentions the need for speed—hence the rapid-fire "push-the-button-to-speak" syndrome we all tend to fall into. I see/hear a very pronounced tendency toward clipping the first half-word from many controller transmissions. The switch not closing quickly enough or the transmitter not at peak power when the first word is uttered can have very much to do with who is going to be listening to the remainder of the first phrase. A missing identifier causes many repeats every hour of every day.

"However, this is by no means a one-sided fault and as a whole, the boys with the spoked eyeballs do a very creditable job. We couldn't leave home without them!" Thoughtful advice, offered enjoyably.

Clipped

"Approach control advised us that there was a commuter on the frequency with the same flight number as ours. . . . We were told to descend to 3000. We acknowledged with our full sign and began descent. As we passed through 10,000 Approach asked our altitude. We told him 10,000 and he said to stop descent there. We had received and verified a clearance to 3000, but the clearance had been intended for the commuter!"

How come? Everybody in the act knew there were two airplanes around with the same numbers and that vigilance was called for. Reporting pilot thinks the company name could have been garbled and feels that similarly designated flights should not be operating in the same area at the same time. Pretty impractical, though, with all the traffic there is, and all the possible combinations of airlines and flight numbers. Maybe there was a little "hearback" problem, with the controller not catching the full ID during the clearance readback.

Maybe there was another little hex at work here, though. Hear the words of Methuselah: During the dark ages, students at the world's greatest flying school (name on request from the Editor) were subjected to a course (among many others) called "Com-Pro," intended to teach communications procedure. Besides wiggling semaphore flags, the fledglings were taught the rudiments of the new-fangled ground-to-air wireless (sometimes known as "radio"). One of the useful bits of lore imparted was that, perhaps for various reasons, there was a noticeable time lag between the keying of a transmitter (pressing the microphone button) and the actual emission from the antenna of an intended communication. There was talk, which may or may not have been technically correct, of "antenna loading" and of "clipping" of the beginning of a transmission. Relays had to actuate—things like that.

As a consequence of all that, many pilots of the era always prefaced their transmissions with an introductory word or two. "Hello Tower, hello Tower, this is. . . ." Often they repeated a word or two. "Roger 627, roger 627, understand cleared to land." In other words, we didn't just push the button and rip into our callsign—or the call of the intended recipient.

Anyway, there is still a time lag between the keying of a mike and the transmitter's actual output. Many controllers use a foot treadle to bring alive a boom mike; pilots either press a mike button or, in many cases, another button on the yoke. If you want to ensure that those first important words are not clipped, press and allow a little time for things to commence to happen. Even if you don't have to wait, nowadays, for the vacuum tubes to warm up. Without going into all this detail, the Controllers' Handbook (7110.65) touches on the problem of correct identification of aircraft with similar callsigns. Controllers are directed, in cases of potential confusion of this sort, to restate the callsign after the flight number—like this: "Commuter 627 Commuter. . . ." In any event, as our reporter says: ". . . we pilots and controllers must exercise extreme care and caution when callsigns conflict."

Communication takes other than vocal forms. The proper use of transponders can be as vital to safety as correct voice procedure. Misuse of the "Mode C" feature, which allows ATC to determine altitudes of radar-tracked aircraft for separation purposes, can be serious. In a column headed, "Cheating," *CALLBACK* gave some inexcusable—and saddening—instances:

"I was working Departure radar. Inbound traffic is at 6000'; traffic departing is assigned 5000' by Tower. I identified a light transport and reconfirmed maintain 5000. I noticed inbound traffic at 6000. I called traffic and told the light transport again to maintain 5000. I then noticed his altitude readout as 5300. I asked him his altitude and got no answer and the altitude section of his tag went blank. After the targets merged and passed, the light transport reported level at 5000 and his reading returned (curious!). In the meantime another controller, working the other aircraft, said that his aircraft asked about the traffic—and then stated that the traffic was ABOVE him.

Other controller's report confirmed this one. Fortunately, this sort of misbehavior appears to be rare, but is evidently practiced by some misguided pilots:

"With rumors abounding that pilots will be violated and get fined for altitude variances of 300', it has now become my policy— and that of other company pilots—to turn off the Mode C if an altitude is missed. Aside from the fact that we might hit some jerk doing the same thing, I feel pushed into this situation by controller attitude. . . ."

What about pilot "attitude"? Controllers are charged with the responsibility of maintaining safe separation between aircraft— according to rules that exist for good reason. Reporter's policy is dishonest and unprofessional. We hope he's set straight before somebody gets hurt.

The article continued with another flagrant example, concluding, "I believe the pilot lied to me in telling me he was at 10,000', when he really busted the altitude, as the ARTS readout showed. . . . I had conflicting traffic. . . . The only way this type of error can be eliminated is by more serious awareness by pilots of altitude restrictions." And by more awareness of the integrity demanded by the flying profession.

The ubiquitous—and dreaded—altitude busts are always with us at ASRS and the reasons—and excuses—for these deviations are many and various. Very often the altitude alerting system is cited as the culprit in these violations—a position not usually substantiated by the facts. *CALLBACK* has lectured much on the subject:

Let Back-ups Be Back-ups

"Altitude Alerter malfunctioned prior to departure, but crew failed to institute a 'mental checklist' to compensate. Departure issued 7000—deviation to 8000 occurred. How many times have you heard this one before? P.S. And how many times have you heard a fail-safe solution?"

Answer to question #1: A great many. Question #2: None. Nearest approach to solution for problems of this sort is constant alertness. Awareness and vigilance are the keys to safety. The engineers cannot provide those things, although they have devised many schemes intended to cover their lack. At ASRS we have developed concern that Altitude Alerters, Low Quantity Lights, Ground Proximity Warning Systems, Takeoff Warning Horns, and such things may have engendered excessive reliance on the electromechanical messages to the detriment of proper human attention to the primary instruments. For instance:

"Cleared to FL350. We then requested a routing change to a more direct route. Some discussion occurred. . . . The controller then cleared us via the flight plan route, maintain FL310. We asked if 310 would be our final altitude and he said no. Because of the amount of talk, we failed to crank 310 into the Altitude Reminder and—I hate to admit it—I flew through 310 to 328, at which point the controller asked if we had been cleared to 310. I levelled and began a descent. . . . I of course committed this error. I intend to be more diligent with the Altitude Reminder in the future, since I have learned to depend on it. . . .

"Climbing to FL330, with clearance to deviate as necessary. The Altitude Alert System was completely inoperative. . . . Autopilot was coupled in the climb mode. I recall noting FL315 while making turns; we broke out and I noticed I was at FL337 and still climbing. . . . We had had a malfunctioning Altitude Alert System the day before and this day it was out altogether. I thought I had covered all the bases by asking the Second Officer to be alert and back up our callouts, besides being especially alert up front. . . . It worked for two days except that this time we all three overlooked the FL320 callout, and arrived at 330. I have always tried not to use the altitude monitor as a crutch by calling out altitudes before the warning went off. I missed this one."

In days gone by, pilots often noted altitude assignments on handy knee pads or on little clip boards attached to the yoke. Such primitive systems worked well but, to be fair, other factors served to render today's required precision less necessary in those days. Prop-driven transports didn't gain or lose altitude as rapidly as do modern jets; less traffic meant less chance of conflict; simpler procedures obviated the complex multi-change routings of today; besides, before radar the controllers had no way of knowing about deviations. Unless the pilots told them. Ha! Things are better now in many ways, but the need for altitude awareness still exists— more than ever—and complacent reliance on secondary instrumentation is not a reliable substitute. Back-ups, yes; fail safe, no.

A very candid pilot reported to ASRS that he had flown above his altitude "because he was thinking about the Public Address announcement he was getting ready to make and lost concentration on levelling off." A good many more, as described in the chapter on automation, blame their troubles on the malfunction or failure of some new gadgetry, others on breakfast being served or incorrect altimeter settings, and the like. The rapid climb capability of the new-generation jets has been responsible for many an overshoot in the hands of pilots not yet accustomed to it. An exasperated plaint came from a captain: "I have read many of *CALLBACK*'s altitude bust reports and have always thought that it was an error in judgment on someone's part. I will have to watch the music closer while the other guy is playing the piano."

Since this chapter has dealt largely with communication problems, I'd like to close it with reports of two unusual communications incidents, one in 1985, the other two years later, proving (again) that there is nothing new.

> He That Hath Ears to Hear, Let Him Hear
>
> St. Mark

Today's aviation safety record is made possible in part by the multiple redundancies built into the system. Here's an account of a back-up we hadn't heard of before:

"During the time the First Officer was trying to get the ATIS it was being updated, which took several minutes. While he was off the ATC frequency, the ear piece for my headset disconnected from the headset and therefore I had lost communication with Center for one to two minutes. My passengers were hooked up to the ATC channel of the Audio Entertainment System and had heard Center trying to call us. They reported this to the Flight Attendants who, in turn, came to the cockpit to check on us. We discovered our disconnected headset at that point and re-established contact with ATC. The loss of communication was perhaps very short in duration, but we had travelled 10–15 miles. The design of the ear piece was obviously partly at fault in that the plastic tube is just pushed into a threaded fitting on the headset and not permanently fixed or threaded into it (we carry this earpiece as part of our personal gear)."

Stay Tuned

"Even Captains on Modern Giant Airliners have to leave the cockpit now and then for 'physiological reasons.' My widebody plane was equipped with five astro-potties; it was also equipped with a switch that allows the passengers to eavesdrop on air/ground communications. This switch was ON throughout the flight. When the 'physiological reason' became very pressing I went to the back of the aircraft, as I knew both astro-potties there were working. This also allowed me to check for old buddies aboard and to find out if my knees still worked. Returning up the aisle through the coach section, a passenger stopped me to say (with a big grin and a pat on the back) that 'Center is trying to call you! You'd better get back up there!' I went back to the cockpit to find the copilot talking to a flight attendant. His radio volume had mysteriously been turned off! Did an itinerant gremlin cause this lever to go off, or . . . ?"

No gremlin; no mystery. ASRS analyst, a retired Captain experienced in this type of aircraft, has explained that the advanced-technology aircraft audio selector panel, on the central console, is fitted with unusually long levers to control receiver volume. These can be moved inadvertently—and very easily. Our man says he has done it himself by snagging a cuff while turning in his seat to speak to a flight deck visitor. Incidentally, the Captain who reported this adventure answered the first question on the ASRS Report Form (Reporter's Role During Occurrence?) with "INNOCENT!"

5

He Was Smoking a Big Cigar

Given a choice between a minor altitude deviation and a midair collision I will always choose the altitude deviation.

We are all very happy that we are able to make this report.

CALLBACK often carries brief fragments (usually referred to as "nuggets") from ASRS reports; two of them, submitted by pilots describing narrowly averted encounters with other aircraft, lead off this chapter and set the tone of its theme: closer-than-desired proximity of aircraft in flight. The first quotation was headed "Good Thinking" and obviously expresses a majority view; the heading for the second was "Thanksgiving." Both may remind old-timers of the well-worn remark, "A midair can spoil your whole day."

In the late 1960s the FAA, concerned about the increasing risk of aircraft colliding in flight and the growing number of informal complaints of such events, instituted a reporting program intended to gather formal data. Pilots were supplied with detailed forms soliciting full information about any occurrences the participants thought involved hazardously close spacing between two aircraft. The scheme died an early death because of apprehension among airmen who believed that such information might conceivably prove incriminating, despite FAA's promise of confidentiality and nonpunitive intent; however, the program gave wide exposure to the term "near-miss." Although in use for many years, "near-miss" is viewed by language purists as an illogical contradiction: "Nearly-missed" implies "hit." Thus, the accepted term has come to be "near midair collision" in American usage or, commonly, NMAC (the British term "air-miss" seems to cover the situation more precisely, as does the French "quasi-collision").

Semantics aside, the threat of the coming together in the air of two aircraft has been of concern to aviators since the earliest days of flying, but the "big sky—little airplane" theory ensured that such events would be rare. However—according to a (probably) apocryphal story told by ASRS Project Manager (and ex-Ohioan) Ed Cheaney, in the year 1896 there were two automobiles in the State of Ohio. Inevitably, in due course, the two crashed into one another. Also inevitably, with the steady increase in the number of aircraft, and in the number of people flying in them, some of them do come together—usually with disastrous results. Rules and regulations, and the introduction of ATC systems—with their trained controllers, radio communications, computers, and radar—have worked well to keep aircraft separated, particularly in nonvisual–flight rule weather, but the occasional midair collision still takes place. Thanks to ATC's superb performance, coupled with the efforts of the (mostly) highly trained airmen using the system, the dreaded midair and the corollary NMAC are extremely rare events in instrument meteorological conditions; in the more generally prevailing visual meteorological conditions, the rule is "See-and-avoid." The geography of the United States with great distances between centers of population, the affluence of recent years, and the deregulation-stimulated proliferation of airlines have combined to fill the big sky with a never-dreamed-of swarm of flying machines; the occasional spectacular collision has loomed larger to focus the attention of airmen on the ever-present possibility of an NMAC.

Since FAA's well-intentioned near-miss reporting program failed in its purpose, it fell to NASA's ASRS to become a collection agency for accounts of aerial conflicts. Almost invariably such conflicts are related to human failure to perform correctly; thus conflict accounts fit into the ASRS-mandated study of human factors as they relate to flying safety. For the purposes of analysis, ASRS classifies conflicts into three distinct categories:

1. *Less than Standard Separation.* In LTSS cases two aircraft flying under instrument flight rules come within the ATC-specified separation distance. This varies with altitude, type of airspace, and so on, but is commonly three to five miles horizontally or one to two thousand feet vertically. The failure of required separation may be due to error on the part of pilots or of controllers; more often than not the loss is a technical matter of precise spacing and does not constitute an actual hazard, although it may result in disciplinary action against the responsible controller or pilot.

2. *Potential Conflict.* Two aircraft are flown closer together than good practice would dictate, although not so near as to cause a distinct hazard.

3. *Near Midair Collision.* Aircraft come within less than 500 feet of one another, or drastic evasive action is taken to avoid collision.

In category 1 an ATC "operational error" has taken place, either because a pilot has deviated from the terms of a clearance or the controller has failed to take action to ensure separation. An ASRS report (CYA) explaining the circumstances often ensues but, since pilots have no way of knowing that a merely technical separation standard has been violated, LTSS reports come predominantly from controllers. It should be noted that regulations make clear the obligation of pilots to "see-and-avoid" regardless of controller responsibility. The other categories involve pure see-and-avoid, although ATC advisories may on occasion mitigate risk. Many reports of such incidents are also submitted; often "multiples" are received that describe the event from the viewpoints of a pilot and a controller or of pilots of both aircraft (although a controller may report apparently threatening proximity, the "merged" or "overlapping" targets feature of his radar equipment makes it impossible to accurately assess narrow separation; valid NMAC-classed events require pilot-reported miss distance or the controller's repeat of a pilot's estimate).

CALLBACK No. 58, in April 1984, addressed a new worry—one that impelled controllers, in order to invoke a waiver of the disciplinary action attendant on loss-of-separation incidents, to report marginal LTSS incidents that previously would not have stimulated an ASRS submission. The same worry affected pilots, producing in them an apprehensive sensitivity to relatively minor clearance deviations and vastly increasing the ASRS intake of altitude "bust" reports.

To Err Is Human . . .
To Be Observed Is Now Computerized

Air Traffic Controllers are human too. Most find no glee in calling official attention to the pilot misdemeanors they observe. Reports to ASRS attest that they avoid doing so when possible; nevertheless deviations from mandated performance—particularly those contributing to loss of required separation between aircraft—must be reported and investigated. In the past, such deviations were detected by "seaman's eye"—a controller's estimate of the radar targets on his scope. The "Conflict Alert" feature of the ATC computer/radar signalled a possible impending anomaly in time for application of corrective measures, but no precise mechanism existed for immediate identification of separation loss and accurate measurement of actual distance. Things are changing. ATC has established a stringent Quality Assurance Program (QAP) in an effort to improve performance in general and to minimize separation compromise in particular. A key feature of QAP, known as "Computer Detected Error," is a new application of existing equipment which provides a positive and accurate indication of questionable situations. Many Air Route Traffic Control Centers have instituted the new procedure (all soon will have done so). Controllers have coined ironic nicknames to describe this new capability. It is known, in various ATC facilities, by such sobriquets as "Big Brother," "Squeal-a-Deal," "Lie Detector," and "Snitch Patch." A concerned and thoughtful controller has submitted an ASRS report which illustrates the new era and may provide information useful to pilots:

"Aircraft 'A' was northeast-bound to a nearby destination in another Center's area. Aircraft 'B' was north-northwest-bound to another destination in the same Center area as Aircraft 'A.' Aircraft 'A' came on my frequency at Flight Level 250, Aircraft 'B' at FL180. 'A' was cleared to descend and maintain FL190. Each aircraft was pointed out to the other as traffic. 'A' acknowledged clearance correctly. As 'A' was passing behind 'B' the Conflict Alert was activated and the altitude indicated FL186. Pilot of 'A' was immediately queried as to his altitude and his clearance altitude was reiterated. Pilot acknowledged that he went through the altitude assigned (FL190) and that the autopilot was recovering. . . . Another aspect of this incident is that the receiving Center has, as ATC personnel refer to it, a "Snitch." In case you're not aware of it, this is a computer feature that immediately reads out any situation where there is less than required separation. . . . Conflict Alert merely indicates the possibility of less than adequate separation impending; Snitch says it has occurred. In the past, deviations could be overlooked if nobody complained; with Snitch it is impossible to overlook the situation. Pilots should be made aware of this, since their mistakes could result in action being taken against them regardless of how the controller feels about the situation. In this case there was more than two miles horizontal and 400 feet vertical separation at the closest point so there was no real danger—but who knows what could have happened? As the controller, I was completely in the clear but I think pilots should be made aware of Snitch. . . . As a general rule pilots and controllers have a good relationship. In situations like this it was not the controller who turned the situation in, but Snitch. If pilots suffer penalties in situations like this (suspension, etc.) don't blame the controller. . . . It is out of the controller's hands."

Pilots may sometimes feel that a minor clearance deviation should not warrant a violation action. The report quoted above and others like it illuminate the hazard possibilities in noncompliance. QAP is now on the job. It should be viewed as an aid to ensure professional performance by both pilot and controller communities. Remember—QAP will be observing and noting lapses.

Although LTSS and nonthreatening PC incidents far outnumber NMAC events in the ASRS database (and in the real world), the latter frequently give rise to colorful accounts from the pilots involved. A PC may be alarming and may call for action to prevent closer approach, but it will not affect the blood pressure of an experienced pilot appreciably; LTSS may pass entirely unnoticed (many ASRS reports from controllers display annoyance that, though action was taken to prevent loss, the snitch machine has been activated to nail them with a separation of 4.8 miles instead of the regulation five). The true NMAC is rare, but it is likely to be memorable. Most long-time professional pilots have experienced—and can recall vividly—one or two in their careers. *CALLBACK* has carried some NMAC tales worthy of note.

Issue No. 12 (June 1980) contained a column headed (thanks to the poet Lowell) "And What Is So Rare as a Day in June?/Then, If Ever, Come Perfect Days." The article discussed a number of incidents reported to ASRS in which the reporters blamed the felicitous weather conditions for their failure to perform up to standard. Following a couple of controller narratives of separation losses, the column continued with this comment and a pilot's report narrative:

The Blue Yonder was really wild that day. Not all the altitude deviations involve the dreaded LTSS (Less than Standard Separation); some are merely nuisances. Others are pretty fraught— ". . . The aircraft passed directly underneath me at what I estimate as 100 ft. vertical separation. The pilot was wearing sunglasses, white shirt and black tie, and had a boom mike at the time I saw him. Credit goes to the ATC controller who monitored the situation very well and issued appropriate action." We read of one in which the aberrant pilot was described as smoking a large cigar!

CALLBACK's first NMAC story appeared in issue No. 3 (September 1979) and described an encounter between a light twin and a small aircraft in an airport traffic pattern. The twin's pilot had received clearance through an airport traffic area; unfortunately he was tuned to the wrong frequency and consequently conflicted with traffic in the pattern at an airport not far from the one in which he erroneously thought he was flying. The following month brought a report from an air carrier captain telling of sighting two hang gliders at his altitude on his downwind leg. "We went between them as we had no time for evasive action." Chapter 7 deals with *CALLBACK*'s "Good Grief" series; many of the incidents appearing under that heading (and reprinted in the chapter) are spectacular near-midairs. The phrase was used initially in issue No. 8 (February 1980) as a comment on a report of an airliner and a small jet that had passed within 100 feet of each other; the circumstance causing my exasperated exclamation was that the NMAC occurred in the high-altitude positive control area where all aircraft must be on instrument flight rules clearances and must be equipped with operating transponders. The small jet met neither of these caveats and its presence was consequently unknown to ATC.

Variations and permutations on the NMAC theme seem to be virtually limitless, although many reported to ASRS bear similarities. A number have involved hang gliders and there have been several reports from pilots astonished to discern parachutists hurtling by their windows. A few reports tell of narrowly averted collisions with weather balloons and there have been several complaints of large radio-controlled model airplanes hazardously intruding in airspace that might be thought to be the realm of full-scale machines. In addition to hang gliders, sailplanes occasionally figure in conflicts with powered aircraft. In one *CALLBACK* story the pilot of a small airplane writes,

"Climbing out when out of the corner of my eye I saw something on my left. As I turned to look, I saw a rope dangling above me, just off my left wing tip. Before I could wonder what ropes are doing hanging from the sky, the tow plane showed up, in a steep dive, no more than 25 feet from me. I don't think the pilot saw me, as he almost dove into me. It was impossible for me to see him before, since he came from above and behind me . . . no time for any evasive action. . . . I became worried about the glider that had apparently just been released, and made 90 degree turns to left and right looking for it, and looked up as well as I could, but never located it."

Aircraft performing aerobatic maneuvers often stray into the paths of others bent on more prosaic business. "ATC called traffic at ten o'clock. . . . Directly out of the sun a World War II fighter just missed hitting our aircraft on the Captain's side window. Evasive action." Another from an airliner Captain: "As we emerged from between the clouds the First Officer shouted, 'Look out!' and initiated a left bank. I looked up and sighted an aerobatic biplane about 200 feet above us. He was executing a sharp pull-up; his aircraft was about 90 degrees nose-up in a slight left turn . . . a loop/Immelman entry or a very sharp Chandelle. . . . The F/O stated, 'The other one went below us!' "

ASRS receives enthusiastic support from the U.S. military aviation services, who forward their own internal safety reports to NASA if there is civilian involvement. Naval and Air Force aircraft figure in NMAC incidents with civilian aircraft while inadvertently straying from their own operating areas ("spill-out" in our jargon)—and sometimes with civilians who have strayed ("spill-in") into those areas. And sometimes military/civil encounters happen in unrestricted areas. *CALLBACK* No. 40 (October 1982) carried a feature sermon on the subject:

The Sound of Freedom

That was the caption on an advertisement used some years ago by a well-known aircraft manufacturer. The picture showed a new military airplane in a spectacular climb-out over a sleeping city. It was intended to calm the agitated citizens awakened by the roar of the afterburners. This patriotic message did not get through to the agitated citizens, wide-awake and busy flying their civilian aircraft, who sent the following reports to ASRS. Our country's military services (in which several ASRS staff members have served with pride) have always been staunch supporters of the program, and we are well aware of the superior abilities of their pilots and of their need for constant training. Notwithstanding, the succession of reports we receive like these impel us to suggest to the military pilots that they exercise utmost caution when their training requirements take them near areas where civilians may be flying. A corollary to this is that civilian pilots must exercise the same degree of care if their routes take them close to areas where military activities may be anticipated. Reminder to military pilots: Just missing isn't good enough; try not to alarm. Reminder to civilian pilots: Check the status of military areas and routes; keep away if possible. And all of you: Keep alert!

"I was in a forestry contract helicopter on a recon flight. We were climbing (at 500') slowly while flying down a valley about one mile wide with steep ridges on each side rising above the valley floor for 3–4000'. We observed a military jet on the far side of the valley at about our altitude. We were watching it when another one came around the ridge which extends into the valley and before any evasive action could be taken it was past us. It was in a steep bank in coming around the mountain. It missed us by 200' (below us). . . ."

"On climb at 17,900' I, looking out my right sliding window, saw two fighters at my altitude and less than 200 yards. One rolled inverted over us and the other dived below us. We missed the high one by less than 100 yards as we passed through 18,000. . . . I can't understand why they had to be doing their training in a climb corridor and be VFR at or near the transition altitude. They came so close that passengers heard their engines as they flew by."

"On departure we were advised by Center that military aircraft were operating to the west at 5000'. Level at 4000 we broke out into a clear area 4–5 miles across and I observed one fighter on the deck northbound and as I was about to tell Center this, a second fighter dove through my altitude directly ahead of my aircraft and about 250' away. I informed Center—and started shaking after my arrival at my destination. The military planes were not on Center frequency, common in the area of occurrence."

"I was on a low altitude survey flight, operating between 100' and 500' above the ground. At the moment of conflict I was approximately 100' AGL and 500' below the peak of a ridge, proceeding away from the ridge at 80 knots. I looked up through the windshield; a fighter's wingtips were visible in the side windows. It was VERY close! The fighter made no turns as it passed, leading me to believe I wasn't seen. I had been briefed that the training route was active and was vigilant when I was near it. How can I protect myself from behind from this very dangerous threat?"

ASRS analyst replies: Only answer to pilot's query is for him to be somewhere else when the training route is hot.

A dramatic counterpoint to complaints of military aircraft flying in territory claimed by the civil community is described in a Navy report carried in *CALLBACK* (and reprinted in Chapter 7) under the heading "Good Grief—#31" (May 1986). In this adventure the apparently irresponsible pilot of a light civil airplane, buzzing around an aircraft carrier maneuvering off the coast, came within 200 feet of a helicopter about to land on the ship. *At night!*

A later Navy report is reminiscent:

> Aircraft carrier inbound to port on homecoming visit. Midair collision hazards were created by approximately one dozen light civil aircraft flying in the vicinity of the carrier. These aircraft circled repeatedly while military helicopters were conducting flight operations from the deck of the carrier. At least three civil aircraft were at flight deck level and as close as 100 feet horizontally from the ship. The pilots of these aircraft were a hazard to themselves and to military aircraft operating in the area by creating a potential midair collision situation with other aircraft and a potential collision hazard with the carrier.

The air traffic controllers' strike in the summer of 1981 imposed a serious strain on all participants in the aviation system; while pilots and the curtailed controller staff cooperated mightily to make things work with minimum disruption and hazard, unwished-for anomalies cropped up with frequency. ASRS conflict reports described encounters, hitherto very unusual, between IFR aircraft in the Positive Control Area and others flying without flight plans in an effort to avoid clearance delays. In addition, many well-equipped general aviation aircraft, which before the strike would have been on filed flight plans and clearances, attempted to save delays by flying in the 10,000- to 18,000-foot stratum without filing. This practice placed considerable traffic unknown to ATC in areas of air carrier descent and climb activity and brought frequent queries from the conforming airmen regarding the failure of controllers to provide traffic advisories. There was also substantial misunderstanding concerning why, when conflicting traffic was called out, avoidance vectors were not provided.

CALLBACK No. 29 (November 1981) addressed these topics in several brief articles; one of these (headed "Ask—And Ye Shall Be Given") presented a number of such narratives and explained that not all traffic can be seen by controllers; an operating transponder will help to make you visible. Even if visible to ATC, not all traffic will be called out. It is the responsibility of pilots to take evasive action. A request for vectors-around will bring you suggested headings to keep you clear if the controller can manage it. "But SEE-AND-AVOID REMAINS THE PRIMARY RULE." John Donne's phrase, "No man is an island entire of itself," headed another column in the same *CALLBACK* issue dealing with other aspects of the congestion in the skies.

In the following issue (No. 30, December 1981), the front page was given over to a discussion of multiple reports of a single incident and features narratives from two pilots who nearly collided just as one was rotating for takeoff and the other was performing a late go-around. Each blamed the other for careless operation; they were probably both correct. A few months later I printed a typical account of the classic low-wing/high-wing conflict. It read in part:

*Severely VFR day. Both of us were playing with the radios (I was supposed to be flying; i.e., left seat). Did a quick left-to-right scan and peripheral vision caught something above. Directly overhead, not more than 50 feet, was a low-wing airplane. We were never able to ascertain if he saw us—maybe he did and climbed 50 feet or maybe it was not our time. Of interest here, the combination of courses and wind had each of us crossing from our blind spots. . . . Comment: I guess it is a matter of convenience and/or poor habit pattern that the guys with high-wing planes only look down and the guys with the low wing planes and bubble canopies only look up. Could this be a corollary to Murphy's Law?

CALLBACK commented that "wise old pilots keep Murphy at bay by looking up, down, and around, regardless of wing position." And keep on looking! The double NMAC is not unknown (nor is pilot gratitude for timely ATC traffic calls), as these selections from *CALLBACK* No. 36 (June 1982) and No. 73 (July 1985), respectively, prove:

Bang! Bang!

*Descending, cleared by Approach Control to 3000'. wx was 3500 broken, 10 miles, by ATIS and we were below clouds by 3000. Visibility was generally good except for patchy shadows caused by sunlight and clouds. When cleared to 1500', we began descent. Passing 2900, Approach said there was traffic, 12 o'clock, one mile, unreported VFR at 2800. Just then I saw the plane as it emerged from the shadows into sunlight and I took evasive action. The other plane never deviated and we cleared it by 100'. Then I saw a second plane just behind the first by ¼ mile and again took evasive action. . . . While sky conditions were reported good VFR and were as reported, it is hard to see in patchy shadow and bright light. Credit the approach controller for a timely call. I might not have seen the first one in time, and I was looking, as was the copilot. Contributing to the difficulty was near head-on approach with almost no relative movement. . . . A warning to planes that are under control is worth every bit of the controller's effort. P.S. I have already sent thanks through his supervisor.

Whoosh! There Goes Another One!

*I put the student under the hood and began to vector him for a practice VOR approach. We were just south of the airport and I was busy watching for traffic departing or approaching when I saw a silver-colored small airplane pass about 500' below us. I watched him for a moment to make sure he wasn't going to climb into us and then looked out the forward windscreen. When I looked out I saw an older small airplane 400 to 500 feet away at our two o'clock position. He too was at exactly 2500 feet! I told the student to descend to 2000 and fly heading 070. The other aircraft was moving at about our speed and did not appear to notice us at all.

Mention in *CALLBACK* of "scud running" brought several enquiries as to the meaning of the term. An NMAC account in issue No. 53 (November 1983) was offered in explanation and as an object lesson on the hazards inherent in the practice:

*Began descent in solid IMC. At approximately 7700' we were in indefinite precip with down—but no forward—visibility. Copilot said he had ground; as I looked up he said we had traffic head-on. I looked out through left window and saw a small aircraft pass under the left engine, estimated miss 100–150 feet. He was near base of clouds in light precip. Our forward visibility was less than one mile. The small aircraft continued southeast and we completed our approach, reaching good VFR approximately 6500 MSL. It was an interesting way to start the morning! The small aircraft was scud running over the foothills below radar but on final approach coarse.

Perhaps folly, perhaps inexperience, *CALLBACK* suggested "get-home-itis" may have been implicated, as it so often is in flying mishaps and almost-mishaps. Another sort of lesson was described in an earlier issue, with the comment that the flight instructor may have learned more than he taught:

*My student was a big man, probably 6'3", 210 lbs., with a lot of his weight from the waist up. I am 5'7", 150 lbs., with most of my length in my legs. The result was that, seated in the cockpit, he effectively blocked my vision port-side. When I instruct I have the habit of turning slightly cock-eyed (to the left) in my seat during cruise to facilitate conversation. I was busy instructing from this position when out of my left eye I saw another airplane pass 25 to 50 feet under our left wing (it had been coming toward us from the left). Because I was sitting turned slightly to the left I knew I was blind-sided on the right and frequently checked for traffic there (as well as in front and back). But I really had not realized how much of the left window this student blocked out. Obviously too much. Had we been at the same altitude the other aircraft would have hit us just aft of the cabin on the left side. No evasive action was taken; it all happened too fast. It happened because I failed to account for the need to rubber-neck around a larger-than-normal student in the left seat during a training session. To prevent recurrence: Keep a better lookout!

"Had we been at the same altitude," "There was no time for evasive action," "must keep a better lookout"—these are very familiar comments; they appear in hundreds of NMAC reports. Here is another aspect of the same-altitude situation, as reported to ASRS and printed in *CALLBACK:*

Lucky Error

*All pilots are taught from the time of the first pre-flight inspection to the very last flight that accidents are caused by poor piloting technique or through violation of some F.A.R. The following incident is an example of the direct opposite. . . . Based on the haze, I elected to file IFR. . . . Clearance was to climb and maintain 2000 feet etc. My front seat passenger was a non-pilot and very interested in viewing the area. As we closed on 2000 feet he pointed and asked, "Is that the stadium?" I looked long enough to identify the stadium and when I looked back, the altimeter read 2060. I throttled back, lowered the nose, lost about 50 feet, and the windshield was immediately filled with another aircraft. The other plane was at 2000 feet, crossing from my right to my left. It was so close that I could see the color of the pilot's shirt and see that he wore horn-rimmed glasses and a headset. I was also impressed that his plane must have had a very recent paint job. Had I been precise and on my assigned altitude we would have had a mid-air—absolutely no doubt about it. . . . I certainly am not advocating busting altitudes, but if I hadn't, I wouldn't be here to tell the tale.

CALLBACK commented, "The message is not that you should deviate from your clearance; it is—loud and clear—that constant vigilance is the key to safety in the air." That vigilance applies to—and is often exercised by—controllers as well as by airmen is apparent from testimony in many ASRS pilot reports giving credit to ATC for timely calls clearly averting imminent NMAC's. Some examples:

*We were in the clouds with occasional ground contact. I requested the First Officer to turn off the high intensity strobes in order to alleviate very bright reflection off the clouds. Approach Controller notified us of traffic at 2 o'clock, distance garbled. We did not see the traffic. A moment later she queried, 'Do you have the traffic?' and the First Officer picked up an intermittent target at 1:30 with a distinct red beacon—in and out of the clouds. First Officer asked Captain, "Do you have traffic over here?" I then sighted traffic converging at 1:30 and guessed that it was very close to our altitude. At this moment the Second Officer said in a loud voice, "Drop down!" and I immediately pushed forward at about zero "G," disconnecting the autopilot. The small aircraft was observed to pass directly overhead. . . . All three pilots observed at close range a single-engine, fixed-gear, high-wing aircraft with a bright red beacon. . . . The other aircraft was not using transponder and was close to the TCA . . . operating in controlled airspace in IFR conditions without clearance, thus jeopardizing the lives, in this case, of 231 people. I am convinced that an imminent collision was averted due to the persistence of the Approach Controller. Had she not called our attention to the traffic a second time, we would probably not have been focussing our attention, in IFR conditions at night, in the appropriate direction. Secondly, had we not turned off our strobes in the clouds we would never have picked out the small aircraft.

The captain added a plaintive note to his narrative: "Next day I asked the ATC supervisor on duty, 'How often do unauthorized aircraft penetrate your TCA?' He replied, almost blandly, 'Well, there were four on my shift last night.'" The second officer, also reporting, provided some vivid color: "Controller made a second callout with a lot more urgency in her voice. . . . In the time it took the First Officer to point out the traffic to the Captain, the situation changed dramatically. . . . Our closure rate was very rapid. . . . I clearly saw the rudder, horizontal stabilizer, and left side of the small airplane even though it appeared slightly fuzzy due to the thin clouds. . . . I was astounded at how rapidly the situation changed, requiring severe evasive action to avoid a collision. . . . There is no doubt in my mind that the ATC person saved our aircraft and the lives of all aboard."

*Controller gave us traffic at "11 o'clock, 2 miles, altitude unknown." We queried him, as we saw lower traffic at 12 o'clock, and he said, "No, traffic at 11 o'clock and closing." Simultaneously, my copilot and I spotted the small single-engine aircraft in a left turn at our 11 o'clock position. . . . I had to disconnect the autopilot and initiate an IMMEDIATE sharp pull-up to avoid a collision. He was close enough to read the numbers. . . . Our kudos to the controller, for had he not seen him on radar we would not have been able to pick him out. He blended into the background very well.

At 4000 feet ATC called, "Traffic 5 miles, 12 o'clock, 4200 feet. . . . First Officer and I were both looking and replied, "Negative contact." We kept looking . . . ATC called traffic 2 miles and suggested right turn. . . . At that time we saw the traffic, slightly higher, opposite direction. . . . A small aircraft, white with red trim, passed 100 feet to our right. All of this happened very fast. . . . He was at wrong altitude for his direction of flight. I feel that ATC did a good job of calling out traffic all along."

Approach Control called that we had traffic 11 to 12 o'clock, less than a mile. . . . I spotted the small aircraft as it came out from behind my front window and told the First Officer, who was flying, to pull up. . . . The quick call from the controller prevented us from hitting the other aircraft . . . and averted a major mid-air.

Controller called, "Traffic 1 o'clock, altitude unknown." Captain saw the small aircraft and yelled. I pulled off power, dove, and rolled right. It looked like we were going to hit him. The other airplane rolled hard over to the right—nearly inverted—and dove. . . . In this near mid-air the controller deserves the credit for a quick and accurate call-out.

As the preceding accounts show, NMAC incidents give rise to colorful and graphic descriptive accounts. Here are a few more expressive (and typical) comments culled from ASRS report narratives: "Had we levelled our wings to look for the traffic, you would have read about this in the newspapers!" "He was close enough that F/O saw shock when he looked up and saw us." "Flight Attendant entered the cockpit and stated that several passengers were upset about the near miss with another aircraft." "What is so startling about this is that, despite a vigilant scan, even looking away for just a few seconds can spell trouble." "Suddenly both right side passengers shouted and I looked out. . . . Went directly over our vertical stabilizer by five feet." "The person in the right seat pointed across my face and said, 'There he is!' All he saw was the landing gear go by."

Obviously, all near-midair collisions are undesirable events. A few are inevitable; in an environment full of moving objects, some are bound to move in close proximity. Many can be prevented by awareness on the part of participants; others by careful observance of regulations and procedures. Airborne collision avoidance systems, so long in development, will soon come into service and will doubtless contribute to a lessening of the NMAC hazard. Possibly alleviation of international tensions will eliminate a few frightening incidents—like this one, retold with fragments from flightcrew narratives:

*Oceanic Control confirmed radar contact on center line at FL330
[enroute to a Caribbean island destination]. We observed a large
four-engine aircraft crossing from left to right several miles ahead
at our altitude. . . . While watching, we heard a loud noise of tur-
bines passing aft of cockpit. Asked control if they had traffic; they
had no radar contact. . . . Flight attendants called and asked if
noise was another aircraft . . . particularly noisy in lower galley.
No markings observed. Both aircraft on southwest courses.

It had a long, thin wing with quite a droop, and four engines. . . . I heard a roar like a large propeller-driven aircraft
going by so close that I ducked my head. Looking out, I saw the
second aircraft in the 3 or 4 o'clock position at our altitude. . . .
Silver, with no discernible markings, and of a type I was not familiar with. Best guess is they were large Russian turboprops en
route to Cuba. Whatever they were, the fact that they were flying
through controlled airspace with no clearance and no transponder is totally unacceptable.

Perhaps a suitable subject for summit discussion?

6

Crashing the Gate

Received doctrine tells us—frequently—that a substantial proportion of aircraft crashes occur during the approach or landing phase of flight. Since true accidents are excluded from the agenda of NASA's Aviation Safety Reporting System, they are not discussed in this work. Nevertheless, each day's mail bag of ASRS incident reports bears accounts of potentially hazardous occurrences associated with activities before touchdown. Prominent among these are airman confessions that they failed to obtain landing clearance, usually studded with excuses for the omission. Many of these reported events did not entail actual danger; some were fraught with severe risk. All featured violation of regulations and of good procedure, regardless of the underlying reasons. *CALLBACK* first took note of these aberrations in August 1981, in issue No. 26 with a page of relatively harmless examples, each laid to a separate cause (or series of causes).

Crashing the Gate

Unannounced arrivals on the runways under their jurisdiction seldom receive a cheerful welcome from tower controllers; now and then hackles are raised and salty remarks ensue. The frequency of reports to ASRS confessing these pilot misdemeanors—all inadvertently committed and all caused by distractions that interrupted routine procedures—has been increasing. Time to take stock, pilots. Variations on the theme are many; the usual situation involves failure to switch radios from Approach to Tower frequency for one reason or another.

"Copilot was flying; I was working the radios. Approach Control cleared us for ILS. At 1500 feet we encountered a bird strike. Evidently I did not change over to Tower, as the bird strike distracted me. . . . The first time we recognized that we had landed without a clearance was when Ground Control said, 'The tower says you are cleared to land.' It is obvious that as Captain I should have made sure we were cleared to land, but I also think that Approach should have said something to us."

Now that would be nice, but it just isn't very often practical. Approach controllers are busy with their own fish to fry, are not necessarily—or even usually—located in the same area as the tower people, and do not monitor Tower radio traffic. Once they have shipped you to Tower, their active concern with you is ended. Some reporters claim that Tower could have let Approach know that you hadn't checked in, but that is asking a lot too. The local controllers have their own responsibilities—takeoff releases, landing traffic—and are not concerned with you until you make that vital call as you pass the final fix—usually over the Outer Marker.

"I (First Officer) was flying. The right windshield heat failed en route and the windshield started frosting up on my side. . . . We were cleared for a visual approach to the right runway, to follow a widebody landing on the left. After turning final it was apparent that my windshield was too frosted for me to land, so I asked the Captain to take over. At almost the exact moment he did so we flew through vortices from the widebody, requiring full control deflection to maintain control of the airplane. I then diverted my attention to clearing the windshield and monitoring the balance of the approach, and forgot that my function of flying versus radio work had been switched with the Captain. We landed while still on Approach frequency.

"Thunderstorms in the area and we had been cleared for the approach with a turn to intercept and an altitude to descend to. We were told to contact Tower at the Outer Marker. I was flying the approach and monitoring the radar scope and failed to notice that my copilot had not changed to Tower frequency. After landing we noticed that we were still on Approach frequency. At this time we changed to Tower to ask about taxi routing to the terminal. The answer we got back was: Since we did not bother to get a landing clearance, why bother now? We apologized and did not get a response. . . . Both pilots were concentrating on the approach and overlooked the Tower contact over the o.m. . . . Approach Control did not try to give us a call . . . to remind us to call Tower again."

"Gear, slats, and spoilers were used to accelerate descent for closer turn-in from a 10,000 foot downwind. The gear seemed excessively noisy, so the First Officer tried looking through the peek hole to ensure that the nosegear doors were closed. Captain was flying and responded to the 'cleared for approach, call the tower at the Outer Marker.' Checklists were completed and reviewed, but with the gear already down the normal clue to switch to Tower did not exist. . . . A safe landing was made without talking to the tower."

Get the idea? Uninvited guests are not greeted with joyous cries, even if they have come to the right address. Here's a slight variation: First Officer flying, Captain twiddling the radio knobs. Clearance received at the last minute prevented a violation.

"Unable to contact Tower until moments before touchdown. 118.35 dialed in instead of 118.20. Frequency was obscured by landing data card and the error was noted by Second Officer. Tower was contacted just before touchdown."

And one more example of a late invitation, this time not the fault of the arriving guests:

"Approach advised us two or three times (once after passing Outer Marker) to stay with him for traffic advisories. He had cleared us for a visual approach to follow another large aircraft. We were subsequently cleared to land on the Approach frequency, but it wasn't until we were almost at flare height above the runway. This caused no problems, but may have inconvenienced the Tower controller, and I feel it is not good operating procedure for flight crews to be asked to switch frequencies late in an approach to land. We switched to Tower frequency, made the landing, and during the roll-out the tower called us and asked if we were on his frequency."

A pretty full menu of distractions during those busy last few minutes: Bird strikes, fogged-up windshields, T-storms, data cards in the way, troublesome gear doors. Sometimes traffic evasion and speed instructions so occupy the crews that they just forget.

"At the Outer Marker we lowered landing gear and made a normal stabilized approach and landing. The Approach controller never told us to contact the tower. After landing, I (First Officer)

asked for clearance to cross. Approach controller said, 'I don't
know; why don't you ask Ground?' "

LANDING CLEARANCE should be, perhaps—and with some airlines is—a BEFORE LANDING checklist item.

A few months later, in No. 33 (March 1982), I printed reports
of an occurrence that, in contrast to the relatively innocuous
instances above, emphasizes the danger that can attend the
failure to ensure landing clearance:

Too Late Remembered

*Approach switched us to Tower, who requested we report the Out-
er Marker, but we got so busy with checklists that we forgot it, so
during the flare to land Tower asked if that was us and why didn't
we call the O.M., but we had already touched down. This is the first
low-minimum approach we did for many months so we were a
little rusty on procedures even though we practiced a few times
during good weather and I remember now reading *CALLBACK* on
the same subject.

CALLBACK No. 26 (August 1981) indeed dealt with this sort
of thing in a story called "Crashing the Gate," in which several
examples of arriving uninvited were described. Although not
recommended practice, and inconvenient for controllers, the incidents did not involve actual hazard. Here's a hair-raiser to
show that the gate isn't the only thing you may crash if you fail
to obtain landing clearance.

"We were waiting for departure. The weather was indefinite zero,
sky obscured, visibility $\frac{1}{4}$, RVR at minimum. We were number one
for departure, waiting on arrival of a large transport. Tower asked
us to advise them when he went by the approach end of the runway so we could take position. He landed and we were cleared into
position and hold. Also at this time there was another large transport on the approach. After about two minutes waiting for the
first aircraft to clear the runway, we were cleared for takeoff. After
rolling about 200 feet we were told to hold our position and cancel
takeoff clearance due to the aircraft still on the approach. At this
time Tower advised that aircraft to go around because we were still
sitting on the runway. . . . We never heard an acknowledgment
from the aircraft. Still in position, the next thing we knew he
came right over the top of us, missing hitting us by—it seemed
like—inches. His thrust rocked our aircraft. As he initiated a go-
around his aircraft came within five feet of touching down. After a
minute or two were cleared for takeoff."

Welcome light was shed on this unsettling incident by reports to ASRS from the crew members of the aircraft that made the go-around.

"Approach Control failed to hand us off to Tower for landing clearance. . . . Upon completing our final landing checklist I realized that we had not yet received landing clearance, so I called Approach on my last assigned frequency (that I had not been directed to leave). No response was received and at this time we were in the final and critical phases of the approach. Attention was returned totally to required cockpit duties as decision height, approach light and threshold sighting occurred. A large aircraft was also sighted (fortunately) in takeoff position on the runway. Immediate go-around was initiated. . . . Later . . . I discovered that Tower had been attempting to send us around on their frequency and couldn't understand why I didn't comply.

"Frequently clearance is given on Approach frequency so we weren't assigned to Tower. Also, apparently another aircraft acknowledged our go-around order. . . . We all need to continue work on acknowledgment with full callsigns. If handoff to Tower is to be made, make it far enough outside Outer Marker to allow pilots ample time to make contact and get back on controls and instruments."

That ought to be a convincer to those who don't see any great harm in gate crashing. The incidents in *CALLBACK*'s earlier discussion were all related to cockpit distractions; often complacency is the culprit. The one above involved a series of complex factors. Take heed! Knock before entering—and wait for an invitation.

The back page of *CALLBACK* No. 26 (August 1981) featuring the gate-crashing tales also carried, under the heading "On the Other Hand," an amusing counterpoint about "a flightcrew that didn't forget to call for a landing clearance." In fact their clearance was unusually prompt. "They did, however, forget one other little thing and consequently encountered an outstanding welcoming committee on landing." The first paragraph below is the captain's terse report; the second paragraph gives an amplified account, as given by the captain in a telephone callback conversation with the ASRS analyst.

*Reporting over XYZ (last foreign point before entering USA), the controller asked us to contact the American Center ahead on 125.65, squawking 7500. We acknowledged and complied. The consequence of 7500 went unnoticed until landing, when it became quite obvious.

Center asked me to confirm squawking 7500 and I confirmed without it reminding me that that was the hijack code. The approach was curious in that we received sort of special handling.

There didn't seem to be anybody else on the frequency and everything went very smoothly. Tower asked us to roll out all the way to the end of the long runway, which seemed odd. It was only when I taxied off the runway and was surrounded by a phalanx of vehicles and the whole world was there to greet us and someone asked if I knew the meaning of Code 7500 that it dawned on me what had happened. It was then difficult to convince the authorities that the flight was in no way abnormal. Unfortunately, in the papers the next day they correctly spelled my name.

The reporter declared that the adventure was exciting while it lasted: police cars, airport vehicles, FBI, Border Patrol, M-16 carbines, sirens, lights, Customs people. His airline has provided transponder code refreshment training for all crews and he recommended that foreign controllers undergo a bit also. Regulations say that "Code 7500 will never be assigned by Air Traffic Control without prior notification from the pilot that his aircraft is being subjected to unlawful interference."

The no-clearance reports continue to arrive regularly; several hundred now repose in the ASRS database. They seldom differ in substance from those in this chapter, but one occasionally calls for more than routine notice. The finale to one such did inspire a short *CALLBACK* filler:

> Just One Little Thing Wrong

> The landing, however, was one of the best in recent memory.

> Forgot to call Tower for landing clearance.

While landings without clearance do cause concern among safety professionals, other anomalies of the "airport environment" are often more fraught. An air carrier landing by mistake at an airport other than that intended always involves flightcrew embarrassment, and sometimes hazard, although the hazard described in this *CALLBACK* excerpt is a rare one:

> "Turn was made to intercept the inbound course on the VOR approach as the haze had obscured the airport. . . . The airport environment seemed to fit (the VASI lights were out) so a landing was made. Our mistake became apparent when we noticed the armed personnel along with the abnormal activity of the people on the runway."

> Sure enough, the bird alighted at a military airfield in (as we say around here) "close proximity" to the intended destination. Foreign country, but not so far from home. Embarrassing—and alarming—but perhaps productive of a vivid lesson for others: Use all available aids and stick with prescribed procedures; failure to

do so can be, at the very least, inconvenient for everybody involved—and it may put you eyeball to eyeball with a hostile native.

One morning early in the ASRS program three reports, duplicates and, it developed later, all typed in a lawyer's office, appeared in the pouch. The captain, first officer, and second officer of a large air carrier jet were enjoying a smooth late-night flight to an uncontrolled airport, where none of the three had landed previously, located in a sparsely settled region of a western state. The skies were clear and bright and distances were deceptive. Sighting airport lights dead ahead, the crew landed. Luckily, the landing was a good one and touchdown was accomplished not far beyond the threshold, because it seemed to take a pretty vigorous application of reverse thrust to stop on the runway of the apparently deserted field.

Not deserted for long, even at the late hour. As it turned out, this was the first-ever landing of a jet at this remote high-country village. Unfortunately, it was forty miles south of the planned destination. Buses had to be sent for the bemused passengers and the empty airplane was flown out the following morning to the cheers of the villagers, who thereafter showered the crew with honors for their feat. No honors were received from the crew's employer, nor from the authorities.

Over the years, *CALLBACK* has devoted several columns to problems of this sort. In one of them, separate but matching reports told a story of an incident which gave rise to civic repercussions and led to revised local airport regulations.

Wrong Pew

"Cleared to land," said the controller, and the flightcrew of a heavy jet transport did so. Unfortunately, they did so at Airport "B"; the clearance—and the crew's intention—involved Airport "A," not far away. Not so very unusual—*CALLBACK* has noted similar occurrences before. Certain factors seem to be common to most wrong-airport landings: The two airports are close together; it is night time, so runway lights are conspicuous; the runways are fairly closely aligned directionally; the flightcrews are unfamiliar with the area. Nearly always the errant pilots have failed to use all the aids available to them, and often the touchdown runway turns out to be considerably shorter than expected. This, as our most recent reporter says, ensures good business for tire companies.

Two additional factors lend special interest to this wrong-airport event: (1) A subsequent and coincidental report identified by ASRS analysts as occurring at the appropriate time and place indicates that more than one reportable event resulted from that unfortunate choice of landing site:

"Small aircraft landing on Runway 24 made go-around due to a heavy aircraft landing in opposite direction. . . . As it turns out, the heavy had been cleared for visual approach to a nearby airport."

(2) The heavy jet roaring in over a housing development just off the end of the runway, and then roaring off again a few minutes later (!), ensured a sympathetic hearing for the irate local citizens whose emissaries had only that day petitioned the town fathers for restrictions on the use of the airport by large aircraft.

Lessons: Make sure, especially at the end of a long flight when you may be feeling some fatigue (and possibly boredom), that you are aiming at the proper target; use all available aids right up to touchdown; take another look if the controller reports, "Not in sight," when you report the lights. Even if the landing is smooth, this kind of thing can be embarrassing. . . . We just happen to have another report that reinforces those lessons and mentions the embarrassment. First paragraph, reporter's narrative; second, his comments on callback:

"Vectored toward the airport. Being high, we used speed brakes and broke out of the clouds with an airport directly ahead. We cancelled IFR and contacted the Flight Service Station. . . . We reported downwind, base, and final, only to find we had landed at the wrong airport. . . . We departed VFR and landed two minutes later without further incident . . . near identical runway headings, night, close proximity of the airports.

"Conditions were perfectly set up for the incident to happen to me, who knew I was not dumb enough to land at the wrong airport after twenty years of flying. . . . My first time into the area. After cancelling IFR we lost track of the DME and in fact did not check the NAV facility after spotting the airport. Tower at our destination was very nice—like this happened every day. Apparently, FSS had not really missed us and was surprised when we, for the second time, reported on final."

In a very similar incident, a major airline flight, cleared to land at a southwestern city airport, put down on an adjacent military field. Realizing the error as the airplane rolled out, the quick-witted captain announced to the 150 passengers that, because of the size of the airport, he intended to take off again and to land closer to the terminal.

Commendable concern. . . . The crew gave the occurrence no further thought until, at the completion of their schedule, two days later, they were called into their chief pilot's office to explain why the aircraft's automatic flight data recording system had reported two landings at the destination city only three minutes apart.

So it goes. The database has many of these reports. Many reports also tell of landings on taxiways instead of runways, and of last-minute recognition of airport misidentification in time to break off the approach and divert to the appropriate destination. Another short *CALLBACK* space filler emphasizes another aspect of the genre:

Surprise!

*Other than the final courses, the approaches to the two airports are nearly identical. . . . As we made ground contact I immediately realized where we were. . . . Fortunately, we were in prairie country and not in the mountains!

As you will have deduced, landings without clearance are not uncommon events in day-to-day aircraft operations. Wrong-airport arrivals occur frequently; even more familiar are landings on a wrong runway—usually one parallel to the correct one. Aircraft at times mistakenly land on taxiways, usually when the airport is covered with snow or the visibility is restricted. And once in a while they land with their wheels up. Perhaps because it seldom entails injury (except to pride), this form of mishap engenders much levity; it has been taking place since the first retractable gear aircraft appeared, and is almost always due to pilot complacency ("I just forgot . . ."). Transition by inexperienced pilots from fixed-gear to more complex types is sometimes implicated; professional pilots are not immune from gear-up incidents, but distraction is likely to be the cause.

CALLBACK's first related adventure of this kind appeared in issue No. 10 (April 1980) under the heading, "There Are Those-Who-Have and Those-Who-Are-Going-To. . . . The featured report described a new captain, who encountered a series of unusual and confusing distractions during his landing approach and just missed being one of those-who-have. The second officer's narrative continues:

At 350′ Captain recognized that gear was not down, saying "!@#&, the gear's not down." His response was to begin to initiate a smooth go-around. In the confusion, the First Officer put the gear down anyway. Although there was probably enough time for a safe landing, Captain elected to make the go-around . . . No further incidents."

A short general aviation report is reminiscent of the classic joke ("I couldn't hear the tower telling me to go around because that gear warning horn was so loud"). It is followed by an example of the "unfamiliarity syndrome," which resulted in a narrow escape:

Gear Up and Locked—Head Likewise

"On a normal, seemingly uneventful, landing I inadvertently missed the GEAR item on my checklist and failed to extend it before landing. The damage was quite minor (prop tips). I believe the primary cause of my failure to hear the gear warning horn is that I wear a headset with close-fit 'muff-type' ear pieces. . . . I will have to remove the headset prior to landing sequence or else discontinue use of this type of headset completely."

But then you may miss something else important—controller warning, party line, etc. There are other alternatives. . . . Gear-down lights help.

Reverse Twist

*It had been more than a year since I had flown this small retractable gear airplane. After completing a third touch-and-go, my concentration was broken. Gear was never retracted. I flew downwind and around the pattern. On final I "lowered" the gear by manual movement of the mechanically operated gear handle. Aircraft speed picked up and I couldn't get it slowed down. Close in, I checked the gear handle. It was locked in place. Something didn't seem right, but I couldn't figure out what. Speed was still about 20 miles per hour above normal for this point in approach. I thought to myself, "I'll just land hot and get it slowed up on the runway with a nose-up attitude on this tricycle-configured aircraft." Another aircraft was just clearing the runway when I was about 200 feet in the air. I had already been cleared to land. As I pressed on, fast and about 10 feet off the deck, the tower told me to take it around. Puzzled, I added power, rogered the tower, and reached to raise the gear. As I was trying to figure out why the wave off—the other aircraft had already cleared the runway—I realized the gear was already up. As I turned downwind I called the tower. "I owe you something. . . ." If things don't seem right, go over your procedures to make sure they are.

In *CALLBACK* No. 99 (September 1987), the last but one before I traded the editorship for the lighter duties of monthly columnist, two slightly unusual, but related, gear mishandling reports were featured. They seemed to call for comment based on personal experience and on legendary misadventures recalled from my Navy days:

Check Landing Gear—Whether by Land or Sea

"Pilot was practicing landings in recently acquired aircraft. He was accompanied by pilot qualified in make and model. . . . On the approach phase of the landing, the passenger pilot engaged in a discussion of speed control which resulted in the pilot making an unusually smooth touchdown on the runway. The concentration on approach speed was at the expense of lack of concentration on the requirement to extend the landing gear. Because the aircraft is amphibious, little damage was done. . . . Had this aircraft been landing on water with the gear extended, a reverse situation of the subject incident, the result would have been total structural failure of the airframe and a morbid experience for the occupants."

Something for everybody. . . . A new ASRS report covers that situation, too—with results not as dire as predicted above:

"Landed amphibian in the water with gear down. Aircraft flipped upside down. . . . I was wearing a seat belt and shoulder harness and was not injured."

Both reporters noted that use of a checklist would have averted the mishaps. ASRS confidentiality policy (and Editorial reticence) dictates nonidentification of pilot who experienced similar upside-down flip even though checklist was used and gear was up. Pilot was injured when he went through windshield (complete with seat, belt, and harness) during maneuver. Fatal to sea-lion which surfaced in front of aircraft just at touchdown. This interesting (?) event occurred pre-ASRS.

These tales recall a couple of old sea stories: (1) Pilot of an amphibian was making an approach for a water landing and was waved off because his gear was down. Rejecting the landing, he decided to put down on the adjacent airfield. Retracting the gear during the go-around, he made a smooth landing on terra firma— with wheels retracted. (2) Pilot (possibly same one?) landing amphib on airport realized just in time that gear was up so he elected to alight on nearby body of water. Smooth landing; taxied up to nicely sloping beach, stepped out onto lower wing, and jumped nimbly off—into water up to his waist.

Perhaps the last word(s) on this regrettable sort of airman performance was provided by an ASRS reporter who was frustrated by having to extend his downwind leg unduly in order to follow a slower airplane ahead. *CALLBACK* emphasized the final sentence of his report: "The gear-up landing was caused by the pilot apparently failing to lower the gear."

7

Good Grief—And Good Humor

A new Captain, upon bidding into Miami, asked advice from an experienced Captain on how best to fly Florida thunderstorms. The sage advice was, "In the morning, when you are heading north from Miami and encounter thunderstorms, always turn west, but in the afternoon, when you are heading south, always turn to the east."

The newcomer then asked, "Will this always avoid the storms?"

"No," said the Voice of Experience, "but it will keep the sun out of your eyes."

That little tale appeared (under the heading "Experientia Docet") in *CALLBACK* No. 18 (December 1980) as a preamble to a discussion of the text borrowing that goes on among aviation publications. In this case the anecdote was lifted from Delta Air Lines's flightcrew bulletin *Up Front,* which labeled it "an old story, but worth repeating."

Earlier *CALLBACK*s had purloined items from various sources and we had received a number of requests to reprint our own material. Such use is, of course, strongly encouraged; we merely noted that a "from NASA's ASRS *CALLBACK*" credit would be appreciated.

The adjacent column in the same *CALLBACK* emphasized the point. Headed "Neither a Borrower nor a Lender Be," the article admitted that even the heading was borrowed—from "Hamlet," ignoring Shakespeare's advice. Gilding the lily, so to speak, our page, normally bereft of illustration, was brightened by a clever cartoon borrowed from *Air Force Magazine.* The drawing, by Bob Stevens, was in two sections; the first depicted a controller in front of his radar scope with the caption, "Air Force 1234, you have traffic at two o'clock, six miles." The following panel showed the controller with a befuddled expression; the caption read, "Control, can ya give us another clue? We've got digital watches." Sure enough—beneath the cartoon was the *CALLBACK* credit line. *Air Force* and artist Stevens had indeed borrowed the joke from *CALLBACK,* but we too had borrowed it, as this article, reproduced verbatim from *CALLBACK* No. 20 (February 1981) explained:

Traffic Watch—Credit Where Due

The Christmas *CALLBACK* carried a cartoon lifted from *Air Force Magazine* illustrating that digital watch joke. We acknowledged our debt, at the same time pointing out that the idea had been borrowed from us, we in turn having borrowed it from Continental Airlines' flightcrew bulletin *Golden Contrails.* We expressed curiosity as to Continental's source; a recent letter helps us trace the matter further. Doug Wood of Air Canada informs us that he was the originator of the joke by way of a cartoon he drew for his company's publication *Intercom* in October 1978. In August of the following year British Airways' *Air Safety Review* reprinted the cartoon with no credit. Four months later it turned up in Air France's *Securite des Vol,* with credit to British Airways. In June of 1980 the joke appeared in *Golden Contrails* (no cartoon, no credit). *CALLBACK* was next, running the thing (no cartoon) with acknowledgement to Continental in our August issue. Next to check in was *Air Force,* crediting *CALLBACK,* followed by our reprinting of their Bob Stevens cartoon, with proper attribution. So belated credit to Mr. Wood and Air Canada and our thanks to him for setting the record straight. If it really is—maybe the ubiquitous story has surfaced elsewhere, unknown so far to him and to us. Prize to the first reader who sends us Aeroflot's version—if and when. It will have been originated by them, of course.

Coincidentally, and as a postscript to this topic, I reprint a short item from another *CALLBACK:*

An airline friend has written to us about his days as a copilot, when he flew with a salty character who enjoyed startling controllers with his responses. Like this:

Controller: You have traffic at twelve o'clock.

My Captain: We have one at eleven o'clock, but then you're on daylight saving time, aren't you?

CALLBACK No. 1 (July 1979), in a preface describing its purposes, stated, "Safety is a serious subject, but we hope you will find this bulletin interesting, instructive, and even—sometimes—entertaining." It seemed a reasonable premise that thoughtful selection and judicious editing of ASRS reports to be reprinted in the bulletin would provide the hoped-for interest and instruction. Entertainment may have been an unattainable—and even inappropriate—goal; I did, however, resolve to make *CALLBACK* readable.

Readability, it seems to me, is in the eye of the beholder. The *CALLBACK* beholder is the aviation community, a constituency whose tastes I believe I understand and share—in general—after fifty years of active involvement. In general! To generalize about such things may be viewed as pure folly. Psychologists claim to have defined a "profile" of the average pilot. Pilots make up the largest segment of *CALLBACK*'s circulation; ergo, a study of the profile should establish pilot preferences in reading matter. I suspect the profile is about as accurate as the stereotype Hollywood aviator popular in the 1930s talkies.

Not all pilots are tall, trim, clear-eyed, laconic, fearless. But most of those I have known share certain characteristics: Optimism is a common one—faith that things will work out, and in one's own indestructability; self-confidence (it has been said that every pilot, even the most modest, knows in his heart of hearts that he is the best); and sense of humor. And the most prevalent, and most engaging, of these is surely the last. The joke may be broad or bawdy, it may be subtle or sophisticated, but the ability to find amusement in life—and in flying—is eminently present in the pilot population. This admirable quality seems to have been part of the aviator's standard makeup from the earliest days and has been declared by the erudite analysts to represent a form of compensation—and a cover-up for apprehension—for the risks to be faced by those who go aloft. Maybe. But regardless of the pundits' reasoning, flying people tend to be light of heart and to laugh readily, especially at themselves or their fellow airmen, notwithstanding the stern-faced public image of the breed.

The practical joke is not unknown in airman circles, as any attendee at Quiet Birdmen festivities can testify. According to Brendan Gill's fine biographical *Lindbergh Alone,* the hero himself was a lover of this dubious form of wit and was the ringleader in certain Kelly Field cadet barracks escapades not suitable for more polite society.

At any rate, two requisites of readability for *CALLBACK* were to be: (1) brevity (despite some pressure to increase its content we have maintained the one-page, double-sided format from the beginning), and (2) humor (or at least the avoidance of solemnity). The humor has taken various forms: ASRS reports of amusing incidents—or of unamusing incidents amusingly described; tall tales of early adventures told around the coffee pot by the old eagles; anecdotes heard or read, often contributed by writers of letters to the editor; the only requirement is that the humor must be connected in some manner to a *CALLBACK* article, which is to say that it will be, if only peripherally, related to flying. The tales we have told have been often true, often prevarication or pure fiction, sometimes apocryphal anecdotes or venerable legends. Here is a story told by a visitor at an early ASRS Wednesday pizza session (it was set aside to hold for just the right *CALLBACK* occasion and has not yet appeared):

> ATC: Flight xxx, turn 45 degrees right immediately!
> Captain: Roger, turning right. (pause) Center, what was the reason for the turn?
> ATC: xxx, your turn was for noise abatement.
> Captain: Noise abatement? We're at 41,000 feet over Northern Utah!
> ATC: Roger, Sir, but have you ever heard two 747's hit head-on?

Probably apocryphal, but you never know. . . . The ASRS database contains a good many examples (although some wayward pilots might dispute the possibility) of controllers' wit. Here are some controller stories from various issues (all in some way highlight an accompanying serious passage):

> *The airport was off our left about four miles; I told the copilot to tell Approach Control that we had the field in sight for a visual. Approach asked us if we had a jet in sight coming up on our left between us and the field. Just then, off to our left, here comes this jet going *considerably* faster than ourselves and we were doing 250 knots! Before I told the copilot that I did indeed have the jet, Approach initiated the following contact: "Airline A, what's your speed?" "Two hundred and fifty and slowing," we said. "Airline B,

what's your speed?" he inquired of our traffic. "Two hundred and fifty," he said (no way!). After a pause, the controller said, "Slow to ninety." We all got a laugh out of this as we followed him to the airport.

"Center, we've just taken a bird strike and are declaring an emergency." The controller . . . acknowledged the call and, after making radar identification of the aircraft, asked for additional details on the bird strike. "It was a northeast bound chicken hawk," the Navy pilot said. "He was a big _____ too. He hit our canopy head-on at 300 knots." Maintaining his composure, the controller responded, "Roger, and how fast were you going, Sir?"

CALLBACK by no means aspires to replace Joe Miller's Joke Book as a compendium of knee-slappers, but a funny story has often served to add point to a discussion of some prevalent problem appearing in ASRS reports. Consider, for instance, an article from *CALLBACK* No. 7 (January 1980):

Matters of Interpretation

Responses to queries or instructions, though well-intentioned and carefully thought-out, sometimes differ substantially from the expected. We heard recently (not via an ASRS report) of a Central European pilot who, when asked to report his height and position, responded at once with, "I'm five feet seven and a half, and I'm sitting down."

One of our reports last month reflected a not-dissimilar misunderstanding. A pilot, cleared for a "Maspeth climb" (Maspeth is a fix in the New York Metropolitan Area), was observed on radar to be somewhat higher than called for in the procedure, and flying in the wrong direction. Unfamiliar with the local geography, but eager to cooperate, the pilot was trying his best to execute a "massive" climb.

Some months later a *CALLBACK* article featuring reports of distractions caused by flightcrew meal service provided a good excuse to quote from a letter I had received from a captain who had reported to ASRS on several occasions:

He writes "of the very bumpy ride we and several other flights were experiencing. . . . I asked the copilot to inquire of Center how the rides were at other altitudes."

Center: "How's your ride at 350, XYZ 123?"

XYZ 123: "Well, we're eatin' dinner and the Captain's stabbed himself with his fork three times!"

Silence.

Center: "ABC 456, how's your ride at 290?"

ABC 456: "We don't know; we haven't eaten yet."

An article about maintaining a sharp visual lookout over geographic points of interest was illustrated with a letter from another airline pilot correspondent:

*During the heat of summer, our chief pilot passed along a complaint received from a nudist camp along one of our routes. It appears that they don't like aircraft over their facility and have complained to the FAA to try and get it stopped. The FAA in turn has passed this along to their offices and the airlines have received copies too. The letter from FAA to all pilots was posted on the bulletin board with a cover letter from our chief advising compliance. An enterprising pilot paraphrased the advisory with bold letters underneath saying,

ABSOLUTELY NO FLYING OVER THE NUDIST CAMP ON THE XYZ VOR 356 DEGREE RADIAL AT 19.6 DME!

Please deidentify the actual location, as I'm in enough trouble already!

Another feature on communications misunderstandings was illuminated by a short story borrowed from a flightcrew bulletin:

The flight attendant told passenger Groucho Marx that it would be all right for him to smoke his cigar if it didn't annoy the ladies. He replied, "I didn't realize there was a choice. In that case, I'll annoy the ladies."

Another flight attendant encounter with a celebrity suggested this introduction to an article on pilot physical condition (standard ASRS deidentification of the champion):

A story—told to us as true—deals with an alert flight attendant who enjoined a modern-day media hero, renowned for his ego as well as his athletic prowess, to fasten his seat-belt before takeoff.
Hero: "Superman don't need no seat-belt."
F/A: "Superman don't need no airplane. Buckle up."

Not from *CALLBACK,* but included here as a sort of high point (150 miles or so!) in aviation humor, is a short story that will ring a bell with all pilots who have endured that seemingly endless climb through black, rainy, turbulent clouds, waiting for the always-dramatic breakout into clear skies:

Spacecraft rocketing up toward the moon; one astronaut says to his companion, "Another thousand feet ought to top it all."

Let us consider now those rare actual events, as reported to the Aviation Safety Reporting System, in which the participants have displayed irresponsibility or otherwise bizarre behavior, or the circumstances are so unlikely as to generate surprise—and usually disapproval of the conduct of their fellow airmen—in the ASRS staff members (who tend to fall into the trap of thinking they have heard it all). A column from *CALLBACK* No. 8 (February 1980) became (although not by editorial intention) the first in a continuing series that readers have evidently found, as we hoped in the beginning, "interesting, instructive, and even—sometimes—entertaining."

Dumb—And Dangerous

In the normal way of business, ASRS does not assess blame nor attempt to judge. Reports like those following tempt us, though:

Large aircraft was on departure. . . . A small aircraft passed directly under just beyond the end of the runway. Enquiry established that neither approach nor local controller had contact with the errant pilot. Tower reported that "the aircraft was crisscrossing back and forth across the departure end of the runway. Controller made a call in the blind on tower frequency and the pilot replied that he was looking at real estate and was now leaving the area. The controller asked for the callsign but the pilot refused to give it." (Dumb maybe, but not that dumb!) "The aircraft departed west." Efforts to track the culprit failed; he was too low. ASRS analyst predicts that a new housing development will soon appear off the end of the runway. Don't they always?

"VFR aircraft called Center at 17,500 feet, advising that he was climbing to 21,500 VFR. Controller advised the pilot that above 17,500 was Positive Control Airspace. . . . He next noticed the aircraft at 18,500 feet, climbing. Controller advised him his altitude readout showed him at 18,500 and to descend VFR to 17,000 feet." He had been crossing a high altitude route luckily, at the time, unoccupied. Maybe just ignorant—but difficult to excuse.

"Going through FL 290 we encountered a small jet, level, opposite direction. We passed within 100' of each other; it was so fast no evasive action could be taken. Both of us were in the clouds. Center said they did not see any other aircraft; they had no transponder return nor did they see a skin paint. They also said they could not find any other person controlling any aircraft at that location or altitude. GOOD GRIEF!

That was *CALLBACK*'s first use of the exasperated cry uttered so often by Charlie Brown, Snoopy, and the other "Peanuts" characters (possibly the Red Baron sequences in the popular Charles

Schultz comic strip subliminally suggested my choice of exclamation). No other comment seemed appropriate, and I fell
back on it again in December 1980 in issue No. 18, this time in a
heading to a report by a helicopter pilot who, approaching the
airport in level flight, was buzzed repeatedly by a light plane
that came within "10 to 15 feet. Upon landing . . . the other pilot
advised us that he had seen us and the pass was intentional."
Only two months later came:

Good Grief—#3*

*A pilot drove down an active runway. He was sitting on top of his
sunroof-equipped car, steering with his feet. His young daughter
was operating the gas pedal. He was driving erratically—swerv-
ing from side to side of the runway. I was on base for landing in a
sailplane. As I turned final, the car and driver turned onto the
runway and drove in my direction at about 25–30 miles per hour.
There was insufficient room to land behind the car at my speed
(60+ MPH). With no engine (sailplane), I could not abort. I had to
close my dive brakes and zoom over the car, landing beyond same
at far end of the runway. Obviously this is a gross safety violation.

The asterisk in the heading referred to a footnote explaining,
"Good Grief—a category assigned by *CALLBACK* to reports of
occurrences that defy us to append any other comment." *CALL-
BACK*'s circulation had increased mightily by the time this appeared and many readers took the trouble to write that they did
indeed enjoy reading these accounts of dangerous foolishness
and would profit by vicarious observation of the errant behavior
of the participants. Number 4 came in June of 1981, describing
an air carrier's sighting head-on of a large radio-controlled
model airplane at 3,000 feet, requiring evasive action on the part
of the airliner's crew. Unaccountably, a review of back issues
does not reveal any Number 5. The next to reach print came in
December:

Good Grief—#6

*The small transport on VFR TCA clearance was not happy with
being vectored 40 miles out of his way for traffic in the metropolitan area. When he came on my frequency he made many
coarse remarks, then finally would not reply to my control instructions or do as he was instructed to do. This caused him to
come to be in Less Than Standard Separation with an air carrier
aircraft. I tried to turn both aircraft but only the air carrier would
comply. This is all that kept the situation from being worse than
it was.

By this time the Good Grief stories seemed to have established themselves as a permanent *CALLBACK* feature. An earlier continuing series of Memorable Lines, taken from "hangar talk, from flying novels, most of all from old aviation films" (You wouldn't send a kid up in a crate like that, would you?) had run its course. The heading "1″ = 1000′" dealing with altimeter setting errors turned up in *CALLBACK* No. 5 (November 1974), was updated a year later, and has been used a few times since at irregular intervals. Reports judged suitable for Good Grief treatment continue to flow into the ASRS post box, and their frequency suggests that they will continue to run as object lessons as long as the ASRS bulletin is published.

While most Good Griefs describe incidents of irresponsible or unprofessional flying, poor judgment, carelessness, and the like, an occasional unusual occurrence may serve as a model of how things should be done. Exemplary performance ". . . in which the flightcrew very ably converted a hazardous situation into a happy conclusion" was the subject of No. 9, in the April 1982 *CALLBACK:*

> *We had just received a visual approach clearance. First Officer called out a power loss on No. 2 engine at the same time I was trying to determine why we had an abnormal yaw condition to the right. Confirmed no power available from No. 2 by moving the throttle. No response. I feathered No. 2 and we told the tower of our condition and to have emergency gear stand by the runway. Being high I called for gear down and flaps. . . . We had an adequate rate of descent to not overshoot the runway. When I added power to No. 1 to stabilize the approach we heard several loud noises from No. 1 engine and felt a power loss, with smoke smell in the cockpit. We were approximately 1200 feet above the ground. I brought the flaps up, turned final, and had the First Officer try to get a relight on No. 2. Negative results. The runway was not obtainable without some power! We turned left about 90 degrees and landed on the river ice. The aircraft stopped in about half a mile. All passengers and crew exited the aircraft. No injuries.

The period April to July 1982 provided a moratorium on the sort of spectacular or unusual events judged to be suitable Good Grief candidates, but an excellent example turned up for the August *CALLBACK;* this was followed in November by another classic. To each of these was appended a short bit of editorial moralizing.

Good Grief—#10

"Arriving from southwest with vectors from Approach Control at 8,000 feet. Approximately 10 miles southwest of the airport a deadheading crewmember in the jump seat sighted, through a break in the clouds, a powered glider-type aircraft at our one o'clock position—estimated less than one mile, at our altitude. Momentary sighting due to cloud density. Called traffic to Approach Control—they did not paint it on radar. Weather was estimated 6,000 broken with tops about 10 to 11,000. My estimate— 80% coverage with towering cumulus. Ideal soaring weather!"

Reporter: Captain of widebody jet. Location: Smack over one of our largest metropolitan areas, with TCA top of 7,000. Hazards (among others): to vehicle and its pilot; to widebody and its passengers and crew (and to other aircraft in the neighborhood); to persons and property on ground. Calls to mind a vivid line from a popular ballad of some years back: "Young man, quoth Abdul, has life grown so dull/that you wish to end it so soon?" As the Captain said, it was ideal soaring weather, and no doubt quite beautiful among those spectacular cloud canyons, but— . . . As we said, "Good Grief!"

Good Grief—#12

"My instructor felt I was ready for my CFI check ride, so he had me fly with another instructor to find any weak spots. . . . While I was going through the pre-start checklist (I was in the right seat) he quizzed me about the pressure switch in the nose gear (aircraft was a small retractable gear type). When I indicated that I didn't know how to test it he said, You can test it this way, as he turned the master switch ON and pulled the gear lever to the UP position. In accordance with Murphy's Law, the pressure switch didn't work, and the nose of the aircraft crashed to the pavement."

CALLBACK's primer for those unfamiliar with retractable undercarriage aircraft: Most such are equipped with a "squat" switch installed on one of the landing gear struts to ensure that when the weight of the aircraft is on the gear (strut compressed), inadvertent retraction is prevented ("Oops, I meant to retract the flaps"). Airborne, with the weight off the gear, the switch closes, allowing movement of the gear lever to actuate the retracting mechanism. There are better ways of testing the system—for example, with jacks under the aircraft. See last month's *CALLBACK* for remarks on the value of "imagination."

In August of 1984 (*CALLBACK* No. 62) a noteworthy entrant in the "How could I do that?" sweepstakes appeared. It was an ASRS first, one we did not expect would be repeated. We were wrong; just over a year later we received a match (obviously from a nonreader of *CALLBACK*) described briefly in a short article, which follows (*CALLBACK* No. 75 , September 1985) the thought-to-be-unique adventure reprinted below:

Good Grief—#19

*On this morning I arrived at the airport before daybreak. My copilot was there, in the hangar pre-flighting the aircraft. . . . Preflight was completed under the hangar lights and the aircraft was towed out onto the ramp. It was dark and the sky was overcast. My copilot disconnected the tug while I closed the hangar doors. . . . We received our clearance over the landline, with release time and a void time only five minutes later. The aircraft was situated on the ramp so as to be approached from behind. Little did I know— and I didn't ask—if the towbar was disconnected. I failed to do a final walk-around because of the pressing time to release. . . . While taxiing I noticed a slight vibration in the rudder pedals and asked my copilot to taxi and see if he felt anything. It felt all right to him; I had not flown this aircraft in several weeks and at this point felt it to be insignificant. I did not want to lose our release time by shutting down to send the copilot out to take a look. . . . We launched with three minutes to spare. The aircraft tracked smoothly and with no vibration in the pedals down the runway. We rotated, got the gear up and completed the after t.o. checklist. We had no indication that anything was wrong; the gear came up smoothly and we had no warning lights. The gear was cycled four times as we tried to get into our destination airport, but we were unable to because of ground fog. Each time, the gear went down and came up smoothly. . . . We had no idea that the towbar was still attached to the nosewheel. We diverted to our alternate and initiated the ils. Upon lowering the gear in a shallow right turn I felt a slight nose-right yaw which was easily corrected. . . . A smooth nose-high landing was made. After clearing the runway, a ground vehicle came on the frequency and said we had a towbar attached to the nosewheel. . . . As a team, there must always be an avenue of communication—not just in the cockpit, but during all aspects of the operation. We hope this report can help in preventing others from allowing the same circumstances to pile up on them and allow this sort of thing to happen.

History Repeats

A year ago *CALLBACK* carried a report from a pilot who took off with towbar still attached. First time we heard of such a thing. Read on for second time:

"Left a light electric towbar attached to the nosegear. . . . Tower advised. . . . A safe landing was accomplished."

Sure cure: On walk-around inspections, walk ALL the way around! We'll bet no *CALLBACK* reader will ever do this again.

While not a repeat, a Good Grief report (No. 27) in *CALLBACK* No. 77 (November 1985) displayed similarities to an earlier story

(No. 13) in issue No. 44 (February 1983). Both dealt with traffic pattern misbehavior and, as in most of the series, there were lessons to be learned by readers.

Good Grief—#13

*Final with gear down and full flaps. I noticed a movement out of the corner of my eye. Another aircraft was turning final ahead and to our left. We took evasive action and went around. The aircraft took forever to get off the runway and we thought we might have to go around again. We didn't, but on short final right before we landed the pilot of the other aircraft said, "Tower, were you trying to call me?" We decided that we ought to talk with this pilot about the close call. He must have known we'd be looking for him, because he disappeared. We stayed out of sight for a few minutes and sure enough he reappeared. . . . He was apologetic. His excuse was he had his personal tape player headset on and couldn't hear the tower over the music.

Perhaps the music lover learned his lesson and will be able to resist the temptation to play video games on the weather radar when he grows up to fly larger aircraft.

Good Grief—#28

*Circled airport and made left hand standard pattern. . . . So much talk on UNICOM that I couldn't talk. People talking about airport celebration. I told people talking to talk trash on another frequency. One pilot said, "Amen," another said, "Plane on final is talking to nobody." I replied, "I don't have to." Another pilot told me to stick it in my ear. I told that pilot to stick it in his. Other pilot stalked me to the ramp where I picked up two waiting passengers. The other unknown and unwanted pilot tried to board my aircraft in what appeared to be anger. My engines were both running so I blowed him off the wing to protect me and my passengers with max power and took off. Was very courteous to traffic in pattern.

All the examples in the continuing series demonstrated unusual aspects. None seemed more unusual than these two, appearing only a month apart in the spring of 1986: The plane in No. 30 in No. 82 (April 1986) plowed into a snow bank; No. 31 in No. 83 (May 1986) was adapted from a Navy report to ASRS:

Good Grief—#30

"After obtaining a weather briefing and pre-flighting the aircraft I loaded my one passenger and secured all baggage. I departed and climbed to an altitude of approximately 1000 feet above the ground. I took up a heading following the coastline and continued to follow the coastline for 10 to 12 minutes. At this time there was a sudden flash of strobe lights reflecting inside the cockpit. Thinking that I might have inadvertently entered a cloud, I lowered the nose of the aircraft a bit. Almost immediately we experienced a deceleration of the aircraft. We had inadvertently hit the ground, sheering the nose wheel and bending the prop. We slid to a stop and both pilot and passenger exited the aircraft. Neither of us was injured."

Good Grief—#31

Paraphrased from official Navy report to ASRS: Scene is an aircraft carrier underway at night, not far from an island airbase. Commanding Officer's comments cover the situation nicely and display admirable tolerance. This is not the recommended procedure for joining the Navy.

"While maneuvering for landing on the carrier the helicopter was forced to make an emergency descent to avoid a mid-air collision with a small civilian aircraft. Closest point of approach was 200 feet, with the small airplane directly over the helicopter, which had descended. The small aircraft was sighted one minute prior to evasive action. No evasive action was taken by the civilian plane, which proceeded up port side of the carrier, then turned off its exterior lights and departed from the carrier. The small airplane had been ordered by a nearby Navy tower about 20 minutes earlier to clear the Base Airport Traffic Area."

This chapter of amusing and/or alarming tales closes with a particularly choice Good Grief candidate; I chose an alternative heading because I couldn't resist it (*CALLBACK* No. 50, August 1983):

Ole! Toro!

The aircraft in the following Wild West adventure had fixed landing gear before the event. A few days afterward it had landing gear fixed. The reporter's ASRS narrative was somewhat terse, suggesting to our analyst that a callback might be productive. This transcript of the pilot's tale during the 'phone conversation is considerably more graphic than the original report:

"I was supposed to spray this field and I saw that two Black Angus bulls had strayed out of their pastures onto the field. On my second pass attempting to herd the bulls out of the field I reckon I got too low. This one bull made a lunge at me and my left gear hit him in the head. He knocked my left gear off but I killed him dayed. I flew around to burn up some gas and then flew over to another airport and landed on the soft sod alongside the runway. Wiped off my left spray boom on the landing but otherwise no damage to me or the aircraft. I retrieved the gear, got some new parts, and was flying again in a couple days. After talking with various people I am now in heavy discussion with my insurance company."

Good Grief!

8

Brave New World

Any sufficiently advanced technology is indistinguishable from magic.

Arthur C. Clarke

Of the people who gave us our first flying machines, some were engineers (self-taught or otherwise), and some were mechanics or scientists, or plain visionaries, but all were master tinkerers. And it is the way of tinkerers to be forever unsatisfied. No sooner did vision become reality than it had to be improved or made easier to operate or simplified ("Simplificate and add lightness," was the formula for aircraft design prescribed by John K. Northrop, a notable self-taught engineer-tinkerer—and founder of the aircraft company named for him). But unfortunately and paradoxically, simplification often complicates. Thus it has been with the trend known these days as "cockpit automation." While *CALLBACK* had carried an occasional ASRS report of automatic flight control malfunction, the bulletin's first acknowledgement of impending major changes came in an article in No. 48 (June 1983). Comment was not offered; I merely reprinted two reports that seemed to speak for themselves and foreshadowed many that arrived thereafter. These accounts from air carrier pilots provide a typical glimpse into the confusion that existed during the transition by airlines to the new Advanced Technology Aircraft:

Brave New World

*Caused a potential ATC problem. Performance Management System (PMS) is a new installation used on this aircraft on a trial basis. I am unfamiliar with its operation. I was given a short course about six months ago; since that time I have seen it on the aircraft only twice. A subsystem of the PMS consists of automatic throttles to be used from takeoff roll throughout flight, including landing. On T.O roll the autothrottles were armed and T.O. power was set. Departure Control told us to level off at 4000'; I did. I expected the autothrottles to reduce the power; they did not. I retarded them manually but they once again advanced to climb power. While I was fighting a battle with the throttles ATC told me to turn to heading 230° and intercept the 335° radial, which I did. At this time I disconnected the autothrottles by means of a button on the side of the throttle knob. This caused a bright red light on the panel to begin flashing. It is necessary to push the light to extinguish it. While trying to push the light I accidentally and unknowingly pushed the switch/light adjacent to the flashing red one. This was the Omega NAV engage switch and it immediately caused the VOR needle to center. . . . When I saw the needle was centered I made a left turn to intercept what I thought to be the 335° radial. Shortly thereafter Departure questioned this action, informed me I was in another ATA, and directed me to turn back to heading 230. This of course was a potentially dangerous condition, caused by unfamiliarity with the aircraft system. Actually, the autothrottles will not retard automatically unless the autopilot is engaged, which I was not aware of. To prevent a recurrence, or similar incidents, I recommend that more emphasis be placed on potential hazards associated with PMS while in ground school . . . further, that the Omega switch/light be moved from its close proximity to a warning switch/light or guarded so it cannot be inadvertently activated.

I put the landing gear handle down and pulled out the checklist card. At this time I reported one dot low on glideslope. LOC was in CAPTURE position. The landing gear amber light stayed on so I recycled the gear. This time we got the green light. I turned on my map light and completed the pre-landing checklist. As I returned the checklist card to the holder the GPWS sounded, "PULL UP, PULL

UP, GLIDESLOPE; PULL UP, PULL UP, FLAPS; PULL UP, PULL UP, TERRAIN";
and I also yelled at the First Officer to pull up, which we did. We
then crossed the Outer Marker in climb and made a hand-flown
attempt to capture the ILS but we were unable to do so, and then
flew a missed approach. When we reached to set Missed Approach
Altitude we found the PMS altitude set to "0". Neither of us think
we set it there—how did it get there when the last altitude set was
2700' MSL? The autopilot did not capture the glideslope since we
were below the G/S on the approach. . . . Innumerable traps. . . .
Needs constant visual scan by both pilots. . . . Very dangerous
situation and we were possibly saved by the GPWS.

Enthusiasm often induced a sort of myopia blinding the early-
day tinkerer/inventor to possible undesirable secondary consequences attendant on the success of the original bright idea,
thus necessitating further tinkering to refine the concept. As
the increasing complexity of flying machines led to the meta-
morphosis of the solitary tinkerers into large industry design
groups, so escalating airline operating costs induced economy-
driven pressures. Presto! Let's reduce flightcrew work load (and
size) by making some duties automatic. The radio operator disappeared some time ago, followed by the navigator. Now for the
flight engineer. . . . By the late 1970s manufacturers' drawing
boards specified the two-pilot cockpit in response to the market-
ing department requirement (and aided by new technologies) to
offer labor-saving aircraft to the air carriers. Transports of the
eighties were projected minus the engineer's station. The buzz-
word "automation" was heard throughout air-transport land.

A different word resounded throughout the pilot/flight engineer community: furor. Amid boasts of economy and efficiency from the manufacturers and airlines, and protestations of
safety deterioration and technological unemployment from the
labor groups, and with new-generation certification of aircraft
imminent, a presidentially mandated task force was asked to
investigate the opposing claims and resolve the emotion-ridden
"crew complement" controversy.

To the credit of the agency, FAA officials anticipated this issue
and early in 1980 requested a special ASRS search of relevant
database material in an effort to shed light on the various safety
problems foreseen. The result was the largest response (a stack
of computer printouts several inches thick) yet produced (under
the Freedom of Information Act, as are all such searches) by the
project. More than 1,200 incident reports were retrieved in
which the size of the crew (two- or three-person) was noted as

being relevant to the occurrence, either as a positive or negative influence.

John Lauber, now a member of the National Transportation Safety Board but at that time a prominent NASA human factors researcher and an adviser to ASRS, had been coopted to serve on the crew complement Task Force and had requested a copy of the FAA search response. As hearings progressed and became more heated, so did the Air Line Pilots Association, the Flight Engineers' Union, the Air Transport Association (representing the carriers), and at least one major aircraft manufacturer. Emphasizing the diversity of views and the impartiality of the ASRS data, the same information was used in the Washington hearings to buttress the testimony of the opposing factions.

A not entirely relevant, but interesting sidelight on the issue of crew complement versus safety is the fact that in 1957 the Aerospace Safety Division of the University of Southern California published a revised version of an earlier—and provocative— paper by Benjamin O. Howard, identified as "Consultant, Aviation Industry." "Benny" Howard was also a famed air racer, a widely respected test pilot and aircraft designer, and an iconoclast with strong opinions.

> *An important decrease in crash rates can be expected with decreases in the number of crew members involved in the operation of the airplane. . . . The ultimate in this respect is, of course, an airplane so designed that all operations affecting safety are handily done by one pilot. A landing gear is never prematurely retracted by a pilot as a result of his nose itching during a takeoff, but many DC-3 gears have been so retracted by the copilot when he interpreted the pilot's hand going up to scratch his nose or adjust his headphones as a signal for upgear. . . . It appears that the more help the pilot has in flying the airplane, the greater will be the probability of a crash. . . . The expectancy of crashes resulting from flight crew deficiencies is considerably increased when, *with respect to safety,* the management of the airplane requires the assistance of a flight engineer or third crew member.

The ultimate decision of the Task Force to approve the two-crew concept was accepted, albeit grudgingly by some parties to the argument, and early in the 1980s the first of the ADVTECH aircraft, with two-person flightcrews, made their operational debut on the airways. But, as *CALLBACK* commented, not without "growing pains and teething troubles" (No. 68, February 1985):

2,4,6,8—Everybody Automate

"It is questionable if all the mechanical inventions yet made have lightened the day's toil of any human being." So said the British philosopher John Stuart Mill about a hundred years ago. His American contemporary, Henry David Thoreau, agreed: "Lo! Men have become the tools of their tools." Both were expressing their contempt for the increasing pace of technology. This is a *CALL-BACK* essay dealing with the new problems associated with the "advanced cockpit," highly automated, aircraft now starting to occupy a prominent place in the skies. Early day pilots, forced to remove both hands from the controls in order to hold their fluttering road maps, learned to grip the stick with their leather-clad knees. The "gyro-pilot" soon came alone to make life somewhat easier for pilots of transports, and did a pretty fair job of keeping the aircraft on an even keel, but required almost constant attention to heading and pitch knobs to compensate for directional gyro precession and longitudinal trim changes (passengers occasionally walked down the aisle!). The old-timers around here (that takes in most of the ASRS staff) remember well the do-it-yourself "semi-automatic pilot" which eliminated the need to lean forward frequently to make the corrections. Grasping a long stick with a clip at one end, you could lean nonchalantly back in your seat and twiddle the knobs at arm's length without disturbing the box lunch in your lap.

In the 1940's the electronic autopilot appeared, providing automatic trimming, coordinated turns, and altitude hold; in due time course and approach couplers were added. Despite the 19th century gloom, these things did relieve flightcrew workload and helped to make flying smoother and safer. Now, as a consequence of advances in electronic knowledge and because of the emerging prevalence of the two-pilot crew and the high performance of the new-generation aircraft, we enter the world of the "glass" cockpit and the Flight and Performance Management Systems.

But not without some growing pains and teething troubles. . . . As new aircraft—and older ones retrofitted with new devices—have increased their proportion in air carrier and corporate fleets, so have ASRS reports of aberrant performance with the new equipment. Analysis of reports and frequent callbacks to reporters suggest that, as is the case with all such gear, some glitches do exist. In many instances problems seem to have arisen because of insufficient experience. Flightcrew training has sometimes been reported as less than optimum; maintenance difficulties may not have been identified; occasional allusions to design deficiencies have cropped up. On balance, it is the opinion of the ASRS staff that, as pilots gain actual flight experience with the complexities of advanced cockpit systems and their idiosyncracies, and as they adapt to the performance capabilities of the new aircraft, workloads will be eased and safety and efficiency of flight will be enhanced. Some examples of difficulties (or perceived difficulties) being encountered:

"Aircraft on autopilot climbing to 5000' MSL with Flight Guidance armed to level off at 5000. Flight Mode Annunciator indicated altitude capture approximately 4800, but did not transfer to altitude hold. By the time recovery was initiated (considering passenger comfort), aircraft went to 5600. Re-established flight path at 5000. Digital Flight Guidance System appears to have difficulty capturing altitudes with very high climb rates (5000+ FPM) immediately after takeoff below 10,000 MSL."

"We were descending to 16,000 feet. The autopilot was selected to level the aircraft. It was a quick descent and as we approached 16,000 the First Officer and I were briefing the approach. The altitude alerter interrupted us and I saw that we were at 15,600 and descending. We went to 15,400 before returning the aircraft to 16,000. One of us had apparently bumped the yoke enough to disengage altitude select. The lesson is obvious. When levelling at an altitude, automatically or manually, full attention must be paid. We allowed ourselves to get rushed. I no longer try to do several things at the same time."

"We were climbing out of FL380 for 390 (called by F/O). Vertical navigation system was climbing aircraft at about 2500 FPM (this was noted by crew as being excessive for last 1000 feet). At 38,800 we realized the altitude capture and hold wasn't going to function properly and Captain attempted to control (stop) the rate of climb with the vertical speed control knob (this is usually smoother than disconnecting the autopilot and pushing over . . .). Anyway, we overshot FL390 by about 500' by the time we got the ascent stopped."

"Both crew members were new to the aircraft. Descent was made on autopilot in the PERF mode. We marvelled as the autopilot levelled us at 10,000, slowed to 250 knots, descended to and levelled at 8000. We were then vectored for the approach and the F/O asked, "How do I get it out of PERF?" I replied, "Just punch something else." I was involved in the checklist and failed to see that the F/O selected IAS HOLD for the pitch channel. This did get the autopilot out of PERF and did keep our indicated airspeed at the requested value, but of course wiped out ALT HOLD mode of the pitch channel. I was made aware when the altitude alert sounded at 7750' and we then returned to 8000."

"Flight Director Annunciator indicated ALTITUDE CAPTURE. The reason the aircraft failed to level off automatically is that I accidentally touched the vertical speed wheel and it switched from ALTITUDE CAPTURE to VERTICAL SPEED mode."

"On autopilot, Flight Management System, DESCENT mode, and changing program to slow to holding speed. Neither pilot noticed that ALTITUDE CAPTURE was not activated. Aircraft descended through 350 to 337 before Captain took over manually. . . . Problem caused by both pilots being involved with reloading computer. Captain was showing F/O how to make FMS slow down and descend at the same time."

"Once it is recognized that the intended level off is not going to be affected by the autopilot/autothrottles, manual control will still result in a several-hundred-foot excursion due to the negative "G" injury-risk factor to Flight Attendants and passengers."

Etc., etc., etc. Most of the reported incidents involve climb/descent/level-off problems, but there are others.

"Received FMC (Flight Management Computer) message on CDU (Control Display Unit) of IRS NAV ONLY (inertial Reference). We noticed that the DME's were not being tuned by the FMC. Tried tuning different VOR's remotely through CDU but FMC would not lock on DME display (tuned). Continued using LNAV and aircraft showed on track. . . . Tuned VOR manually and noted full scale north of course. . . . FMC worked perfectly after being realigned . . . be aware that HSI map may develop significant errors when DME is not being tuned by FMC and on IRS NAV ONLY."

All ASRS pilot staff members had coped with the growth of cockpit automation over the years (although we hadn't thought of the new gadgetry appearing in our airplanes in such elegant terms), but it now appeared that with the new wave—the two-crew cockpit and truly advanced systems—we had been out of school too long; a refresher course was in order. The airlines and aircraft manufacturers of which we are alumni, cooperated in providing familiarization sessions, including flight deck passes and simulator sessions. Led by the enthusiasm of Old Eagle Capt. Harry Orlady, ASRS attacked the ADVTECH subject with gusto, initiating several research studies.

In a paper delivered at a Flight Safety Foundation International Air Safety Forum in Vancouver, in October 1986, Captain Orlady discussed one approach:

*Fortunately ASRS has temporary access to the pilots and controllers who submit reports. This access is unique, and permits our analysts to contact reporters by telephone to solicit additional information regarding their incidents before the reports are "de-identified" by removing and returning the reports' identity strips. From a research standpoint, this access to its reporters is one of the ASRS's greatest strengths. In this study of cockpit automation from the pilot's viewpoint we used telephone callbacks to supplement the initial data reported. We also used the callbacks to secure a great deal of organized general survey information that went well beyond the incidents reported. . . .

Unlike many safety-oriented studies whose purposes are primarily to identify faults or deficiencies, this ASRS study was concerned with both the positive and negative aspects of cockpit automation as they were perceived by the pilots flying ADVTECH airplanes. We believed it was as important to identify the automatics that increased safety and efficiency—that worked well in the system—as it was to identify those that didn't help the operation or that created problems. The rationale was that the positive responses would help identify the subsystems that should be automated and the automation principles that didn't work. Those that created problems, and that pilots didn't like or didn't use, could help identify the automatics that, for any reason, were not working well in the real world.

Over a period of sixty days, Captain Orlady and his analyst cohorts made forty-eight of these "structured" callbacks, lasting from 45 minutes to more than 2 hours, and averaging 1 hour and 20 minutes. "Without exception, the reporters were more than willing to discuss their incidents and answer the questions in the general survey. They also provided their professional opinions regarding many of the issues that had been raised and volunteered a wealth of supporting anecdotal detail . . . 90% of both captains and copilots changed from a three- to a two-person crew when they transitioned to ADVTECH airplanes."

Further and more detailed studies of the subject continue as a growing number of routine ASRS reports deal with the new generation of aircraft—and pilots. In concluding this preliminary examination, the author summarized, "There is no question that the responding pilots like the ADVTECH airplanes—and they like *most* of their automatics." Some frustration was noted by the pilots over their interaction with the ATC system. This point is discussed in detail in the paper; it relates to the inability of the present ATC system to allow optimum use of ADVTECH airplanes—"primarily because of the amount of traffic in busy centers and the wide variety of performance in their traffic mix."

Reporters in this survey expressed "considerable concern over their ability to maintain an adequate traffic watch and to monitor effectively." SOPs and the allocation of duties were frequently mentioned as areas of concern in connection with the transition to the new airplanes.

At Captain Orlady's request, *CALLBACK* carried a brief article entitled, "Automation—How Goes It?" appealing "to the

Troops. . . . Have you encountered a situation or been involved in an incident in which cockpit automation has helped or hindered you? Do you have any comments?"

Plenty of comments ensued, both in regular ASRS reports and in the letters to the editor, which have, from the beginning, brought so much pleasure and so much insight into the human aspects of safe flight. One of the first responses came in the form of a letter from

> *a brand new Captain in [one of the earliest ADVTECH airplanes] with only a month on the airplane (50 hours on the line). Automation has not been a problem; it has helped more than hindered—and I think I will have an even stronger positive opinion when I get more time. The only negative I can see is the possibility of too much heads (both) down-time messing with the Flight Management Computer when at least one of you, if not both, should be looking for traffic. This becomes very important as we no longer have the luxury of that third set of young (usually) and sharp eyeballs. . . . Flying long transcontinental legs direct at Flight Levels of 390 and 410 really makes things easy—and saves gas.

The correspondent confirmed the findings of the Orlady structured callback campaign and pointed out that the new airplanes were not only new in their automated features; their performance capabilities represented a considerable improvement over the older generation: "ATC doesn't seem to be very aware of the FMC capabilities and often we can't use them as they were designed (particularly on descent) due to altitude and airspeed restrictions. Late descents (normal for other aircraft but late for us) mean using speed brakes during a significant period on almost every descent; maybe this will improve as more "clean" airplanes get in the system."

A minor side effect of the high tech revolution has been the introduction of a whole new lexicon of initial and acronymic nomenclature. An ASRS report printed in *CALLBACK* No. 94 (April 1987) offered some translation aid:

High Tech ABC's

> "Captain was flying aircraft on autopilot using Indicated Airspeed (IAS) hold mode of the Flight Guidance Computer (FGC) to descend to assigned altitude of 7000'. I was checking approach plate information when I heard 'ALTITUDE' from the Central Aural Warning System (CAWS). I immediately pressed 'Altitude Hold' mode on the Digital Flight Guidance System (DFGS) and at the same instant Approach called to enquire about our altitude. He (ATC) reported us

through 6600'. . . . We climbed back to our assigned altitude (7000). . . . This is another perfect example of the Altitude Alert system working at its best to tell you that it's time to file another NASA report."

Tell the Aviation Safety Reporting System (ASRS) right away (PDQ) and protect yourself (CYA).

In reporting a similar problem, a pilot wrote, "at about 250' low the altitude warning sounded and the 'girl' started saying, 'Altitude!' " (for the meaning of "girl," see translation of "CAWS" in paragraph above). The reporter also voiced a frequently heard plaint: "It was one of those high tech glitches that was not a 'gotcha'—this time. But when that high tech stray electron gets loose next time?" Another reporter echoes, "Transient malfunctions of this type have occurred previously. They do not occur again for many flight hours and cycles. . . . We refer to these episodes with some element of humor as a case of 'bad 'trons' (bad electrons). I'm sure these episodes also occur in other computer-controlled aircraft."

Erratic behavior of the new systems has drawn frequent critical comment. "For some reason the computer erased the crossing restrictions and continued to descend. . . . I have never had any incidents such as this until the computers came along. I think I'll fly the airplane and they can use the computers in ground school."

The merging of airlines (and establishment of new ones) since deregulation has encouraged the purchase or lease of basically similar aircraft often differing in degree of cockpit automation. ASRS analysts refer to the result as "fleet inconsistency"; it can bring its own brand of trouble, as the finale of this report illustrates: "Contributing is the fact that my airline now has four different cockpit configurations, uses a fifth for training, and is planning to buy additional transports with a sixth. . . . On a given day one can fly two or three different types of flight director systems."

No doubt flightcrews will become accustomed to the new aircraft and their systems as time passes and as they learn through experience the idiosyncracies; bad 'trons, too, will decrease as designers and manufacturers refine their products. During this transition period there will be conflicting opinions on the new era and some cries of regret for the passing of the good old days, but the spread of ADVTECH is inevitable.

High technology will indeed continue its spread throughout the aviation industry, but the words of the late distinguished British Royal Air Force flight surgeon H. P. Ruffell Smith seem applicable to the situation:

Lest We Forget

Man is not as good as a black box for certain specific things; however he is more flexible & reliable. He is easily maintained & can be manufactured by relatively unskilled labour.

9

Great Catches

Dark and stormy night. Deep stack of aircraft flying around and around west of O'Hare. Harassed Approach Controller transmitting almost nonstop: "Global 25, cleared ILS, report the Outer Marker; Universal 762, descend to eight thousand, report leaving niner, etc., etc., etc." Impatient voice breaks in: "What's our expected approach time? If we hang around here much longer, we'll have to go to Minneapolis." Controller, without stopping for breath: "Roger, cleared to Minneapolis; Universal 762, you are now cleared for the ILS, etc., etc." One of our analysts, until recently a very senior Captain on a very major airline, and a fellow not given to fantasy, says he heard this little interchange. Recognized the impatient speaker's voice, too, as that of a newly-checked out widebody Captain on his own line.

That little anecdote appeared sandwiched among more serious matter in *CALLBACK* No. 1 (July 1979) under the heading "ORD Controller Aims to Please." It was intended to make good on my announced editorial hope that readers might find the ASRS bulletin "interesting, instructive, and even—sometimes—entertaining." At least it entertained the small group of pioneer Old Eagles gathered in my office for the daily brown-bag-lunch-and-hangar-flying session, reminding one of them of an earlier (and less credible) story about a busy night at La Guardia in those good old days: A pilot, near the top of a deep stack of holding giant DC-3 airliners, became apprehensive about his reserve fuel and, according to our man, quietly departed and flew to Syracuse. After refueling there, he returned to La Guardia, surveyed the tiers of circling running lights, and resumed his proper place in the stack.

Although not so identified, the story in the premier issue was the first of many in later *CALLBACK*s to deal with a prominent aspect of the flying world. A column in 1981, using the ASRS in-house term, discussed the matter. It is followed by another, with the heading provided by a more eminent writer.

Party Line

Everybody in the neighborhood talking on the same frequency: Annoying sometimes; sometimes very useful in providing clues on the activities of others. And sometimes productive of problems. First, a report from an alert and responsible pilot to illustrate party line value. Second, instances of the opposite. Some faulty "hearback" appears, too.

"We (in Aircraft 'A') were proceeding south on the Airway at Flight Level 370 when we heard another aircraft ('B') report on the frequency at FL 430, so we assumed this might be opposite direction traffic. A few minutes later we heard an unidentified voice on the Center frequency saying things like, 'Hello, hello, hello . . . Test, one, two, three, hello, hello, hello . . . Do you hear me? I can't hear you, George. . . . Test, one, two. . . .' Shortly after this the following conversation (to the best of my recollection) took place:

"Center: Aircraft 'B'. descend at pilot's discretion to maintain one six thousand. Altimeter XXXX.

" 'B': Roger, Aircraft 'B' cleared to six thousand.

"(Shortly thereafter)

" 'B': 'B' is leaving 430 for six thousand.

"Center: Roger.

"Me (Aircraft 'A'): Center, this is 'A.' Just out of curiosity, we thought we heard you clear the other aircraft to ONE six thousand and he read back SIX thousand twice and you acknowledged. Which is correct?

"Center: ONE six thousand! Aircraft 'B', maintain sixteen thousand; that's ONE SIX thousand.

"'B': 'B', descending to one six thousand. We were just about to ask you about that.

"Center: 'A', thank you very much. I had you on the overhead speaker because maintenance was running some checks on the headphones, and that sort of confused the issue. Thanks again.

"I don't know for sure that 'B' was on the same airway, but there's a 6500 foot mountain on the centerline and that day the cloud bases were about 2000 feet and the tops about 10,000. . . . Had things gone differently there might have been a CFIT ['Controlled Flight Into Terrain', discussed in an earlier *CALLBACK*]. This is, perhaps, a classic example of the start of a snowball effect—a series of minor occurrences each insignificant by itself but cumulatively disastrous. I think history has shown distraction or changes in routine are often associated with snowball-type accidents. I suggest that pilots and controllers be especially alert whenever there's something unusual going on, however minor it may seem."

People who study the human factors involved in aviation safety think of this sort of thing as a chain with a number of links. If the chain is broken at any point short of the end, the otherwise inevitable result will be averted. Our conscientious reporter broke one of the links—and all was well.

The Babbling Gossip of the Air

Shakespeare wrote that. He wasn't thinking of our party line, but this controller was:

"Busy issuing instructions to aircraft arriving and departing when a pilot asked another how his ride was at his altitude and to tell him how it had been. The flight that initiated the conversation did not ask me if I had anything going on and if he could use the frequency to talk to another aircraft. This delayed instructions to other aircraft. . . . This is an example of disregard and is a dangerous thing to do. This is not just limited to air carriers. . . . I had two General Aviation aircraft do the same thing. At least when a pilot asks permission to use the frequency the controller can tell him to keep it short."

It's a good idea to remember that there are other aircraft up there—and that some of them may have call signs much like yours. It's easy to get a wrong number on aviation's party line.

"Airport using Runways 10 and 19 for takeoff. We were cleared for takeoff on 10. As we rotated, another aircraft was passing over the departure end at about 100', heading south after taking off on 19. Because of our configuration and speed, we could continue only straight ahead. We passed about 1000' behind him. Our flight numbers were somewhat similar. From information I received later, the other aircraft also took our clearance for takeoff."

"Maintaining Flight Level 250 (had requested lower and been

told descent would be forthcoming). We heard controller tell another aircraft, 'Maintain 260, turn left account traffic to the right.'
We were eastbound and about to start a right turn. Out our left
side was an aircraft apparently southbound . . . felt that a right
turn was best action. The second aircraft reported, 'Traffic in
sight.' Clearance was then issued for my flight, 'Descend on present heading. . . .' Upon arrival I contacted Center and the other
flightcrew. Apparently the other flight answered a clearance
intended for our flight (but not received or acknowledged) and
started descent, whereupon the controller issued the 'Maintain
260, turn left' instruction."

Listening carefully before acting is another good thing to
remember.

"We took evasive action to avoid a small aircraft that had been
instructed to follow us. He had acknowledged and reported us in
sight. I believe he saw another aircraft and ASSUMED we had mis-
represented our position."

We think that if the pilot of the small aircraft had been listening
to the frequency he would have realized there were two aircraft
inbound.

As some of these narratives illustrate, eavesdropping on aviation's party line can be an important safety aid; conversely, inattention to what's happening on the frequency can jeopardize a
flight. On several occasions, *CALLBACK* has reported on incidents in which the availability of the party line, even for nonin-
tended purposes, has prevented serious consequences. From No.
51 (September 1983):

Commendation Column

The two flightcrew narratives that follow deal with two situations
of extreme hazard which, happily, were brought to safe conclusions by the quick reactions of observant, not otherwise involved,
bystanding pilots. Their alertness, vigilance, and prompt responses to perceived danger—in the words used by the armed
forces in the award of medals—". . . upheld the highest traditions
of . . . ," in these cases, the flying profession. Well done, Fellow
Members!

"Our widebody aircraft was moving on to the active runway for
takeoff when the crew of another aircraft informed us that we had
two spoilers on our left wing in the FULL UP position. We aborted
takeoff and returned to ramp for maintenance inspection. Two
spoilers on left wing were jammed in full up position and would
not return to normal position. Cycling controls, switches and systems was no help. . . . Trying to push spoilers down manually was
no help. . . . There is no cockpit indication of this condition and

horn will not sound. Follow-up from maintenance: control rods from spoiler mixer were dry and lacked lubrication. . . . Recommendation: Pre-flight inspection of top of both wings to ensure spoilers are flush."

Spoilers are very useful devices, intended to spoil the airflow over aircraft wings when such is desirable. They can also spoil other things—like your whole day—when they fail to operate as they are supposed to do.

"Widebody air carrier was on final approach and cleared to land on Runway 25R. A small aircraft had been cleared to land on Runway 24R, but mistook his runway in restricted visibility and headed for 25R. The runways are 6000 feet apart and the respective tower frequencies are not common. The small aircraft was below and slightly ahead of the widebody—both headed for the same runway. As it looked like a possible collision would occur, the crew of another air carrier parked at the end of the taxiway for 25R broadcast a warning on tower frequency. No reply. They then broadcast for the widebody to take it around—as the small aircraft had landed just ahead of it. At about 100 feet AGL the widebody went around. The tower was unaware of the incident until they saw the small aircraft on the ground and the widebody going around. There is no question in the minds of the parked aircraft's crew that had the widebody landed he would have demolished the small aircraft."

Excerpts from reports carried in later *CALLBACK*s are reminiscent of the two above. The second was headed, "Who Done It?" and included editorial comment:

"Pilot from another airline behind us advised that we had a panel on the right wing extended. Visual check by Second Officer confirmed that an outboard roll spoiler was fully extended. Our flight control position indicator showed a very slight extension. Returned to ramp. . . . I seriously doubt if this crew would have noticed the very small indication. . . . I can only guess we would have had our hands full in flight with this panel stuck full-up. My sincere thanks to the alert airline crew on behalf of myself and crew and 245 passengers who didn't have to experience this in-flight incident!"

"We were cleared for takeoff on Runway 18, while an aircraft on short final for 36 landed. Did not see other aircraft until well into takeoff run. After rotation we immediately moved to the right of landed aircraft."

Seemed a straightforward report until ASRS Analyst checked the airport and found that it lacked a tower. UNICOM operators, other pilots, bystanders may give informal advisories in trying to be helpful ("Hell is paved with good intentions," it has been said)

and Flight Service Specialists can offer suggestions, but nobody—
NOBODY—can "clear" an aircraft for takeoff except a qualified
and authorized Air Traffic Controller. "Pilot's Discretion" is the
operative rule under any other circumstances.

As has so often proved to be the case in the ASRS program, a
reported occurrence, seemingly unique, is soon followed by a
reply. A *CALLBACK* account in 1985, describing a variation on
the party line theme, had an echo two years later. The echo was
reported by a captain whose several earlier reports, like the one
here, displayed an unusually droll outlook:

> He That Hath Ears to Hear, Let Him Hear
>
> St. Mark

Today's aviation safety record is made possible in part by the multiple redundancies built into the system. Here's an account of a
backup we hadn't heard of before:

"During the time the First Officer was trying to get the ATIS it
was being updated, which took several minutes. While he was off
the ATC frequency, the ear-piece for my headset disconnected from
the headset and therefore I had lost communication with Center
for one to two minutes. My passengers were hooked up to the ATC
channel of the Audio Entertainment System and had heard Center
trying to call us. They reported this to the Flight Attendants who,
in turn, came to the cockpit to check on us. We discovered our
disconnected headset at this point and re-established contact with
ATC. The loss of communication was perhaps very short in duration, but we had travelled 10–15 miles."

Stay Tuned

"Even Captains on Modern Giant Airliners have to leave the cockpit now and then for 'physiological reasons.' My widebody plane
was equipped with five astro-potties; it was also equipped with a
switch that allows the passengers to eavesdrop on air-ground
communications. This switch was ON throughout the flight.
When the physiological reason became very pressing I went to the
back of the aircraft, as I knew both astro-potties were working.
This also allowed me to check for old buddies aboard and to find
out if my knees still worked. Returning up the aisle through the
coach section, a passenger stopped me to say (with a big grin and
a pat on the back) that 'Center is trying to call you! You'd better go
back up there!' I went back to the cockpit to find the copilot talking to a flight attendant. His radio volume had mysteriously been
turned off! Did an itinerant gremlin cause this lever to go off,
or . . . ?"

No gremlin; no mystery. ASRS analyst, a retired captain experienced in this type of aircraft, has explained that the advance-technology aircraft audio-selector panel, on the central console, is fitted with unusually long levers to control receiver volume. These can be moved inadvertently—and very easily. Our man says he has done it himself by snagging a cuff while turning in his seat to speak to a flightdeck visitor. Incidentally, the Captain who reported this adventure answered the first question on the ASRS Report Form (Reporter's Role During Occurrence?) with "INNO-CENT!"

Another matched pair, again separated by two years, points up still a different aspect of Everybody-on-the-Same-Frequency. Second reporter offers sensible advice:

@#&*!

"Annoyed that Approach Control kicked me off a practice ILS approach (inside the Outer Marker) for following traffic and gave me extensive delaying vectors, I roundly cursed the controller, thinking only my safety pilot could hear me. After several minutes Approach Control asked us, rather pointedly. '. . . have you heard someone on the frequency doing a lot of cursing—using a lot of profanity?' 'Ah, negative,' I stammered, immediately wondering (silently, for once) if I'd had an intermittent stuck mike. Moral: ANY aircraft can have a stuck mike; if you're gonna cuss in the cockpit, do it at your own risk. . . . As I told my safety pilot—in a diatribe liberally salted with invectives—I thought the separation vectors, though prescribed by ATC rules, were not necessary. . . . I also had roundly cursed the flightcrew of an arriving airliner. . . . Again, this is a hobby I enjoy in the (so I thought) privacy of my own cockpit. . . . I was flying with a hand mike, which I usually drop into my lap when busy. Might I have squeezed the side button on the mike with my thighs? Might I have unconsciously depressed the mike button on the yoke and thus activated the hand mike? I don't know."

Tsk, tsk—three days suspension from the Fellowship of Flying. Try counting to ten slowly next time.

"X" Rated

Or at least Parental Guidance Advised before listening to the Tower tapes. . . . This is the second ASRS report carried in *CALLBACK* of earthy comments transmitted via an inadvertently open microphone. Watch your language, Troops—or watch that mike button!

"Somewhere during the BEFORE-TAKEOFF checklist (challenge and response) my mike button became stuck. This disabled the intercom. The F/O and I (after investigating several other reasons as to why the intercom wasn't working) finally discovered the problem. Of course our conversation was transmitted on Tower local frequency. I have no doubt a few mild obscenities were transmitted also. . . . Tower never mentioned the problem but we were quite embarrassed. Any transmit problem should first be assumed to be a stuck mike (to avoid disabling ATC). Also, keep cockpit language relatively clean (or at least 'PG' rated) in case this event occurs."

Air Traffic Controllers appear as the principle figures in many ASRS reports of narrowly averted disasters, often acting well beyond the requirements of duty. In one case, an alert controller doubtless prevented the loss of a military plane and its pilot but, as *CALLBACK* said, "Local citizens may thank him for keeping their favorite TV program on the air."

*Fighter was on instrument training route, but was off course about 17 miles East. He descended below the limitations of his route and was descending directly toward terrain with a TV antenna charted at 3098′ MSL. Aircraft had left 4000′ and was not talking to Approach Control. The controller working that radar sector transmitted in the blind to aircraft on VHF Guard to IDENT if he received Approach. When he idented the aircraft was about five miles from obstacle. When controller advised him of his position and the elevation of the terrain the aircraft was less than three miles from the mountain and the antenna. He made an immediate turn to the West, still descending, and went below 3098 MSL. No one knows for sure whether the pilot would have turned, but if not he surely would have wiped out the crest of the mountain and TV Channel 12 off the air.

In an incident reported by a grateful—and now wiser—general aviation pilot, a center controller and an approach controller teamed to prevent another Controlled-flight-into-terrain (CFIT) accident; the report is followed by one from a second grateful pilot, who describes a not untypical controller "catch."

*Conscientious and alert Center Controller still observing aircraft on radar after handing it off to non-radar-equipped Approach Control. . . . Approach instructed aircraft to maintain 10,000 until 21 DME, then cleared for the back course approach. Everything trimmed up, tracking inbound right on the button, autopilot switched to ILS (and ILS DME), pilot verified he had a few miles to go at 10,000, flipped the autopilot on, and blithely went about cleaning up the cockpit (putting away maps, other approach plates, etc.) . . . diverted his attention for at least a full minute. When he next glanced at the DME readout he was just inside the 21 miles checkpoint and began the descent.
What he failed to observe is that he had placed the autopilot in

'NORMAL' tracking instead of 'REVERSE' or 'BACK COURSE' tracking and, while his attention was diverted, the autopilot took the aircraft through a beautiful coordinated 180 degree turn. He was now heading due wrong!

Center Controller noted the course reverse on radar, phoned Approach, who contacted the aircraft, verified the incorrect heading, then asked, "Give me your best rate of climb immediately . . . ," very calmly. The back course approach is characterized by very high terrain within very close proximity to the descent profile.

The pilot was taught a great lesson, and fortunately survived to remember it. NEVER, NEVER DIVERT YOUR ATTENTION FROM THE INSTRUMENTS ONCE YOU ARE POTENTIALLY BELOW TERRAIN ON AN APPROACH! Thank you, Center, and thank you, Approach, for calmly getting me out of danger. I'd like to think I was just beginning to recognize the problem when you saw it and hollered. But the truth is, you probably saved my life!

Bang! Bang!

*Descending, cleared by Approach Control to 3000'. WX was 3500 broken, 10 miles, by ATIS, and we were below clouds at 3000. Visibility was generally good except for patchy shadows caused by sunlight and clouds. When cleared to 1500', we began descent. Passing 2900, Approach said there was traffic at 12 o'clock, one mile, unreported VFR at 2800'. Just then I saw the plane as it emerged from the shadows into sunlight and I took evasive action. The other plane never deviated and we cleared it by 100'. Then I saw a second plane just behind the first by ¼ mile and again took evasive action. The second plane also turned away and we cleared by 1000 yards.

While sky conditions were reported good VFR and were as reported, it is hard to see in patchy shadow and bright light. Credit the Approach Controller for a timely call. I might not have seen the first one in time, and I was looking, as was the copilot. Contributing to the difficulty was near head-on approach with almost no relative movement. . . . A warning to planes that are under control is worth every bit of the controller's effort. P.S. I have already sent thanks through his supervisor.

A *CALLBACK* column in 1983 headed "Matched Pair" contained reports from two pilots who "blundered into the same pickle: Caught on top without the instruments required to execute safe descents; rescue was effected by fortuitous join-up with other aircraft for shepherding down." In the first incident controller intervention aided the safe outcome; reporter's comments follow the second.

1. "Flight was planned . . . VFR on top, dead reckoning . . . , no NAV gear. . . . Received wx briefing calling for 4000 scattered at destination. Filed VFR flight plan and departed for a planned 2:30 flight with 3:00 fuel. . . . Proceeded to destination area VFR on top at 11,500′. Checked destination wx en route and forecast was amended to 7000′ overcast. By this time it was too late to return to departure point and the best wx forecast within my range was still the original destination. Contacted Center 150 miles northwest and destination wx was given as 2500 overcast. I then declared an emergency as I would have to descend through 5000′ feet of clouds with no gyros. I requested Center to send an aircraft to intercept me and they provided a small plane that was in the area. I descended in very close formation on him as he made an approach and landed with no further incident."

2. "I was pilot-in command, aviation manager was in left seat. . . . Weather was approximately $\frac{3}{4}$ mile visibility, with fog and stratus right down on the ground. We were cleared for takeoff; aviation manager began T.O. roll. . . . I checked engine instruments on his side . . . and noticed his airspeed indicator begin to indicate forward airspeed. I then focused on engine instruments on my side and called their readings as OK. At the same time I saw my airspeed indicator still reading '0'. I called to him that my airspeed was reading zero and glanced back to his airspeed. As it reached V_1 I called it. He rotated and, as the airplane left the ground, all pitot/static instruments failed. When this happened we climbed on attitude instruments to VFR conditions and told Departure Control of our problem. We remained VFR, checking wx one more time, then proceeded to an open airport. We joined up with a light twin who we followed to flare point in loose formation (for speed control) and landed uneventfully. After landing we discovered all static ports taped closed (airplane was washed the night before)."

This reporter suggests several things; red streamers under tape when washing; remove tape after washing; more thorough preflight inspection; most important, remember the alternate static source selectors. Both pilots expressed embarrassment and felt, particularly, that their failure to remember the alternate static procedure reflected on their professionalism.

Timely warnings from heads-up controllers have prevented many a belly landing, gaining many a commendation. Typical:

*This is supposed to happen to the other guy. "No excuse," pretty well sums it up. It was a visual approach on a beautiful clear day. . . . At approximately 500 feet the tower advised us of no gear.

I started to flare the airplane, when the tower controller came to my rescue with, "Go around; no gear"—classic case of distraction and complacency. . . . Fortunately the controller was not suffering from the same affliction. His job includes all the aforementioned hazards plus boredom due to the light traffic load at this airport lately. His professionalism, as the saying goes, saved my bacon.

Bacon-saving by ATC folk is not restricted to potential gear-up landings. Modern radar and altitude-reporting transponders allow early detection and notification to errant pilots of altitude assignment deviations, eliciting more commendations—and more self-criticism.

*Controller caught our overshoot, not us, and apprised us of our error. Needless to say, my ears are still burning. The controller was professional and a gentleman about not turning the knife, for which I thank him. Personal recrimination and soul-searching is enough.

The system works. A very sharp, alert controller was watching and notified us of our transgression.

*Only real explanation seems to be that awful word—complacency (Hiss!). Score (another) one for the controller and modern radar. Looks like the system works.

Aeronautical operations are no more immune to oversights and errors than are most other forms of endeavor. Fortunately, many of these mistakes are trivial; some may have disastrous consequences. It is encouraging that most are caught by pilots themselves, on preflight inspections or otherwise; by other observant pilots; by controllers; by ground personnel. The errors may involve nonextension of wheels; extended spoilers or not extended flaps; covered static ports; ignored gear pins or control locks; altitude or course deviations—the list is infinite. Few are unique, but the ASRS database contains a few narratives of rare catches. Here are two *CALLBACK* stories; both refer, coincidentally, to buckets of ice in an uncommon context:

In Martinis, OK—On Wings, No!

*Cold night at the airport. Captain decided to take a look over the right wing while the catering truck was up at the galley door. When he stuck his head out the galley door he noticed ice cubes on the inboard portion of the wing. When quizzed about the ice cubes, the catering people said that they were throwing extra ice on the ramp and some (two buckets worth) happened to land on the wing.

They also said, "It was no problem." Solution: The Captain called ramp service and had them de-ice the right wing. I liked his decision, since the aircraft manufacturer never did ice cube tests on airfoils. If more pilots took precautions as this captain did, we would all have fewer accident reports to read. I learned from it!

Encore Hazmat

CALLBACK No. 81 4/86 discussed examples of hazardous material shipped—innocently or otherwise—on aircraft. We now borrow from Transport Canada's "Safety Letter," which borrowed in turn from "Professional Pilot," an account of a very innocent, yet potentially hazardous incident.

"The manifest for the charter listed three executives and some tasty cargo—several large containers of their company's ice cream—all bound for an exposition on a neighboring island. It was a typically hot September day in [the area] and we had the air conditioning on while we taxied to the active. Even so, as we trundled along I noticed that breathing was becoming difficult. Probably just an insignificant something or other, I thought. No need for alarm, or mention. I turned the [twin turboprop] on the runway and was about to shove the power levers forward when my copilot said, 'I wonder if they packed that ice cream in dry ice.' The alarm finally went off in my head. I aborted the takeoff, popped open the cockpit vent windows and went back to investigate. The ice cream containers were being cooled by two or three buckets full of dry ice. We heaved the dry ice overboard and then resumed the journey. . . . When I queried the passengers after the discovery, all three admitted they, too, had experienced breathing difficulty while we were taxiing out, but each had assumed the problem was unique to himself (as had I). Were it not for my copilot speaking up. . . ."

"Professional Pilot" quotes from an FAA Advisory Circular that states that dry ice (solid carbon dioxide), while not poisonous, "is an asphyxiant which can be life-threatening in high concentrations" such as in confined spaces with poor ventilation. Open the windows and throw the stuff out. And beware of the Good Humor Man!

An editorial in *CALLBACK* No. 74, in August 1985, offered some advice for avoiding situations like those in this chapter: "Beware, Be Wary, Be Aware."

10

Checklist—Or Check Out

I am writing this book on a word processor—a device that has become almost as necessary to a writer as an aircraft to a pilot, and about as similar to a typewriter as a modern advanced-technology airliner to a Ford Tri-motor. Among the features of my machine is a built-in computerized dictionary, which defines "checklist" as "a complete list." Not very helpful. . . . Nor is the related thesaurus, which flashes, "There is no entry for checklist," and suggests as possible substitutes(!): "chuckles," "cheekiest," "catchiest," "chattiest." "Reminder" does better: "Something that keeps a person or thing in mind." Synonyms: "expression," "gesture," "indication," "sign," "token."

Everybody who flies understands the meaning of "checklist" and most recognize the concept and importance of the "reminder." In aviation's early days there wasn't much to forget, but increasingly complex machines soon began to make demands on the operators which, if ignored, often led to disaster—or at least to serious troubles. Written reminder lists and placards on vari-

116

ous instruments and controls became the first reminders, and an assistant pilot served the cause in the larger aircraft. Ingenious tinkerers and well-meaning experts devised an astonishing array of solutions to the "I forgot" problem; I can recall a popular 1950s transport equipped, on many airlines, with a roller contraption on which the pilot could rotate small knobs to reveal detailed printed checklists for every phase of flight. A popular mechanical marvel relied on a board with a series of sliding plates covering the check items, which were unveiled as the checking process proceeded. A variant of this one had a row of small lights which were illuminated as the accompanying item was ticked off. Still another featured small pegs which fitted in holes beside each check entry. In time manufacturers provided printed cards or pages in manuals to cover all aspects of preflight, takeoff, climb, cruise, descent, approach, landing, and postflight procedures, with sections to cover all imaginable emergencies.

Today's pilots rely on a combination of memory, SOP, and printed lists, with the challenge-response system used by most multiperson crews. Air carrier aircraft are equipped with a multitude of bells, whistles, horns, and lights to warn or remind, including the attention-getting ground proximity warning system (GPWS) that uses a human voice (sometimes irreverently referred to as "the girl") to warn of danger. Many pilots flying simple aircraft resort to memory-jogging mnemonics such as the well-known GUMPS check (gas; undercarriage; mixture; prop; stabilizer), and many small aircraft have their own warning lights and horns. Accordingly, nothing should be overlooked—should it? But, regrettably, something often is—the oversight usually induced by one (or both) of those twin demons, complacency and distraction. And ASRS often hears about it. *CALLBACK* has carried many tales of overlooking; here's the full text of an early one, summarized briefly in Chapter 6:

There Are Those-Who-Have and Those-Who-Are-Going-To . . .

The pilots in this true-to-life adventure story fortunately escaped joining the Those-Who-Have Club; we'll bet they never will after this lesson. We like to think that all reports to ASRS are of equal interest but, as the late George Orwell said in a somewhat different context, "Some are more equal than others." The narrative that follows is considerably more equal than most. In fact, it is almost a textbook in itself on how individual factors can compound to lead innocent flightcrews down the garden path.

Captain was in his first 100 hours in type. We now turn it over to the First Officer: "At 6000′ MSL, heading southeast, 10 miles from the airport, Captain accepted a visual approach to Runway 21R. Just outside the marker he called for 25 degrees flaps, as the aircraft was very high (recommended OM altitude—2300′). After catching the glideslope from above, a stabilized approach was established at 500–600 feet per minute, gear up. A headwind of approximately 40 knots caused abnormally high power settings, not allowing gear warning horn to sound. The final vector from Approach Control caused turn-on to be inside the marker. Also, traffic was called by Approach, paralleling to land on the left runway (no contact by crew). Tower was contacted in vicinity of marker. Our aircraft was to the right of the localizer because of traffic (not sighted). Inside the marker, Tower called parallel traffic.

"This prevented Captain from making his normal gear call and caused First Officer and Second Officer to be diverted outside cockpit. Shortly thereafter, Tower called that helicopter traffic would be passing under approach course at 1300′ MSL (550′ above ground). All crew then again searched for traffic (no contact). By this time, aircraft had descended to 550′ AGL, where Ground Proximity Warning sounded, 'Improper Landing Configuration'. This was confusing and caused a delayed response, since crew then thought that helicopter had passed under our aircraft.

"At 350′ Captain recognized that gear was not down, saying, '!@#&; the gear's not down.'† His response was to begin to initiate a smooth go-around. In the confusion, First Officer put the gear down anyway. Although there was probably enough time for a safe landing, Captain elected to make the go-around. Doing so smoothly, the aircraft descended to about 150′ AGL. Go-around was successful. No further incidents." Just as well, too. . . .

†What the Captain really said was just what all the thousands of Those-Who-Have said under similar circumstances (What else is there to say?). *CALLBACK* regrets that, as a family publication, it must dilute slightly this forceful narrative. Shucks!

The reporting first officer appended a detailed list of the multiple complexities and distractions leading to this almost-incident. *CALLBACK* added, "Sort of reminds you of that old, old, old story of the pilot who couldn't hear the tower tell him his gear was up because that blasted horn was making so much noise. Don't feel too badly, Captain and crew; most of us have been there ourselves."

Coincidentally, that same early *CALLBACK* discussed an article from Pan Am's flightcrew bulletin *Crosscheck* in which Editor Arnold Reiner described a number of occurrences of faulty flightcrew checking. Mr. Reiner wrote that the airmen, "harboring feelings of guilt and inadequacy, should be welcomed back to

the human race with understanding. They and the crews they
fly with should accept their experiences as milestones of re-
discovered vulnerability rather than as blots on a flying record."
He points out that time and success breed complacency, "a mal-
ady as insidious as hypoxia. No one is immune." *CALLBACK*
expressed the hope that pilots "will resist complacency through
learning of others' experiences," and printed some confessions of
carelessness and attendant humility from recent ASRS reports. I
preached, "Let us not be complacent; pride goeth before a fall."

ASRS has received reports of many gear-up incidents, usually
caused by flawed checking procedures; some resulted in belly
landings, in some this sequel was narrowly avoided. *CALLBACK*
No. 89, in November 1986, carried a typical pair of the former
class:

> . . . Not Best to Swap Horses
> When Crossing a Stream
>
> A. Lincoln

"I was invited to go along with a friend to check out his new
airplane. I wanted to fly it around the pattern and as we took off
my door flew open. I was in the right seat and cleaned up the
airplane as required (lifting gear, etc.). The other pilot tried to
close the door from his side with no luck. He then took the airplane, which he had been checked out in, and told me to try to
close the door. The noise was deafening—could not hear the tower.
I heard my friend say, 'GUMPS,' and start the check but I was distracted by the door and continued to try to close it. I could not see
the gear lights and we had no horn alarm so I assumed he had put
the gear down. . . . We entered the flare and the props ate the
ground. . . . The distraction of the open door and the switch from
one P.I.C. to another in mid-stream caught us off guard. HE did not
put the gear down because HE did not put it up. *I* put it up and that
didn't register."

> Here Comes Another One

No mid-stream change here, but one more mishap caused by that
old devil, preoccupation. . . . The emphasis on the final sentence is
CALLBACK's.

"Normal gear-lowering and checking sequence was interrupted by the exceptionally long downwind leg of a small aircraft
ahead, causing the pilot to concentrate on increasing spacing and
dividing attention. By this time the pilot was out of his landing
sequence and failed to notice gear was up. No warning horn was
heard. THE GEAR-UP LANDING WAS CAUSED BY THE PILOT APPARENTLY
FAILING TO LOWER THE GEAR."

Inattention to detail in preflight preparation, by ground workers as well as pilots (referred to by my friend Bob Parke as "the danger of the runaround instead of the WALKAROUND"), is a common prelude to trouble. A pair of *CALLBACK* paragraphs illustrate typical instances:

> *Five seconds into the start-engine cycle the right main landing gear collapsed, followed rapidly by the nose gear and left main landing gear. Though all the landing gear checks required by the Originating Checklist had been performed normally, it was subsequently learned that maintenance personnel had performed a periodic check of the landing gear extension/retraction systems. Presumably, a mechanic left the gear handle up while checking the emergency extension handle operation.
>
> Nose gear would not retract on takeoff. Returned for landing. Removed nose gear pin. Nose gear retracted normally.

Most of us on the ASRS staff served time on the doughty old DC3 and recall vividly the importance attached to the pins installed in the landing gear assembly after each landing as a precaution against failure of the down-locking mechanism. Check lists called out "pins and battens" and most operators followed a prescribed procedure that required a groundcrew member, standing beneath the left-hand (captain's) cockpit window, to hold up the two landing gear locking pins and the three "battens" used as external control locks to prevent windbattering of the surfaces. Generally these had red cloth streamers attached; the groundling would display the pins (and battens) for the captain's inspection, after which he would wrap the red streamers around the pins and toss them into the baggage compartment before securing it, pulling the wheel chocks, and giving the farewell salute.

When the DC3's were replaced by the four-engined DC4 the external control locks were replaced by an internal system, activated by the flightcrew in the cockpit, but a new feature was added: a tail stand. This was a stout metal tube—about the height of a man—installed beneath the aft cabin of the airplane immediately after parking to prevent the shifting weight of the disembarking passengers from causing the tail to bang on the concrete. More than one of these aircraft took off with the stand still dangling; it too became a checklist item. In these more sophisticated times most such archaic devices have been superseded by high-tech solutions but, as noted above and in the following *CALLBACK* column, gear pins remain an occasional tribulation.

Pinned Down

"During the Flight Engineer's preflight I noticed the nose gear down pin was installed. I looked around and couldn't find any station personnel to notify. On return to the cockpit I got busy with some small cabin problems and overlooked calling maintenance or informing the Captain. . . ."

"After normal takeoff we attempted to retract the landing gear. The in-transit light stayed on. The landing gear was cycled up and down and up and the in-transit light remained on. The gear was selected down and all functions indicated normal. We returned and made a normal landing. After arriving at the gate maintenance personnel found the landing gear safety pins were still installed. The pins were removed and the flight continued."

"Commenced" might be more accurate. No further information was revealed by the reporter in the first tale. Presumably the result was similar to the other. After dumping a few thousand pounds of fuel.

While the external control locks of the DC3 era went the way of the tail wheel (in the context of modern airliners), to be replaced by internal mechanisms, a short ASRS report indicates that there can still be problems and emphasizes careful use of the pre-takeoff checklist after a long wait to go:

Won't Unstick—Oops!

*High-speed abort in a small corporate jet! Northwest winds of 30–40 knots required use of same runway for takeoffs and landings. We were #8 or so for departure, approx 35 minute wait in line with mixed large airliners. Winds buffeted controls, which can't be locked once engines are started. After 15 minutes or so I decided to let the autopilot hold the controls for me. I didn't realize the wind loads caused the autopilot to roll the trim to the forward stop. TRIM comes earlier on the checklist. Reached V_2 plus 15–20 knots and used 4500 feet of runway before abort completed. 7000 feet of runway and strong headwinds gave me plenty of safety margin; sure glad it wasn't a 3000 foot runway! Autopilot does a great job holding controls, but if you use it, put TRIM at end of checklist.

A popular novel (and motion picture) was based on an incident in which a cup of coffee, accidently spilled in the cockpit, caused the crash of an airliner. A 1982 ASRS report, carried in *CALL-BACK,* confirmed that checklist performance should not be attempted while the flightcrew is diverted by other activities—such as eating or drinking.

Too Much Vitamin C

Captain reports an incident which has happened many times before; First Officer adds a note on prevention. A word to the wise. . . .

"We were in the process of doing our preflight checklist when a glass of orange juice inadvertently got spilled on the center console. We immediately grabbed some paper towels and napkins and mopped up the spilt juice, being careful to blot out all around the switch holes and cracks between the radios. About the time we had finished this operation, I heard a loud buzzing in my headset which I traced to the No. 1 audio selector panel. . . . I asked the s/o for a screwdriver and proceeded to pull the panel out of the rack and disconnect the plugs. The buzzing stopped, so it was apparent this was the problem."

By good fortune the Captain held an A&P mechanic's license; he continued with a series of remedies to rectify things and the flight went off with no further problems (the mishap occurred at a station lacking proper maintenance facilities). To avoid having to learn the hard way, attend the F/O's words:

"To prevent this type of incident from recurring, it must continually be stressed that no liquid of any kind ever be placed on the central console of any aircraft. Had this occurred in flight, a loss of radio communication could have resulted."

CALLBACK adds that radio NAV capability might also have been affected.

Several *CALLBACK* stories have dealt with cockpit memory lapses leading to neglect of standard operating procedure and unintended engine shutdown, fortunately on the ground (there have been a few in the air, as well). The opposite can happen, too, as the first tale below testifies. It appeared under the heading, "Have You Forgotten Anything?" In the second, I fell back on personal experience to highlight the message.

*Several days after the alleged incident, I was advised that maintenance personnel allegedly found Number 2 engine still running after our crew had parked the aircraft at the gate and departed. . . . Although it was also alleged that the aircraft parking brake was not set, ground personnel did confirm that the aircraft had been chocked before crew departed the flight deck.

Beware of (Too) Quick Reaction

Many issues back *CALLBACK* described the plight of an air carrier flightcrew, landing at a pre-dawn hour, who rolled to the end of a long runway, turned off, and inexplicably shut down all four engines. They were marooned for more than an hour out in the

South Forty and effected rescue finally by despatching the Flight Engineer (who else?) down the escape hatch rope, to run a mile through the black night for help. Now we have a report reminiscent of that one:

"Clearance for takeoff received. Very shortly after applying takeoff power we got an EEC (Electronic Engine Control) aural warning and failing light for left engine. Intention then was to turn off control switches for both EEC's, as per procedure, but made the error of turning off both engine fuel control cutoff switches. Aircraft was coasted off runway, APU (Auxiliary Power Unit) started, engines restarted, and flight continued normally. My mistake was realized immediately and why I cut both fuel control switches is just unexplainable. Lesson Learned is that the warning was only a caution and did not require immediate action. Just abort, assess the problem, and go on from there."

Not unexplainable to us. . . . One reason why we're pretty good at what we do here is that one (or more) of us has been there before. Our anonymity policy (and Editorial diffidence) precludes identification of the pilot who, in the long-ago, responded to the checklist call, "Fire Warning Test," by discharging the fire extinguisher bottles in both left engines. Wouldn't have been too serious except that it scratched a days-in-preparation night takeoff of a complex test aircraft. And it took place with an audience of about 100 assorted mechanics and engineers out to watch the proof of their work. The unfortunate pilot was compassionately removed from the cockpit after an hour of quiet sobbing. Comes back to haunt us when we read tales like that above. We do understand.

Two articles from *CALLBACK* No. 50 (August 1983) tell of the afflictions of the flight engineer position; the second relates to the engine shutdown events mentioned above.

Who's That Knocking at My Door?

Barnacle Bill

"We were approx 14 miles out at 6000', being vectored for approach. . . . The NO SMOKING sign had been turned on about a minute before. Almost simultaneously, we were cleared for the approach and a Flight Attendant came into the cockpit and informed the Second Officer of a problem in the cabin. She was unable to remove the bassinet from the forward bulkhead. FAR's require this item to be stowed for approach and landing. The S/O asked if it would be ok for him to take care of it; I said, 'Yes.' He returned about a minute and a half later. At this point I thought the problem was solved—but he got a tool out of his bag and left the cockpit again. As we passed the Outer Marker there was a knock on the door. At this point the gear and flaps were down, the checklist was complete, and the s/o panel was set for landing. I landed and taxied to the gate. After clearing the runway; the First Officer got up and let the s/o into the cockpit. At the gate the s/o reinspected the location where the spare cockpit key is kept. It was there, but maintenance had installed the key in a different location than normal. The s/o had left his key at his station when he returned for the tool. Spare key location in the cabin is a pre-flight item for the Flight Attendant. At the time of the knock on the door, I had gear and flaps down, checklist complete, clearance to land, and runway in sight."

This unusual occurrence prompted the ASRS analyst to initiate a callback to the Captain, who explained his reactions. "My first thought was to ask the F/O to unstrap from his seat and reach the door to unlatch it—but then I had the thought that if there was trouble in the cabin, anyone could come through that door. Further, it did not seem like a good idea for the F/O to be out of his seat too, so I went ahead and landed. . . . I had a quick decision to make and I landed rather than change aircraft configuration, pull up, get back in the traffic flow, sort things out, and work another approach."

More Woe for the Poor s/o

Certain similarities here—vacant seats, etc. Number 2 engine flameout in cruise at FL310.

"Required checklists were performed and it was discovered that the No. 2 fuel shutoff switch on the Flight Engineer's panel was closed . . . performed a normal airstart. Readings were normal and the flight proceeded uneventfully. When this event began, I was eating a crew meal. The captain had just returned from the cabin and the First Officer was stowing his oxygen mask. . . . It should be noted that the Flight Engineer's seat was very difficult to move and had been written up previously. When the Captain left the cockpit I had to move the seat, which was stuck. I shifted around in my seat and propped myself against the panel for better leverage. Although I did not notice it at the time, I must have inadvertently hit the switch in a downward motion. . ."

Lax cockpit coordination can induce insufficient checking and is often responsible for takeoff-associated errors, as illustrated by the *CALLBACK* story below. It is followed by a tale of an unusual takeoff error in which the pilots were quite blameless. The item appeared originally in *Up Front,* the flightcrew bulletin of Delta Airlines.

Gross Weight—Gross Error

Not many incidents involving tail-draggers come our way. Of those that do, this one is NOT typical: "During takeoff, stick-shaker was encountered at approximately 12 degrees nose-up. Nose was lowered and go-around thrust added. Due to unknown stick-shaker cause, speed was increased to approximately $V_2 + 30$. During climb it was reported that a stewardess seated near a rear door heard a noise that could have been the tail contacting the runway (this was later confirmed). Cockpit analysis of the problem revealed the V speeds for 460,000 pounds takeoff gross weight were used instead of 660,000. Upon fuller review, it was revealed that the check Captain flying as First Officer had pointed to the speeds used in the aircraft operating manual and the Captain on line familiarization confirmed the speeds without referring back to the TOGW column."

Reporting Captain suggests that each pilot make his own computations with no looking over the other pilot's shoulder. ASRS analyst (who used to be a check pilot on the same aircraft type) points out the subtle difficulties for a Captain on a line check in maintaining his command status in the presence of a dominant—and probably senior—check pilot flying as his First Officer. In addition, the Second Officer, who would usually make out the takeoff card, must have been dazzled by all that gold braid in front of him. A little too much "Yes, Sir, if you say so" in that cockpit must have upped some pulse rates.

Loaded

We frequently borrow incident accounts from the airline flight-crew bulletins we receive, and reprint them in the interest of informing our readers of unusual operational events:

"On takeoff the aircraft demonstrated the performance of a lead sled. The Captain's concern prompted a check and double check of fuel, cargo, and passenger weights. It took a bit of doing to determine that most of the passengers were attending a coin-collectors' convention and had carry-on bags which weighed 60 to 75 pounds. Collectively, the collectors' collections caused considerable cockpit crew consternation."

Summary comments often appear in the reports of errors submitted to ASRS. These seem quite pertinent to the discussion in this chapter:

*I allowed myself to be distracted and not monitor the flight. I am especially embarrassed because I have told many First Officers that this is a two-person crew, not two people taking turns flying solo.

I have been at fault in the past. This time I was not; however, the controller, my copilot, and I all have the same problem. WE ARE HUMAN!

11

The Editor, Sir:

Completely absent from my mind was any thought that *CALL-BACK* would become an instrument for fostering international relations. Thus when letters from foreign countries began to turn up in the daily mail, they came as a distinct surprise. As a matter of fact, what the secretarial staff referred to as "*CALLBACK*'s fan mail," foreign OR domestic, was entirely unexpected. Early issues, which carried a small coupon offering a free subscription and requesting comment on the bulletin, brought a prompt, encouraging, and very agreeable response. A good many readers, too, having encountered "NASA's blue sheet" in some airline operations office or in the lobby of a fixed base operation, took the trouble to indicate their approval via letters.

Most of these early correspondents expressed the gratifying view that *CALLBACK*'s reprinted reports to ASRS were helpful, as this excerpt from one letter illustrates: "By reading the back issues of *CALLBACK* I have been able to learn lessons that probably would have taken years of flight experience. Thanks for all the help. I know that you are saving some lives. Who knows? Maybe you have already saved mine! P.S. I was exposed to *CALLBACK* because the operator of our airport puts his back issues out for everyone to read."

The international aspect is exemplified by the inauguration in several foreign nations of programs similar to, and based on, the principles pioneered by ASRS. Copies of *CALLBACK* were carried home by international airline aircrew members and helped to publicize the concept and value of voluntary, confidential incident reporting. Inevitably, word filtered to foreign aviation authorities and, since the bulletin was the most visible manifestation of the NASA program, I began to field overseas requests for subscriptions, copies of ASRS research reports mentioned in *CALLBACK*, and program information in general. After considerable correspondence and some visits to Moffett Field by British officials, *CALLBACK* was able to announce in No. 49 (July 1983):

C.H.I.R.P.

We're delighted to welcome a new kid on the block—and a new ally in the battle for increased flying safety. CONFIDENTIAL HUMAN FACTORS INCIDENT REPORTING has entered the fray in England, incorporating many of the features of ASRS here. CHIRP was instituted at the behest of the Civil Aviation Authority (British equivalent of our FAA) and will be run by the RAF Institute of Aviation Medicine, acting the middleman part between CAA and the aviation community as NASA does here between FAA and our own community. The new group's first bulletin, *"FEEDBACK #1"*, has reached us and we find some parallel ideas there, too. An English friend of ASRS involved with the new program writes, "Any similarity with ASRS is entirely deliberate! No doubt you will find *FEEDBACK* just as fascinating as we find *CALLBACK.*" We are pleased that ASRS was considered a worthy model, and *FEEDBACK* is indeed fascinating. As its title indicates, CHIRP will concentrate on study of the human aspects in flying safety and will thus complement England's long-standing mandatory reporting program.

Two factors reduce CHIRP's report intake to only a fraction of the ASRS volume: The United Kingdom, with its relatively small area, has a much smaller airman population and many fewer aircraft than the United States and the level of flying activity is greatly reduced; government enforcement activity is far less stringent. Admonishment is a more likely outcome to be faced by an inadvertently errant British pilot than the American threat of certificate suspension or fine, reducing the immunity moti-

vation for reporting. Notwithstanding these differences, the aim
of the British program corresponds with that of ASRS; *Feedback,*
with fewer incident reports available than *CALLBACK,* is published somewhat less frequently. Making the point that we have
the same objectives, one issue articulated its credo by offering its
interpretation of "human factors":

> *We are interested in all the ways that people can make mistakes in
> an air traffic environment and on flight decks. You may make an
> error where you can see that a set of circumstances or the design
> of equipment made it easy to make the mistake. You may just do
> something silly for no apparent reason, or you may see somebody
> else make an unaccountable mistake. You may even find that an
> unusual combination of normal procedures presents difficulties
> for you. Please let us know all these sorts of events. It may seem
> like a 'one off' to you, but you never know for sure if you don't tell
> somebody about it, and it is certain that nobody else can benefit
> from your error while you keep it to yourself.

CALLBACK commented: "Well said, CHIRP; we've been at it longer, but we couldn't have explained it better ourselves."

The cordial hands-across-the-sea relationship has continued
and been strengthened by personal visits between those of us
concerned in these endeavors ("endeavours" to our British
friends); our friendly welcome of the CHIRP emissaries at Moffett
Field was warmly reciprocated on my visits to Farnborough.
Canada, too, expressed an early interest in the ASRS project.
CALLBACK had acquired many readers among Canadian airmen
and within the national agency Transport Canada, which has
now joined the club with its own version—announced in due
course by *CALLBACK:*

Insight/Aperçu—Welcome/Bienvenue

Canada's recently inaugurated Confidential Aviation Safety Reporting Program (CASRP) has produced the first issue of its own
safety bulletin, joining the British CHIRP's FEEDBACK and our
own *CALLBACK.* Our North-of-the-Border colleagues have coped
very cleverly with their nation's two-language policy, giving the
bulletin a dual name. On one side, "INSIGHT" appears at the top of a
handsomely-designed (blue on blue) page, followed by three pages
(in English) of safety reports; reversed and turned top to bottom,
INSIGHT becomes "APERÇU" with the complete text duplicated in
French. *CALLBACK* bids this new kid on the block a hearty "Good
Luck/Bonne Chance."

Impressed by the industry-wide approval of voluntary incident reporting, and its success in the countries establishing it, missions from other nations have visited the ASRS offices for briefings. The project has provided information and guidance to officials from Brazil, New Zealand, Ireland, Japan, and Australia, all of whom are considering—or implementing—similar programs in their home countries. Australia has long had a mandatory reporting system that has worked well in collecting data on flight control problems, engine difficulties, collisions, and the like, but, according to one official of the Bureau of Air Safety Investigation, "a certain class of incidents are not being reported, however. These are incidents that happen on the flight deck, which are known only to the crew." It is thought that fear of punitive action has stifled the free reporting of such incidents. In an effort to gather the missing human performance information, the bureau has introduced a program entitled Confidential Aviation Incident Reporting, similar to ASRS and the systems operating in England and Canada.

With ASRS cooperation and advice, the U.S. Air Force is likewise experimenting with a modified version in order to gather more data on human factors than provided by its existing reporting systems, which deal predominantly with hardware involvement in safety. The concept has proved itself so useful, in fact, that it has spread beyond the parochial confines of aviation. An adaptation has been tried by the maritime industry and is under study by the nuclear power industry. In all these cases, the lure of confidentiality as a reporting inducement is paramount.

Foreign interest in ASRS has not been restricted to countries wishing to establish their own systems; requests for *CALLBACK* subscriptions have come from more than fifty countries around the world (from Algeria to Zimbabwe, *CALLBACK* reported in 1985)—in addition to all U.S. states and possessions and Canadian provinces. Pen pals from many lands have helped to brighten my days (and stamp collection). In many cases, a comment or query to *CALLBACK* from an overseas reader has inaugurated a continuing correspondence, which I have found both pleasurable and gratifying.

A short *CALLBACK* filler item from an ASRS report brought the first of a series of letters from a high-ranking Scandinavian aviation official, who wrote that he enjoyed *CALLBACK* and wished that he might contribute. In reprinting his letter, I prefaced it with, "Now he has." "OK you guys, cut it out, you are destroying my good reputation," ran the letter. "Here I am, sitting in the early morning shuttle train from my suburb to the city on my daily chores at the Board. Surrounded by morning-eyed serious fellow countrymen, I am reading *CALLBACK:* 'The Captain was flying the leg, but nobody was flying the airplane.' " (For the benefit of readers not fluent in pilot jargon, the reference is to the fact that airline flightcrews customarily exchange the primary flying duties between captain and first officer on alternate trip segments.) "So I start snickering and people start looking. Who is this nut, laughing so early in the morning, reading a plain turquoise paper, and not only that, he is reading it upside down!" (The back page of *CALLBACK* is reversed top-to-bottom so that it can be easily read on bulletin boards.) "The guy must have gone off his rocker."

Incidentally, two other "leg" fragments from bulletin articles inspired illustrator Bob Stevens to draw a page of his typically amusing cartoons for *Professional Pilot* magazine: Two showed a chortling captain, in his left-hand cockpit seat, reading *CALLBACK,* with the captions: "The First Officer never did see the other plane, as he was looking in his flight kit for an item. It was his leg," and "The Captain was flying the approach with a brand new First Officer with only one leg in the right seat under his belt." A third picture depicted the First Officer saying, "Let ME read this one! The Captain was busy reading the ASRS blue sheet and busted his altitude."

I replied to a justified complaint from another foreign reader in one of my periodic articles discussing *CALLBACK*'s correspondence; several excerpts from domestic letter-writers also appeared in the column.

Our Correspondents—God Bless 'Em

38,000 people receive *CALLBACK* each month [that was in 1985; the number is approaching 60,000 as I write this in 1988]. No doubt quite a few more read borrowed, posted, or circulated copies. Many of these readers take the trouble to write us with their comments. At times the press of workload prevents a personal reply, but all letters are read, and gratefully acknowledged herewith. [Actually I have acknowledged nearly all letters.] Sometimes interesting illumination of *CALLBACK* articles appears. . . .

Finally, in a letter from a European reader, we are taken to task for our use of too many acronyms and initials. . . . "We encounter enormous difficulties here with the phenomenal amount of 'shorts' you use instead of words." He suggests that we give the meaning of the "shorts" in brackets. Well, the point is taken; we sympathize. The same complaint comes at times from non-aviation people who come across our bulletin. The problem is to strike the proper compromise between clarity for lay readers and those not entirely at home with American technical vocabulary and condescension toward those (the majority of *CALLBACK* subscribers) who use the seemingly mysterious terms constantly. IFR, VMC, FAR, SID may seem jargon to the uninitiated; translating them would be presumptuous and a waste of space for the bulk of our readers who are members (USA Branch) of the Fellowship of Flying. We do attempt to clarify the esoteric terms peculiar to parochial segments of our constituency: LTSS, QAP, APPREQ have meaning to ATC troops, but not to the general reader. GPWS says a lot to air carrier pilots but not to most GA (General Aviation) flyers. NMAC is clear to FAA statisticians, but the British say, "AIR MISS." We're sorry if we sometimes obfuscate; we shall try to clarify if there seems to be doubt.

Of the thousands of letters to *CALLBACK,* a clear majority have been written by airline pilots—not surprisingly, since they form the bulk of ASRS reporters (and supporters) and *CALLBACK* readers. Surprising, though, are the letters from other writers and editors in the aviation writing fraternity (the Aviation/Space Writers Association is the professional society of toilers in the field). These have been encouraging and in many cases have led the correspondents to reprint *CALLBACK* material in other publications or to write articles about ASRS. The *Air Line Pilot,* journal of the Air Line Pilots Association, for example, carries a monthly selection of ASRS object lesson reports. *CALLBACK* has been quoted often by Roger Bacon, who writes the "Straight and Level" column in the authoritative *Flight International;* equally appreciated by me was a graceful compliment by distinguished writer (and wartime fighter pilot) Edwards Park in an early issue of *Air & Space/Smithsonian* magazine.

And of the letters filling the ASRS box in the Moffett Field post office, a large proportion have included the phrase, "Keep up the good work." These manifestations of goodwill have, naturally, been very cheering, as have those expressing approbation for both substance and style. "Please send *CALLBACK* to me each and every month, without fail, until eternity," read an early postcard. A letter, professionally typed on heavy bond paper, echoed: "This is a fan letter. . . . Keep it up and continue my name on the mailing list forever." A good many correspondents apparently appreciate the efforts to make *CALLBACK* readable through frequent reliance on humor and brevity. "The safety message gets across more effectively through good writing and an occasional touch of humor than through officialese and finger-pointing."

"Seems like the issues get better each time. Particularly liked the comparison of *CALLBACK* to hangar flying as a sharing of experiences we can all benefit from—never thought of that association, but it's true. Thanks," wrote a retired pilot, now an official in the Department of Defense. The comparison of the bulletin's informality with the hangar flying of old has been evoked repeatedly by veteran airmen. One wrote, "In years past, hangar flying was part of the aviation scene. The exchange of info, problems, goofs, and incidents encountered was a very important educational or alerting factor benefitting all pilots. That situation or opportunity does not exist at the present time due to several factors such as tight schedules and other facts of life. The *CALLBACK* publication is doing a great job of replacing the free exchange of the type of info normally acquired in the hangar flying of previous years; *CALLBACK* should be sent to all pilots."

Not surprisingly, the informality and light touch in the early *CALLBACK*s generated serious objections from some NASA and FAA officials, but they were defused by the unanimously expressed approval of the ASRS Advisory Committee and the volume of favorable mail. Dr. Billings and Bill Reynard at NASA, and Battelle's Ed Cheaney, were staunch defenders, and in the end, though subject to review and occasional suggestion, I was given by and large a free rein.

Requests for complete sets of *CALLBACK* back issues have come from schools and librarians, and from many pilots simply interested in maintaining files on safety. "I learn a lot from *CALLBACK* and wish it was published more frequently. Until it joins the ranks of the *New York Times* as a daily (and since I am a new subscriber) I will be satisfied with receiving back issues. What do I have to do to get some or all of the 69 *CALLBACK* issues I haven't read? Unlike the daily papers, I do keep *CALL-BACK* issues for future safety reminders and refreshers. Thank you." A note from an internationally known safety authority read, "Many thanks for the extra copies of *CALLBACK*. I have made up a selection of items and use them in a Human Factors in Transport Aircraft Operation course which I conduct." Similarly, "Up here at 7000' I'm a flight instructor busy earning a living. I wanted you to know that *CALLBACK* has become an invaluable tool in the aviation training process. . . . I begin each ground school class with readings (a sort of aviation epistle) from my stack of *CALLBACK* back issues. They generate much discussion and interest."

Editorial ego in the face of so much goodwill has been kept within bounds by a few serious-minded readers. One disgruntled pilot scribbled on a copy of *CALLBACK*, "More and More desk people are trying to tell operating crewmembers how to act. Most of what you write is of little value to competent pilots. . . . Please don't waste taxpayers' money sending this junk to me." In a similar vein, another airline pilot wrote, "Please do not add my name to your mailing list. I fly an airplane 80 hours a month and take exception to the manner in which you desk pilots oversimplify a large proportion of the accidents and/or incidents that you furnish commentary on." This one had a happy sequel when, following my letter outlining the qualifications of the ASRS staff and pointing out that "We think we've paid our dues in the cockpit; in retirement we are trying to give back a little of what flying has given us," I received this gracious response: "Perhaps I was a bit hasty in referring to you gentlemen as desk pilots. I have read the list of staff qualifications you sent [see Chapter 2, on "Old Eagles"], and I see almost everything but lunar landings. I would be naive or a fool to be unimpressed by the experience level of your staff; I am neither. I offer my apology, and request that my name be put on your mailing list." Several readers have accused us of being "bureaucrats." No lunar landers among us, but we've been around the pattern a few times.

In a similar vein, a military pilot reader commented on a *CALLBACK* summary of the ASRS staff: "Your staff has a glaring deficiency if you expect to cover the entire spectrum of aviation. No fighter pilots." I responded, on behalf of myself and my colleagues, "Don't bet on it, Friend. Several of our old tigers can show extensive combat experience and, in test work, have flown a good many fighter—and other military—aircraft. The small group in the ASRS office does, in fact, cover that 'entire spectrum.'"

Seeking comments on *CALLBACK,* an early issue carried a coupon with this appeal: "(1) Do you think we have written effectively about aviation safety and stimulated your safety consciousness? (2) Have you profited from learning of others' problems?" One reader responded, "(1) Absolutely. (2) If I had not, it would be time to call the undertaker to remove the body for, in truth, I would effectively be dead." Another reply, from a private pilot, read, "I want you to know how much help I get out of

CALLBACK. It helps me to understand flying in ways I had never understood, but knew existed. I thought I was the only pilot who made mistakes. I have three friends I would appreciate your placing on your mailing list. Thank you!" Still another wrote, "In my own circumstances as a commercial airline pilot, the timeliness or almost psychic aspects of *CALLBACK* are phenomenal. I read *CALLBACK* as soon as possible because it appears the lessons to be learned or reminders to be heeded are usually helpful on my next flight. Keep up the great work!"

There have been a few poignant communications: A copy of *CALLBACK* was returned with a short note reading, "My husband just completed his final flight plan and soared off into the heavenly skies. Please remove his name from your mailing list. Happy tail winds!" Two others, from readers presumably no longer flying, indicated satisfaction with our publication, but mentioned that the onset of failing eyesight made reading difficult; they asked if *CALLBACK* could be made available in a large-type edition.

A Florida subscriber wrote,

> May I call back *CALLBACK* for a few comments? This is not a "Captain" with years of airline flying—it is instead an old lady who flies low and slow in her Grumman Tiger (Pussy Cat?). The "low and slow," however, relates to what she does, for the most part—and that's Auxiliary Patrol and Search and Rescue for the U.S. Coast Guard, Search and Rescue and check rides for the Civil Air Patrol, and whatever comes my way. . . . For several reasons I am very safety conscious: 1. I am very chicken. 2. I think one tends to live longer—airborne or ground-bound—if safety tenets are observed, and I enjoy living. . . . And probably most important, 4. I am an OLD pilot, not a BOLD pilot. Didn't learn to fly until I was 42—am "going on" 78 now. . . . I enjoy *CALLBACK* greatly and learn from it; safety seems to be much the same necessity whether one is flying an F-15, a 1011, or a —well—Grumman Tiger!

A reader in Alaska stumped me, but I passed it on: "NASA has announced that space is being made on a Space Shuttle flight for a writer. Where can I obtain an application? I also wish to write an article in my weekly column about the application requirements, so I'll need plenty of information."

The comments of subscribers have often served as *CALLBACK* material, and many articles have, I think, gained in interest through the use of familiar quotations gleaned from memory or, more often, from the invaluable *Bartlett's Familiar Quotations.*

Shakespeare has been the most frequent of these contributors—
"The Bubbling Gossip of the Air," as an instance, formed a fine
heading to an article dealing with frequency congestion—although many others have appeared in the blue sheet. The poet
Lowell provided an appropriate heading for a series of reports of
incidents in which fine early summer weather induced error-
making complacency: "And What Is So Rare as a Day in June?
Then, If Ever, Come Perfect Days." Cervantes, in "Don Quixote,"
offered the perfect summary to an article about a pilot who refused to carry out Air Traffic Control instructions: "I would have
nobody to control me, I would be absolute." John Donne's "No
man is an island, entire of itself" seemed to fit the case of a traffic
conflict.

The ubiquitous Shakespeare, who seems to have covered all
bases, offered the perfect preamble to a report from a pilot who
prematurely, and with hazardous effect, reset his altimeter: "I
haste now to my setting." A report of a TCA penetration by a day-
dreaming pilot seemed to call for one of the many biblical allusions I used over the years: "Behold, this dreamer cometh." Distracting intracockpit conversation produced this, from John
Milton, "with thee conversing, I forget all time." "To dumb for-
getfulness a prey," from a Thomas Gray poem, seemed to fit well
above a report of a pilot who forgot to close his flight plan. In one
quotation-studded issue, my exuberance, in retrospect, may
have overcome my sense of moderation. Thomas Hardy contributed "blinded ere yet a-wing" to a case of strobe-light dazzle;
"who's that knocking at my door?" from Barnacle Bill, worked
well for a report from a flight engineer who was inadvertently
locked out of the cockpit. I am embarrassed now to confess that
there were two more on the same page. Lewis Carroll has produced several headings, as have Samuel Johnson and John
Keats, and popular songs have played their part in my efforts at
catching readers' attention.

Perhaps my favorite among the sayings of the famous that I
have appropriated in the cause of flying safety was used to head
a report of a controller's callsign mistake. James Thurber was
credited with the admirable line, "Well, If I Called the Wrong
Number, Why Did You Answer the Phone?" (This has been
matched by my editorial successor, Rowena Morrison, who
quoted Lily Tomlin's classic line, "Is This the Party to Whom I
Am Speaking?" to introduce an article on radio discipline.) Even
Abraham Lincoln played a part in this international collabora-
tion, when his "not best to swap horses when crossing a stream"

was used to lead into a report of two pilots attempting to exchange seats in flight.

CALLBACK has been an amalgam of reports from members of the aviation community, selections from readers' letters, perceptive quotations from eminent persons past and present, my own comments and, occasionally, contributions from recognized authorities. Notably, we have used several times, with his permission, extracts from articles by Gerard Bruggink, retired NTSB investigator. Mr. Bruggink, a loyal early supporter of the bulletin, is one of the most eloquent writers on air safety and has provided *CALLBACK* with editorial material dealing in particular with the important and often overlooked factor of character. Jerome Lederer, president emeritus of the Flight Safety Foundation and surely the dean of aviation safety authorities (often called "Mr. Aviation Safety"), has lent his staunch encouragement from the beginning, and his frequent and oft-quoted letters have offered historical perspective on many of *CALLBACK*'s concerns.

The unsolicited offerings from the widely assorted sources listed in this chapter have made the *CALLBACK* job a very rewarding experience. All of us associated with the ASRS project have been gratified by the approval expressed by our peers in the flying world, and have been proud of the project's contribution so many have mentioned. This note, addressed to the staff, is typical: "Just a note of thanks. As a General Aviation pilot never flying above 10,000 feet or more than 500 miles at a time, I don't consider my forays very complicated. And yet . . . almost every excerpt you print catches me right in the conscience. I'm proud of the privileges I have as an airman, of our ATC system, and of your efforts to contribute to our safety. Because of the experiences you share, my safety consciousness is heightened and I'm a safer pilot. Thanks again."

12

You Don't Have
to Kill People. . . .

"Hey, ASRS, what do you folks do with all that data?" A good question, frequently asked. With nearly 100,000 reports in the database, and new ones arriving each month at a rate approaching 2,000, the ASRS computerized files represent a unique and impressive resource for studying the human fallibilities that lead to unsafe flying occurrences. After analysis and preparation by the staff of retired professional pilots and controllers (the Old Eagles), the "input" is transferred to the giant computer.

Thereafter, searches may be conducted under a myriad of subjects and in great detail to answer information queries from the print and electronic media; from such public agencies as ICAO, FAA, NTSB, congressional committees; from aircraft manufacturers and operators; and from others interested in particular aspects of flying safety. The ASRS *Alert Bulletin* is usually issued to FAA, but also to others who may be in a position to take necessary action (armed forces, airport managers, charting organizations), based on reports of continuing hazardous situations, con-

ditions and procedures. The bulletin *CALLBACK* is published
monthly.

And we produce topical research studies based on various aspects of the accumulated data. New additions to the list appear in
CALLBACK as they become available. These are distributed to
anyone interested in them. Since the papers are usually lengthy
and replete with tables, graphs, charts, statistics, and notes on
research approach and methodology, they are not recommended
as light reading. For those interested in the subjects but not
requiring detailed scholarly treatment, *CALLBACK* has provided digests of many of the studies. Condensing forty pages
into two columns on the bulletin's back page may seem an in-
justice, but an attempt has been made to retain the meat, without
the condiments. A selection of these digests is presented as an
appendix to this book. Readers whose appetites are whetted by
CALLBACK's "Capsule Commentaries" and who wish to savor
the complete meal may request the full reports by writing to
ASRS, P.O. Box 189, Moffett Field, CA 94035.

What is the meaning of it all? Is the support of the Aviation
Safety Reporting System a profitable expenditure of taxpayers'
money and of the energies of many dedicated—and even tal-
ented—people? Have we accomplished anything worthwhile?
Demonstrably, yes (it has been remarked that if you think safety
is expensive, just try having an accident!).

Thousands of letters testify to the perceived value of ASRS in
providing an outlet for members of the aviation community to
vent their concerns over observed safety-related events and situations. It has lent a sympathetic ear to confessions of airman
error and sent many back to their duties grateful for absolution
and with reinforced resolution to go and sin no more.

More important, it has given wide circulation to accounts of
hazardous procedures and behavior, and has enabled the community of aviation people to benefit from the experiences reported. Through *CALLBACK* and published research reports we
have been able, without being accusatory or aggressive, to pass
to others the accumulated lore and wisdom gained by participants in the program.

The ASRS *Alert Bulletin,* based on incoming reports, has
served to alleviate—or eliminate—unsafe situations and procedures. In an early issue of *CALLBACK* I wrote, "Situations and
conditions incompatible with safety are often called to our attention by concerned reporters. If we agree that alleviating measures are practical, we let fly an AB to the proper quarter. Recent

ones have helped to fix a few problems: A complex profile descent has been clarified; helipads have been marked and lighted; required communications have been simplified in a congested area; new standardized procedures have been put into effect to improve arrival and departure sequencing under certain weather conditions in another." In a later issue I tabulated some results of AB's issued during the previous year:

> Stimulated the re-surfacing of a runway at a major airport that was reported to us as dangerously slick in wet weather.

> Caused chart revisions of obsolete or incorrect information.

> Been responsible for improved runway and taxiway marking.

> Pointed out some navaid and communication abnormalities.

> Noted ambiguous or confusing aural identifiers and intersection names.

> Called attention to garbled ATIS broadcasts.

Still another *CALLBACK* gives an example of a successful *Alert Bulletin:* "Consider the implications of a fix named 'TOUTU'! A pilot told us of a clearance 'TO TOUTU TO MAINTAIN TWO TWO ZERO' . . . rectifying action has been taken; 'TOUTU' is now 'POLER.' "

The ASRS database constitutes a valuable resource for the study of human factors in aviation safety and has provided detailed safety information to government agencies, the media, the academic world, professional groups and associations—to any legitimate inquirer, in fact. We believe we have fostered and encouraged professionalism among members of the airman fraternity. Most significantly, we think we have succeeded in our efforts to enhance safety awareness throughout the world of flying. A *CALLBACK* year-end sermon expressing our credo appeared in issue No. 54, in December 1983:

Noblesse Oblige

This is a *CALLBACK* sermon—and what better time for it? Year's end is a time for retrospection, a time to reflect on those things we wish we had done, or done better, or not done at all: And it's a time to formulate those good resolutions which, if followed, will leave us with a sense of accomplishment. We, participating members in The Fellowship of Flying, owe an obligation to our fellow members and to those not-so-fortunate non-participants. Most of us who inhabit the world of aviation, whether aloft or in the essential ground jobs of controlling traffic and supporting aircraft operations, feel a sense of privilege. More than that, we should feel that we have been endowed with qualities and opportunities not always given to those in more mundane occupations. We should be grateful for these gifts and we should remain always conscious of the debt we, the privileged ones, owe to those not so lucky. In short, we must remember that, in the military phrase, while rank has its privileges (RHIP), it has, to an even greater degree, its responsibilities. Let us all, professional and amateur, tyro and veteran, resolve that in the year to come we will strive for excellence—give it our best shot—and endeavor to live up to the obligation entailed in privilege. Let us, in 1984, pay our membership dues by performing in the highest tradition of the aviation community.

Augmenting the established ASRS functions, staff members often participate, on request, in seminars, forums, conferences, and various aviation group meetings. Bill Reynard, NASA's ASRS chief, has frequently testified before congressional committees considering air safety and has delivered numerous papers on the subject of incident reporting. At a prestigious foreign conference he made some interesting points that were summarized in a *CALLBACK* column:

> "Program participants have expressed the notion that the act of having to organize and express the relevant facts and issues associated with a given event or situation has proved to be an extremely valuable learning experience for the reporter. . . . The event analysis and performance critique that takes place at both ends of the reporting process is clearly a significant, but unmeasurable, benefit of the ASRS program." Continuing, Reynard said, "The most obvious, as well as the most undocumentable, category of ASRS achievements is the element of accidents avoided and deaths prevented; it is impossible to document a non-event. However, given the array of research, Alert Bulletins, publications, and assistance offered and utilized as a result of ASRS operations, it seems reasonable to assert that the presence and product of the ASRS has prevented accidents and saved lives."
>
> Concerning the first point above, a number of readers have told us that the necessity to write a clear explanation of an event has, in itself, served as a form of discipline and self-evaluation of underlying causes. The thought that our efforts may have aided some flightcrews to bring their aircraft and passengers home unharmed allows our staff members to feel that our work is useful.

Although welcomed by some segments of the community early on, the ASRS was not accepted wholeheartedly by others. Mistrust or disapproval of the concept was occasionally voiced. One of the purposes of the monthly bulletin was to publicize the availability of the program; it has been gratifying to note the influence of *CALLBACK* in overcoming skepticism; dissent has noticeably decreased with the passage of time. The unpretentious little blue bulletin has penetrated deeply into the aviation world and, since all comers are welcome to copy, ASRS material continues to turn up in more impressive publications. *Airline Pilot,* for example—the monthly journal of the Air Line Pilots Association—has been among the strongest ASRS supporters and reprints a selection of *CALLBACK* items each month.

Most of the aviation-oriented magazines, most notably *Flying* and *AOPA Pilot,* have applauded the program in feature articles. Britain's *Flight,* among the most respected periodicals in the field, commented in 1986, "Confidential human-error reporting is the most affordable safety innovation of recent times. So far unique to the aviation industry, it explores the uncharted regions of human fallibility." *Flight's* popular columnist, Roger Bacon, who seems to share my own bemused attitude, frequently does us the honor of quoting from *CALLBACK,* and Edwards Park paid the bulletin a graceful compliment in the Smithsonian Institution's elegant *Air & Space* magazine.

As *CALLBACK*'s editor, I received a "Communications Citation of Merit" by the Aviation/Space Writers Association in 1982 for "Demonstrating the Highest Standards of Creativity, Veracity, and Accuracy." In April 1987, the highly esteemed Flight Safety Foundation awarded its Publication Award to NASA "On the basis of the continued contributions of *CALLBACK* as a widely read and heeded publication within the corporate operator community, even though its influence in the international air carrier community has been already acknowledged" by a previous publication award. The citation for the earlier honor commended NASA "for *CALLBACK,* its monthly bulletin analyzing trends and lessons learned through its Aviation Safety Reporting System that provide valuable insights into the attainment of even higher degrees of flight safety on an international basis."

All of us on the ASRS staff, and particularly those of us who have enjoyed the privilege of lifetime careers in aviation, have found participation in the ASRS project very rewarding. The recognition by our peers has been greatly appreciated and we hope that the project may continue for a long time to come to contribute to the enhancement of safety awareness within the world of flying. It's been interesting, satisfying—and great fun! And we think we have done some good in the world. Perhaps that feeling is the grandest prize of all!

Postflight

CALLBACK No. 100, October 1987, was a banner issue for me, marking a goal established long before; it carried an unprecedented—for my modest brainchild—banner headline: "*Callback's* First Century." Beneath that exuberant blast appeared, in the more sedate normal format and spread over two columns:

And a Farewell to the Troops

100 of anything seems a lot. As you will note, this is *CALLBACK* #100; for 100 consecutive months this little two-page blue bulletin has been launched from NASA's Aviation Safety Reporting System. Comments seem to confirm that *CALLBACK* has succeeded in achieving the objectives outlined at the beginning: To call the ASRS program to the attention of the aviation community; and, through publication of reports of safety-related incidents submitted to ASRS, to enhance safety awareness among the members of the community. And—if possible—to interest and occasionally amuse readers while doing these things.

Not long ago a well-known aviation journal carried a short tale about an airliner, moving slowly ahead in a long queue of aircraft awaiting takeoff, which finally reached the Number One spot. As it taxied into position on the runway the Flight Engineer came on the P.A.: "Ladies and Gentlemen, the Captain has asked me to announce that our time has come!" There is a time for everything and indeed the time has now come for a handoff of the *CALLBACK* editorial responsibility. Finally, after 50 rewarding years of active participation in the wonderful world of flying, my time has come. It's time for me to hang 'em up.

The Editorial Chair will have a new occupant next month. For the first time, availing myself of editorial privilege, I abandon the anonymous "we" and intend to revert to the first person singular in this, my last hurrah as *CALLBACK's* first—and so far only—Editor. *CALLBACK* No. 101—and many more to follow, I hope, will be guided through the editorial and publication process by Rowena Morrison. Dr. Morrison, a member of the ASRS research staff, who will become the anonymous "we" and probably won't see her name in *CALLBACK* until her own time comes (to retire), is an experienced pilot and brings to her task impressive professional qualifications in the field of written communication.

So—I expect to spend a few days each month in the ASRS Office keeping up with things and perhaps to enjoy an occasional Wednesday pizza with the troops. In between times I shall be at home with my new word processor (if I can learn to work the thing) writing my column and maybe, just maybe, finishing the long-promised *CALLBACK* book.

Thank you all—more than I can say: *CALLBACK* readers, whose comments have have brought so much pleasure; ASRS staff members; and especially, my colleagues, the Old Eagles—World Class, all. It's been a great privilege and great fun. . . . Stand by for "STILL SQUAWKING. . . ," commencing next month and, in due time, "*CALLBACK,* the BOOK." Happy landings!

Rex Hardy

In *CALLBACK* No. 101 (November 1987) hot on the heels of my valedictory, the new editor inaugurated her tenure with a bow to my fondness for Latin quotations, commencing with one of her own (translated in a footnote as "The King never dies"), and printing a gracious farewell to her predecessor and a hail to the new columnist; to the left of her remarks appeared my debut in my new role. The two articles follow in order here:

Rex Numquam Moritur

In last month's issue, Rex Hardy announced to the "troops" (more properly, legions) of *CALLBACK* readers his retirement from active editorial responsibilities and transition to other activities. Happily for *CALLBACK,* one of those activities will be a monthly column, "Still Squawking . . ." which makes its premier appearance in the adjacent space. Captain Hardy will also continue to serve as Editor Emeritus of *CALLBACK.* This means we may expect to enjoy his Homeric presence at Wednesday pizza lunches and occasional curmudgeonly asides on the human condition— for a long time to come.

In Rex's first issue of *CALLBACK,* published in July 1979, he described his intention to make the ASRS monthly bulletin ". . . interesting, instructive, and even—sometimes—entertaining." That purpose became, and will continue to be, the editorial credo of *CALLBACK.* With an instinct for the foibles of human nature that James Thurber (whom he occasionally quoted) would have admired, but without ever being unkind, Rex made *CALLBACK* the easel on which all of us who fly or have otherwise succumbed to the fascination of aviation can view our lapses in judgement, vigilance, and patience—and frequently smile.

It is a kingly achievement, and legacy, from a Gentleman of the

Old School. We at ASRS hope Rex will persevere in plans to complete his book about *CALLBACK,* and we take inestimable solace and pleasure in knowing that he will still be with us, in the right seat (and left column).

Rowena Morrison

Still Squawking. . . .

Paraphrasing an old ATC joke, a month ago I couldn't even spell "columnist," and now I are one. I are also an Editor Emeritus and, as retribution for having appropriated for *CALLBACK* the words of so many eminent and not-so-eminent contributors, I are now a contributor myself.

While I've never been an Emeritus anything before, I have been an occasional contributor to this and that and I have just recalled that I was once a columnist. Enthralled, like all small boys of the time, by Lindbergh's 1927 New York-Paris flight only a few months before, I inaugurated a bi-weekly aviation column. This appeared in the "FAR AND NEAR", a publication produced by the pupils of my Junior High School, and carried a "logo" (although the word was unknown to me then) of the "Spirit of St. Louis" carved by the versatile columnist (me) from a linoleum block. In each issue the spectacular exploits of the Lone Eagle and other heroes of the time were related in thrilling detail.

Time has erased from memory the title of that early effort; the name for this one came in a sudden flash during a period of insomnia induced by worry over what to call my new venture. I had discarded "From the Aerie" (defined by my dictionary as "Nest of an eagle or other predatory bird"), and other variations on the old eagle theme. "STILL SQUAWKING . . ." seems to fill the bill, allowing interpretation on several levels. For instance, "still" implies endurance. Obviously, writing an aviation column in 1927 and engaging in the same activity in 1987 marks me as a survivor (although possibly indicating a lack of progress) and of course I have survived 100 *CALLBACK*s.

More to the point, "squawking" is the noise made by old eagles. I plan to continue making noise from this perch about perceived non-observance of flight safety practices. To aviation cognoscenti, it is also what you do with your transponder (called the "parrot" by old eagles—all kinds of birds here!) to identify yourself and your position for the benefit of those concerned. I'm still right here (identified below) and I expect to continue making my position clear. Past *CALLBACK*s have defined that position often: The human is the ultimate factor in safe flight. An anecdote from Harry Combs' excellent Wright Brothers biography, "KILL DEVIL HILL" shows that this was recognized long before my FAR AND NEAR days:

"H. Massac Buist was an ebullient Frenchman. . . . He visited the Wrights at Pau, saw their flights, and described them in *FLIGHT* [magazine] in March 1909: 'There must be a human side to flying, despite the colourless, abstract, and appallingly erudite tomes that teem from the Press and turn and turn about with fancy-free, hair-raising treatises.'"

70 years before *CALLBACK!* Another contributor quotes Wilbur Wright on the subject: "If you are looking for perfect safety, you will do well to sit on a fence and watch the birds."

To which our correspondent adds: "One would do well to equip the fence with a seat belt and wear a crash helmet."

If one were aware one would do that. . . .

Rex Hardy

So endeth my unlikely career as an editor and a regular staff member of NASA's Aviation Safety Reporting System, and the commencement of my new endeavor as a columnist. I think we have fought the good fight in the cause of flying safety. In retirement I plan to keep an eye on my cherished colleagues at ASRS and, especially, on *CALLBACK*. It's been a very satisfying effort and, as I have mentioned before, a great privilege and great fun.

Appendix

CALLBACK's
Capsule
Commentaries

During 1985, 1986, and 1987, *CALLBACK*'s back page was frequently devoted to an abridged version ("*CALLBACK* Capsule Commentary") of a previously published ASRS research study. The original papers were lengthy detailed treatments of their subjects, replete with all the scholarly paraphernalia to be expected in official publications. In condensing these papers, I have attempted to retain the principal points in each and to set them out in brief and readable form. I have also tried to present something for everybody, so to speak, by including in my selection topics considered particularly applicable to various segments of the constituency: professional, amateur, civilian, military, air carrier, general aviation, air traffic control, and so on.

This appendix contains a number of the *CALLBACK* condensations; the full papers, as well as a complete listing of ASRS research papers, are available on request to ASRS, Box 189, Moffett Field, CA 94035.

Readback-Related Errors in ATC Communications:
The Hearback Problem

This is one of *CALLBACK*'s ASRS research study condensations. The paper, No. 34 on the ASRS publication list, was written by a member of the ASRS research staff, a retired international airline captain of great experience, who has contributed other studies to this series. The topic should be of interest to all segments of the flying community—amateur, professional, military, civilian, ATC. It figures prominently in many ASRS reports and has been touched on frequently in *CALLBACK*.

> Controller: ABC, where are you going? Your assigned altitude was one zero thousand!

146

ABC Pilot: XYZ Approach, we understood our clearance was to one one thousand; we read back one one thousand. . . .

Controller: Negative, ABC! Turn right to zero nine zero degrees and descend immediately to one zero thousand. You have traffic at one one thousand, twelve o'clock—miles.

Every week, 3 to 4 "Where are you going?!" hazardous occurrence reports similar to the above have been submitted to the Aviation Safety Reporting System (ASRS). Deviations from assigned altitudes, unauthorized taxi crossings of active runways, non-adherence to DME crossing altitudes, turns to incorrect vector headings, and various flights over the wrong Victor airways—in all 417 such errant actions [in $2\frac{1}{2}$ years]—were attributed by ATC controller and airman reporters to misunderstood, mistransmitted, or unheard numbers in ATC-to-cockpit communications exchanges.

These erroneous actions precipitated hundreds of traffic conflicts, some narrowly missed midair collisions, go-arounds, aborted takeoffs and, as aftermath to many of the incidents, the worrisome potential for administrative punitive action. On a more personal, subjective level, airmen's explanations for their communications failures frequently reflected painful chagrin and keen embarrassment for having made avoidable mistakes in flying their airplanes or in running their cockpits. . . .

So begins the ASRS "Hearback" research report. The substance is based on the old adage, "A clearance is not a clearance until it has been heard, understood, and acknowledged," and the unspoken corollary, "and until the acknowledgment has been confirmed." The study explores in detail "a strong indication that an essential redundancy—the fail-operational double-check procedure recently termed 'hearback'—frequently is missing from controller-pilot-controller dialogue. . . . So far as the author knows, the first use of the term [hearback] in this sense was in the ASRS program's monthly bulletin *CALLBACK*."

Following the usual scholarly description of methodology used, and the approach to the problem, the paper discussed its various aspects.

The absence of the confirmation/monitoring step manifested itself in four ways in the flawed communications sequences depicted in the study data set.

1. A pilot misheard the numbers in a clearance message and repeated back the erroneous units for controller confirmation.

2. A controller did not hear—or did not listen to—the incorrect readback. The airman accepted lack of response as silent confirmation that the readback was correct.

3. A pilot correctly heard and acknowledged ATC instructions, but intra-cockpit mismanagement of the clearance information resulted in a deviation.

4. An additional subset of communications failures consisted of: (a) Controller self-admitted errors in initial transmission of the numbers. These slips, mental and verbal, were not caught by the controller during pilot readback of the erroneous information, and (b) Inadequate "Roger" or "Okay" or "So long" types of pilot acknowledgements for clearances that precluded any controller double check of the completed exchange.

As usual in ASRS research papers, this one contains statistical tables summarizing the findings of error categories, types of hazardous outcomes, and airspace configurations involved in the miscommunication occurrences (for example, 50 percent of reported hearback incidents took place in Center airspace).

One of the dominant themes encountered in the study emerged as the typical airman's overtrustful assumption that the controller always found the time to "listen up" to his readbacks. A number of reports indicated that pilot readbacks of doubtful clearance numbers should include an additional "confirm" preface to the normal acknowledgment message. Some ATC controller reports suggested that, at busy times, radar observation of aircraft movements was being substituted for the listening step in the pilot–controller communications link.

For many years airmen have been required to read back ATC clearance instructions; until very recently no requirement existed specifying controller responsibilities for listening to these readbacks. Now, an amendment to the Controller's Handbook explicitly requires this monitoring function.

The ASRS "Hearback" report includes many examples to illustrate the problem. Most of these prove that the human factor is at the heart of the anomalies. Airmen heard what they expected to hear, heard what they wanted to hear, and frequently did not hear what they did not anticipate hearing. There was laxity: "It was such a beautiful day." The hazards are obvious to all. The cure, simply stated, is to listen up carefully—both pilots and controllers. As *CALLBACK* has so often preached, BE AWARE!

Flightcrew Performance When Pilot Flying and Pilot Not Flying Duties Are Exchanged

This installment in *CALLBACK*'s series of condensed ASRS research studies considers a matter important to all members of multipilot crews: What problems arise when the copilot is the pilot flying (PF) versus when the captain is the PF? The alternating of "legs" in air carrier operations, although not formally mandated, is a widespread custom; the practice has been referred to as "role reversal," but it has been pointed out that the term is incorrect. Certain duties may be exchanged, but the captain's responsibility and command authority remain inviolate and cannot be delegated. ASRS investigated a large number of reports in an attempt to determine if there were differences in the sorts of anomalies occurring when the flying duties were switched between captain and first officer.

> The risk in First Officer flying is not that First Officers are less capable, but that Captains are less efficient in the assisting role. Confronted with the ultimate responsibility, Captains are likely to be monitoring the operation closely . . . and to be so involved that their assisting role may be neglected.
>
> Airline policy statement

> When the First Officer is flying, the Captain often fails to execute normal First Officer functions and duties.
>
> FAA study

> The roles of the pilots during the approach and landing were discussed. . . . In this connection, it has been discovered that coordination between the pilots, which was satisfactory when the Captain landed the aircraft, was often less so when the co-pilot was controlling the aircraft and the captain undertook the duties normally those of the co-pilot.
>
> IATA conference

These quotations form the introduction to the ASRS "Duties Exchange" research paper. The study was undertaken by a staff member who is a highly experienced retired airline captain. The objective was "to determine . . . whether or not there were changes in the character, frequency or distribution of flightcrew performance problems reported to ASRS that seem to depend on which pilot was flying the aircraft." The report provides the usual description of objective, methodology and approach, accompanied by tables and graphs.

Perhaps the single most important factor to emerge from the examination of the 245 reports forming the raw material for this study is that captains were significantly more effective in detecting anomalies than first officers, regardless of which pilot was flying. The captain made 33 percent of the detections when he was the handling pilot and 35 percent of them when the first officer was flying. In contrast, the first officer detected only 10 percent of the anomalies while serving as PF, and only 15 percent when he or she was the primary monitor on the flight deck. It seems clear that the monitoring potential of the first officer has long been an underutilized resource in our aviation system. Of the anomalies considered in the paper, flight path control errors constituted nearly half, with near midair collisions in second place.

An examination of the fight path control errors disclosed that, as might be expected, a large proportion—three quarters— were deviations in altitude. These "busts" represented the single largest group of errors in the study and appeared to be a greater problem when the first officer (P2F) was flying than when the captain (P1F) was handling the controls; 45 percent of the P2F anomalies were altitude deviations; the comparable P1F figure was 28 percent. Most of the deviations were overshoots; these seemed a particular problem for copilots, while crossing under- shoots—reported infrequently—involved the captain.

The number of altitude deviations varied considerably by phase of flight, with the largest number taking place during descent. Approach and departure followed in frequency. Report details were too inadequate to determine the reasons for these unwanted occurrences, but suggest a lowered altitude aware- ness on the part of the first officers. Whether or not that is the actual case, "it is clear that the Captains did a relatively poor job of monitoring during departure and climb. It is also clear that many pilots rely heavily on the altitude alert system instead of on their altimeters and their awareness of their clearance limita- tions." Deviations from course or track were predominantly as- sociated with departures; in these instances there were no sig- nificant differences related to which pilot was flying.

The second largest category of anomalies studied was near midair collisions (NMACs), with the majority of these taking place during departure, descent, and approach. NMACs were reported more frequently when the captain was flying and the first officer monitoring than when these duties were exchanged. In an in- teresting reversal of the PF pattern shown in altitude overshoots: NMACs were a particular problem during departure when the captain was flying, while more of them took place during ap- proach with the first officer flying. The reports studied for this paper suggest that the external vigilance required for the avoidance of NMACs can be degraded by poor cockpit management, poor external scanning procedures, and by preoccupation with instruments within the cockpit.

Few aircraft-handling incidents were reported in the group making up this study material; most of these occurred during approach (5) or landing (12). In these cases P2 was the handling pilot predominantly; the incidents were too rare to produce valid conclusions as to reasons for this distribution.

In summary, the ASRS data show that "when the Captain was flying and the First Officer was responsible for monitoring and radio communications, a greater number of NMACs, takeoff anomalies, and crossing altitude deviations occurred. When the First Officer was flying and the Captain was responsible for the pilot not flying duties, a greater number of altitude deviations, NMACs during approach, and landing incidents were reported." A significant number of handling incidents during landing took place with the first officer flying. Generally, it appears that "the flightcrew operates more efficiently when the Captain is flying than when he is performing not flying duties. . . . The Captains appeared to have a higher level of operational awareness than did the First Officers. . . . Pilot handling skills were a minimal factor. . . . The importance of the monitoring function was not well understood by either pilot."

Problems in Briefing of Relief
by Air Traffic Controllers

This is the third of *CALLBACK*'s condensations of ASRS research papers. The first of these, on the problems associated with misheard clearance readbacks—the "Hearback" problem—offered something for everybody. That was followed by a discussion of cockpit duties exchange, a subject of interest primarily to air carrier flightcrews. We now consider problems in the briefing by controllers of the people relieving them at their duty positions. The first report involving controller briefing of relief was received by ASRS in the very early days of the program—June of 1976. Since then such reports have trickled in at a constant rate of five to ten each month.

A substantial majority of occurrence reports submitted to the NASA Aviation Safety Reporting System by pilots and air traffic controllers contain evidence of problems in the transfer of information among the participants in the National Aviation System. While failures of information transfer between ground and aircraft are most common, there are also many failures within the cockpit and within the ATC system. Such failures are often the precursors of other failures; it is important to gain an understanding of what they are and how they occur.

The briefing of a relieving controller by the controller being relieved is a pure information transfer exercise. It always has the potential for a failure to transfer the necessary information, and thus the potential for later failures of separation. Since the mode of briefing is invariably verbal, the process is subject to the many sources of error inherent in verbal communication. . . .

The objective of this study was to characterize the types of human errors reported in connection with briefing of relief in air traffic control operations, and to examine the factors associated with these errors. . . .

For purposes of this study, a briefing of relief (BOR) problem was considered to be a failure to transfer information completely and accurately from an air traffic controller operating a position to another controller who was to assume subsequent responsibility for the operation of that position.

So runs the introduction to the Research Study No. 13 in the ASRS publications list. It is followed by the usual discussion of methodology and by various graphs and statistical tables. BOR defects are classified as (1) absent, (2) incomplete, or (3) inaccurate briefings. Various factors leading to BOR problems are then listed; these include nonrecall of pertinent information, failures of technique or perception, complacency or distraction, ambiguity, work load, inattention, aircraft misidentification, and a few miscellaneous "others." In many cases more than one factor was assigned to an incident. An attempt was made to identify the root causes of the reported occurrences and to point out methods of reducing these errors.

The ASRS reports show no evidence that controllers misunderstand the ATC mandate requiring that a controller being relieved *shall* orally brief the relieving controller; the content of the oral briefing is specified. The incident reports studied for this paper, although a relatively small number, indicate that, despite controller understanding of the importance of the briefing procedure, the consequences of briefing errors were serious.

Assuming the final position the controller released Aircraft B. When B turned downwind Aircraft A departed and was immediately in conflict with B. A took evasive action to climb above B, passing over him by 600 feet. Probable contributing factor—volume of traffic resulted in an incomplete position briefing.

"Heavy traffic volume" appears as a factor in so many ASRS reports of miscommunication that it is no surprise to note its prominence in BOR errors: "Traffic built to a point where more controllers were needed. The controller who was working all positions was too busy to brief me when I attempted to take radar west and a final position."

About half of the analyzed incidents were the result of incomplete briefings—failure to transfer relevant information—or the transfer of inaccurate information. Here is a typical case:

> The new controller was told that Aircraft A had been stopped at FL330. Tape recordings indicated that A was never recleared to 330. When he reported in he advised climbing to FL370. The controller acknowledged but did not verify the assigned altitude. Later Aircraft B requested descent clearance and the controller noticed the A and B targets merging as A was leaving FL348.

> Aircraft A called stating he was on frequency at 6000. Assuming it was his initial call-up I gave him the beacon code on the flight progress strip. A few seconds later he acquired about one mile behind Aircraft B. It was found in the system error investigation that (1) the relieved controller had been in contact with A and amended his clearance, assigning a heading of 090 degrees, (2) he had forgotten about A at the time of relief, (3) the aircraft had not been assigned his correct code, which would have resulted in auto-acquisition.

In the majority of reported errors the fault lay with the controller being relieved; however in about 20 percent of the cases the relieving controller was to blame! "Controller apologized for the mixup, claiming he had just relieved another controller and was told we had been cleared for the approach."

Naturally, distractions play a significant role in briefing failures; the briefing process itself can often be one of the distracting factors. "Scratch pad" notations can be helpful both to briefer and briefee; possible temporary delay of briefing during busy periods may also help. Although the responsibility for the briefing remains with the relieved controller, his counterpart can be of substantial help in discharging this responsibility. Although briefing errors will doubtless continue to be made, alertness by briefer and careful attention by his relieving counterpart can minimize the errors and reduce unsafe instances.

Operational Problems Experienced by Single Pilots
in Instrument Meteorological Conditions

This "*CALLBACK* Capsule Commentary" presents a digest of an
ASRS research paper. The study was performed by an aviation
professor at a major university who serves as a consultant to
NASA and deals with a subject (commonly referred to as "SPIFR")
of interest to many general aviation pilots. This condensation,
like others in this series of condensations, merely hits the high
spots in the study; a more detailed treatment may be found in
Report No. 25 on the ASRS publication list, available on request.

A large number of ASRS-reported occurrences were examined
in which operational difficulties were encountered by pilots flying alone on Instrument Flight Plans (IFR) in Instrument Meteorological Conditions (IMC). "Ten problem categories observed, in
decreasing order of reporting frequency, were: (1) pilot alle-
gations of inadequate service, (2) altitude deviations, (3) im-
properly flown approaches, (4) heading deviations, (5) position
deviations, (6) below minimums operations, (7) loss of airplane
control, (8) forgot mandatory report, (9) fuel problem, and (10)
improper holding."

The study gives statistics showing that general aviation IFR
flight operations are more than double in number those involving air carriers and that GA IFR operations (and number of IFR
rated GA pilots) will continue to increase.

> Presently many IFR single pilot (SPIFR) operations are conducted
> by highly-trained and experienced pilots flying modern, well-
> equipped airplanes. However, a large proportion of the General
> Aviation IFR operations involve relatively inexperienced single pi-
> lots, often with limited equipment, who are expected by the ATC
> system to perform at the same level of competency as the profes-
> sional air carrier crews. Aviation agencies and user organizations
> have expressed concern that the level of competency expected to be
> demanded of the future SPIFR will not be attained unless signifi-
> cant improvements in the design of the aviation system are
> achieved.

As do other ASRS research papers, the SPIFR study explains the
methodology and search strategies used and provides detailed
data in the form of graphs and tables. Discussions are presented
of each of the ten problem categories identified and examples are
used as illustration.

Altitude deviations make up a large proportion of the SPIFR
problems, just as they do among the air carrier reporters to

ASRS, although in the GA case the majority are reported by controllers rather than by the errant pilots:

> Pilot of small aircraft was assigned 3000 feet after departure. . . .
> Pilot was observed climbing through 4600 feet at which time I
> questioned his assigned altitude. Pilot had filed for 8000 and was
> climbing to that altitude.

> Aircraft A that departed was given vectors to on course and was
> told to maintain 5000 feet. Aircraft A requested 7000 due to other
> aircraft going in same direction. Later on Aircraft A was given
> instructions to climb to 6000 and he advised that he was at 7000
> feet.

"Mind set" is considered to be the predisposing condition for the human errors leading to the SPIFR altitude deviations. Instrument approaches constitute a large subset of the study data; here a lack of proficiency may be inferred from the reports:

> Cleared for an ILS approach, pilot reports following Glide Slope but
> never intercepting Localizer, and overflying airport.

> Pilot reports having incorrectly tracked his Localizer on a Back
> Course approach due to fatigue, resulting in a missed approach.

> Pilot reports experiencing vertigo during night ILS approach, resulting in missed approach.

> After being vectored to the VOR/DME final approach course, pilot
> reports incorrectly turning outbound in order to fly a procedure
> turn.

Heading deviations, sometimes due to misunderstanding but more often to a heavy work load or lack of proficiency, appear among SPIFR problems. The same causes can lead to errors in required (or reported) position—an error related to heading deviations. Loss of airplane control is a small but dramatic part of the SPIFR experience. In the reports studied, an encounter with a heavy aircraft wake and others with weather-related turbulence caused difficulties; there were several accounts of distraction-induced loss of control. Improper flight planning resulted in inadequate fuel supplies in a few incidents; incorrect holding procedures led to other difficulties which could be assigned generally to lack of skill.

The SPIFR report suggests that in addition to improving pilot capabilities through additional training and experience, the "nature of the SPIFR task should be changed through the redesign of cockpit systems and ATC procedures in handling the SPIFR." In conclusion, it is clear that lack of proficiency and of awareness, mind set, distraction, and work load were the predominant factors in SPIFR problems.

Human Factors Associated with Altitude Alert Systems

This study, condensed by *CALLBACK,* was made earlier in ASRS history; it is as relevant today as when it was published. Statistical totals are greater today, but percentages—and event types and consequences—remain consistent. The author, a NASA human factors scientist, reviews the history of the regulation (FAR 91.51) requiring altitude alert systems on all U.S. civil turbojet aircraft, effective February 1972, and the reasons for its later (September 1977) modification (optional), which permitted elimination of the aural warning of approach to selected altitude so that only a visual warning would appear, with aural warnings occurring thereafter if the aircraft departed the assigned altitude. The change was made in response to pilot complaints of too many warnings. There follows a discussion of the differing perceptions of altitude alert systems by pilots engaged in long-haul operations and those flying short route segments.

The paper includes tables summarizing salient points emerging from the examination of reports submitted to ASRS. These cover the types of occurrences reported, the enabling and associated factors involved, and the recovery factors. Given that altitude alert incidents were invariably related to altitude deviations, it was found that 85 percent were overshoots in climb or descent. A small group of reports dealt with altitude excursions in cruise, and an even smaller group featured undershoots.

In almost two-thirds of the incidents examined the flightcrews failed to observe an alert warning; in another third the alert had not been set correctly; a few reports told of alert system malfunction or absence. Of those occurrences in which an alert was not noticed, flightcrew distraction was the predominant cause; crew overload accounted for most of the others, with a few reports of pilots unable to see or hear the warning. In the following report narrative the human factors that permitted the signals to be missed are of interest:

> Cleared from FL220 to 13,000, descending at about 2000 ft/min with the altitude alert set for 13,000 feet. I was flying and did not hear the alert horn or see the light; we descended right on through

13,000. The Captain was talking on another radio and called my attention to altitude. I made an immediate correction and started climbing back to 13,000. . . . I noticed at this time that my seat position was too high for me to see the altitude alert light, which is placed high on the instrument panel. On further checking, we found the warning horn was not loud enough to be heard as I was wearing moulded ear pieces and the horn does not sound through the headset. . . .

Cases involving failure to set, or incorrect setting of, the altitude reminder were found. In [some], a misunderstood clearance appeared to be the reason for the failure. In . . . others, the crew simply forgot or overlooked this task. . . .

Cleared to cross 30 DME east at 10,000 feet. . . . As the flight descended through FL210 at 2,500 ft/min descent we were restricted to 14,000 feet in the descent. Passing through FL180, the before-landing preliminary checklist was completed. While descending through 13,000 (and that was wrong), I applied full thrust and rotated nose-up briskly as Center asked our altitude and said to climb to 14,000 immediately. . . . I noted the altitude alert was set at 10,000 feet.

A report "involving the absence of [an alert system] in a military aircraft being flown by a reserve officer who was an air carrier pilot is interesting because it illustrates clearly how dependent we can become on automatic devices which usually function correctly, and which were intended as backup devices for the flight crew." More than 70 percent of the cases studied for this paper cited "distraction" as at least one of the factors involved. "Distractions were usually due to ATC instructions, traffic, required cockpit procedures, or a combination of these factors." Flightcrew coordination appeared as a problem in about one third of the data sample. There was a tendency for the flightcrew to "go outside" when traffic was called; a related problem occurs when an anomaly is discovered within the cockpit.

Many reporters described deficiencies in the altitude alert system—particularly in "giving too many signals, leading to confusion between the device's alerting and warning functions and a tendency to ignore the signals. It is noteworthy that all of these complaints came from pilots on short haul aircraft and routes." Other factors involved aircraft performance much better (or worse) than usual:

Rate of climb was 4,000 ft/min. . . . We all missed the altitude warning and I missed the callout and we needed both. . . .

It is interesting to note that in 56% of cases a controller first noticed the deviation . . . suggests that within-cockpit monitoring was less effective than is desirable. . . . Several reports made note of decreased flightcrew altitude awareness because of the presence of the alert system. The system was originally conceived as a backup, not a primary means of altitude control. It has become more than that, as do most such aids if they function reliably.

In concluding the study the author writes, "Altitude awareness . . . has been adversely affected by the altitude alert system. It appears that the removal of the aural signal approaching altitudes would assist in enhancing flightcrew altitude awareness. . . . It is also possible however that this change . . . may not be equally desirable in long-range operations involving long periods of low workload."

And finally, "These data also suggest the desirability of an examination of flightcrew procedures and monitoring responsibilities during climbs and descents. It appears that improvements in altitude control are needed and might result from more specific assignment of monitoring duties during these phases of flight."

An Investigation of Reports of
Controlled Flight toward Terrain

The early 1970s were marked by a dramatic series of Controlled-Flight-Into-Terrain (CFIT) fatal accidents (those accidents in which an aircraft, under the control of the crew, is flown into terrain—or water—with no prior awareness on the part of the crew of the impending danger)." One of these accidents, in December 1974, in which an airliner struck a mountain after prematurely descending below a safe enroute altitude, "was a watershed for important accident prevention developments. One such development was an amendment to Federal Aviation Regulation Part 121 requiring that all large turbine-powered aircraft be equipped with a Ground Proximity Warning System (GPWS). Another was the initiation of the FAA Aviation Safety Reporting Program and the related NASA Aviation Safety Reporting System (ASRS), of which this report is a product."

This quotation is from the introduction to an ASRS study (No. 24 in the publications list), augmented by a Special Paper (No. 20) and condensed here in *CALLBACK*'s continuing series. Both deal with the problem of aircraft flying into terrain—or narrowly avoiding that fate. No. 20 deals particularly with the performance of terrain-warning systems. In addition to examining the impact of GPWS and the Minimum Safe Altitude Warning System (MSAW) on safety records, the studies attempt "to identify those human and system factors which facilitate the occurrence of

Controlled Flight Toward Terrain (CFTT) events and those which preclude their termination as an accident."

Like the other studies in this series, the CFTT papers include descriptions of search methodology and statistical tables and graphs. From the data, three broad categories of situations and/or occurrences emerged: (1) those in which except for some intervention, or by chance, the aircraft would have come in contact with terrain or some other obstacle; (2) those conducive to an aircraft inadvertently coming into contact with terrain; and (3) those in which a GPWS or MSAW issued a false or inappropriate alarm. The authors note that "while the third category did not relate directly to controlled flight toward terrain, it was judged important because false alarms tend to influence the credibility of alarms or to create new hazards (e.g., loss of aircraft control due to distraction)."

The reports studied suggested that CFTT occurrences could be classified into separate types, although with some overlap. In general, the problem types refer to flightcrew errors (navigation, altitude control, aircraft configuration); inappropriate ATC vectors or clearances or ATC deviation from standard procedures; interpretation of charted restrictions; loss of communication; airspace configuration; unlighted or unmarked obstructions; inadequate or unreliable approach or enroute aids; and problems arising from false or presumed inappropriate activation of GPWS or MSAW.

Of the ASRS reports comprising the raw material, two-thirds were from pilots, one-third from controllers. The following is a typical controller narrative:

> Aircraft was being vectored to an ILS final for Runway 21 Left. While on base leg northeast of the airport the flightcrew reported the airport in sight and requested a visual approach. Approach Controller issued the visual approach clearance and changed the aircraft to Tower frequency. The aircraft turned southbound and did not call the tower. Tower controllers noticed the aircraft on radar with a low altitude alert. . . . The aircraft was observed at 1700 feet MSL, $1\frac{1}{2}$ miles north of a radio antenna 1300 MSL. At this time the aircraft called the tower. Went in descent to 1400 MSL and flight radar target touched the radar marking of the antenna. Aircraft then climbed to 3000 feet and was vectored for an ILS approach.

Many of the CFTT incidents took place during approach or landing phase of flight; hazards were also noted during departure and missed approach procedures. Occasional controller errors appear; it is encouraging to read of the warning devices serving their intended purpose.

> We were given a discretionary descent and to maintain 13,000 feet. During the descent we were recleared "direct to the VOR". . . . We arrived at 13,000 at 33 DME. Conditions were IFR with tops at 14,000. At 30 DME the GPWS activated with a Mode 2 excessive closure rate. We heard, "Terrain, Terrain, Pull Up." I immediately climbed through 14,000. . . . Upon checking the chart I discovered a terrain altitude peak of 11,918 feet. This ground proximity, coupled with mountainous terrain, suggests that the GPWS operated correctly.

The researchers list a number of conclusions derived from their study of the data; first is that "Human error is the single greatest identifiable cause of CFTT incidents." Errors are committed by both pilots and controllers; these are discussed in detail. A number of the reported occurrences involved the role of GPWS and MSAW in averting serious accidents. Compelling evidence of the efficacy of these systems appears in the record of CFIT accidents in the five years preceding the introduction of the systems as compared with the five following years. In their separate study "of accidents in the United States, or to U.S. carriers, in which air carrier aircraft were flown into terrain with no prior awareness . . . of the impending disaster," the authors provide statistics to show that in the years 1971–1975 (before GPWS/MSAW) there were seventeen such accidents; "In the period 1976–1980 (after GPWS/MSAW) there were two (in one of these a GPWS alarm sounded, but was ignored). The probability of this dramatic reduction being coincidental is less than seven in one million." This is shown graphically on p. 161.

Cleared for the Visual Approach:
Human Factor Problems in Air Carrier Operations

This latest in the series of *CALLBACK*'s capsule commentaries is devoted to an ASRS Research Study (No. 31 on the publications list) of a problem often appearing in pilot and controller reports: the visual approach. The full study was done by a retired international airline captain of great experience, now serving as a research consultant to ASRS, who has contributed a number of papers to our list (and to this series). Consistent with other project research studies, the visual approach paper outlines the research plan and method and carries detailed tables and graphs, as well as examples of relevant reports.

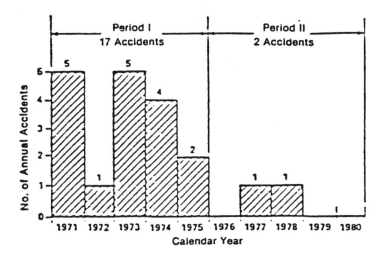

The introduction states:

The visual approach shortcut to the procedural restraints of full-IFR operations represents significant time saving and workload reductions for both controllers and flightcrews. The use of the visual approach unloads the radar controller's traffic separation responsibilities and greatly expedites traffic movements. To the airman, the opportunity to make his own way to the runway is more than a convenience; in these days of soaring fuel costs, no flightcrew is willing, in VMC conditions, to grind through a high overhead arrival routing, in a high drag configuration, to an 8 to 10 mile final.

This legal and desirable simplification of the IFR procedural complexity requires the establishment of appropriate safeguards. The formalized ritual of the controller/airman informational exchange provides them. . . . The "airport in sight" and "traffic in sight" confirmations are as essential to air safety as the "gear down" and "three green lights" cockpit calls prior to landing.

Yet numerous reports to NASA's Aviation Safety Reporting System (ASRS), both from controllers and pilots, narrate a series of serious hazardous occurrences associated with . . . conduct of visual approaches. In-flight traffic conflicts frequently were mentioned but the "what-went-wrong" event list included such incidents as grossly unstabilized approaches, line-ups or landings on the wrong runways, or, at times, on the wrong airports, go-arounds, and the contrary "We made it in but we should have gone around" admissions, landings without tower clearances and a plethora of varied deviations from ATC instructions or clearances.

This research study attempts "to identify and examine the obvious operational hazards and the perhaps not-so-obvious human factor pitfalls reportedly encountered in execution of the visual approach procedure." According to the formal abstract accompanying the paper, "analysis of the report set identified nine aspects of the visual approach procedure that appeared to be predisposing conditions for inducing or exacerbating the effects of operational errors by flightcrew members or controllers. Predisposing conditions, errors, and operational consequences of the errors are discussed. In a summary, operational policies that might mitigate the problem are examined."

"Airport in sight" and/or "traffic in sight" calls are fundamental prerequisites to the visual approach clearance. In an interesting sidelight to the study,

> Comparison of the controller and airman report narratives suggested a fundamental ambiguity in the "airport in sight" procedural response. All controller reports specifically emphasized "runway" while all airman reports utilized the "airport" terminology. . . . To the controllers, airport sighting signifies runway sighting and, furthermore, carries a full expectation that the aircraft would track the shortest, most direct course into line-up in the approach lane. Contrariwise, airmen seem not to apprehend that their airport sighting call precludes any subsequent runway reorientations or flight path realignments to the assigned runway. This airport/runway ambiguity seemed especially significant during operations involving parallel runway layouts.

An ATC supervisor commented, "We take airport sighting to mean that the pilot has the RUNWAY made."

Inadequate accomplishment of the procedural sighting steps led to traffic conflicts, approaches or landings on wrong airports, and descents toward terrain or obstructions. In a typical case,

> While starting a left turn into the runway, checklist was completed. Then I again reestablished visual reference with the runway and made the final approach and landing. As we began to taxi, we realized. . . .

> About 20 miles out the air carrier reported airport in sight and I cleared the aircraft for a visual. Then I got busy with several other aircraft. I did not notice the rapid descent of the air carrier until the MSAW alert sounded. His altitude readout indicated going

> through 5000 feet. I issued an immediate low altitude alert—
> "High terrain at 12 o'clock, 3 miles, at 4700 feet." The aircraft
> climbed immediately. Later the tower told me that the flightcrew
> asked him for the meaning of "low altitude alert."

The presence of uncontrolled VFR aircraft in the vicinity presents an inevitable complicating factor to the visual approach. By definition, visual conditions must exist; thus uncontrolled VFR aircraft must be expected to be sharing the airspace with IFR traffic. In addition, "When the visual approach is accepted by the flightcrew, even the potential 'workload permitting' assistance of ATC is inexorably withdrawn with the (usually) immediate termination of radar services." See-and-avoid becomes the order of the day.

> I pulled up and went over the top of the small aircraft. The miss
> distance was estimated at 25 feet.

> All three of us saw the other aircraft but not soon enough to take
> any action.

"Throughout the study the airman and controller reports suggested a broad, repetitive pattern of complacency." The research "suggested a general call for exact, precise and complete adherence to the fixed procedural steps outlined in AIM and in the Controller Handbook for ATC issuance and airman acceptance of the visual approach." With that adherence, "the visual approach procedure is cost-effective, time expedient, and essential."

Human Factors Associated with
Potential Conflicts at Uncontrolled Airports

This *CALLBACK* capsule commentary deals with Study No. 6 on the ASRS publication list, which was conducted by an aviation professor early in the program. It examines traffic conflicts at airports lacking control towers; in view of the increasing air traffic density, the paper's relevance is, perhaps, greater today than at the time of the study. A quoted NTSB report sets the theme: "Uncontrolled airports present a serious hazard to aviation safety in that [a large proportion] of midair collision accidents occurred at airports where there was no control tower. . . . The principal means of avoiding conflicts in the traffic patterns at such airports is the see-and-avoid concept; it follows that breakdowns in the functioning of that concept were the immedi-

ate causes of those . . . collisions." This report represents "an
effort to help pilots reduce the risks of midair collisions."

After a description of research methods and approach, tables
and graphs are presented to illustrate a discussion of results
and conclusions. For purposes of this study, a potential conflict
is defined as "a situation in which at least one pilot perceived a
potential for a midair collision. Nontower airports fall into three
broad categories: 1. Airports with a published unicom frequency . . . ; 2. Airports with a Flight Service Station (FSS)
Airport Advisory Service located on the field; 3. Airports with
neither a published unicom frequency nor an FSS located on the
field."

The reports studied were "analyzed with regard to where the
potential conflict occurred and the relative motion between the
aircraft. About two thirds of all the reports involved situations
where both aircraft were on final leg, or one aircraft was airborne and one was on the runway. [This is] compatible with
NTSB's findings that 'most of the . . . accidents occurred at or
near the uncontrolled airport at low altitudes (100 ft or less) at
low closure rates.'" Further analysis shows that in 22 percent of
the incidents "neither pilot was reported to have used the radio
to communicate the aircraft's position and/or intentions. In approximately 54% of the reports only one pilot used the radio.
However, if one pilot used the radio but the other pilot was not
listening, that had the same effect as if no radio call was made.
Thus, in 76% of the reports there was no aural exchange of
position information."

The abstract accompanying the ASRS paper emphasized this
point and "the importance of providing aural transfer of information as a backup to the visual 'see-and-avoid' mode of information transfer. . . . It was also found that a large fraction of pilots
involved in potential conflicts on final approach had executed
straight-in approaches, rather than the recommended traffic
pattern entries, prior to the conflicts." In about a quarter "of the
occurrences the two pilots did use the appropriate radio procedures, but still had a potential conflict." Since this study, airline deregulation has increased the incidence of straight-in approaches and introduced new problems; new-entrant carriers
(and some of the older) are serving airports, many of them uncontrolled, that hitherto lacked scheduled service. Economic,
competitive, and schedule pressures combine to render the traditional traffic pattern unpopular; flightcrews feel obliged to take

the shortest route to the runway. In addition, larger and faster aircraft using airports previously the domain of light planes introduce a potentially hazardous speed mix.

The author points out that adherence to procedures recommended in the Airman's Information Manual (AIM) would reduce significantly the incidence of uncontrolled airport conflicts. AIM provides detailed advice on radio usage and traffic pattern practices (since this study the Common Traffic Advisory Frequency (CTAF) concept has become a formal part of communication procedure; it is outlined in AIM and shown on current charts). The paper includes ASRS report narratives. Here is one example:

> Right traffic is standard for Runway 35. I was turning final off right base, when over the unicom I heard, "Two aircraft turning final for 35." I then saw another aircraft low turning final off left base. I initiated a go-around. What I didn't see was brought to my attention by the alert unicom observer, wherever he was located.

"In addition to the apparent lack of observance of standardized radio procedures, there was an apparent lack of consistency in following standardized traffic patterns" intended to ensure "a systematized flow for aircraft." The straight-in approach figures in many potential conflicts. "It is difficult to explain why the pilot of an aircraft on straight-in does not see the other aircraft. It may be suggested that once a pilot is on final, his concentration is on the runway and the 'see-and-avoid' concept failure is the pilot 'not looking' combined with 'did not see' since an aircraft on collision course has zero relative movement and is harder for the eye to see." For example,

> I was turning final on 34. . . . Aircraft B was making straight-in approach. I saw B and made a 360 degree turn to avoid collision. I made calls stating my position on downwind and base on 122.8. Aircraft B pilot later told me . . . did not see me until I made an evasive turn.

Possible reasons for failure to see fall into two categories: human and mechanical. Under "human" are listed the inability to perceive relative movement or aircraft/background blending: simply not looking or tunnel vision; misjudgment of distance; and intentional maneuvering. "Mechanical" reasons include structural obstructions to vision; blinding by sun position; visibility impairment by cloud or precipitation; and dirty (or reflecting) windshields. The low-wing versus high-wing situation appeared in the "not-seeing" context, but there were insufficient data to permit valid conclusions. "Not seeing" is self-explanatory; "not looking" is not so obvious and is accounted for by "cockpit work load, fatigue, or inattention due to other pressures."

In summary, the study stresses the AIM admonition that "combining aural/visual alertness . . . will enhance safety. . . . Behavioral factors . . . in potential conflicts were (1) the lack of use of recommended radio procedures and (2) the use of non-standard traffic patterns. . . . It is suggested that an . . . educational program may be useful in motivating pilots to practice safe procedures that have proved their effectiveness and have been recommended for universal application."

The Go-around Maneuver in Air Carrier Operations: Causes and Resulting Problems

A go-around maneuver is neither difficult nor demanding; in pilot jargon it is a "no sweat" procedure. The typical flightcrew reaction to go-around is annoyance at the waste of fuel, time, and effort in pulling out of the approach and a semicynical expectation of long vectors, delay, even holding, prior to resequencing into the pattern. However, when placed into the context of the near midair collision risk picture, go-arounds, as reported to the Aviation Safety Reporting System (ASRS), are frequently avoidance or evasive maneuvers in breakouts from traffic conflicts. Furthermore, these pullouts from approach often channel the aircraft immediately and precipitously into conflicts with other aircraft in the airport traffic area. With respect to conflicts, a go-around can be a transition phase—from the frying pan into the fire.

This passage is from the introduction to an ASRS research study dealing with "the go-around maneuver." The paper was written by a retired airline captain, now a research consultant to ASRS, who has contributed several reports to this series. This one, like those previously condensed in *CALLBACK,* contains a description of the data set and methodology utilized in the study; detailed tables augment the text.

According to the study, "Traffic conflicts with other aircraft, either converging during the approach or situated on the landing runway, directly caused 80% [of the go-arounds]. 18% were reportedly caused by nonconflict operational problems, such as bounced landings, crosswinds, wake turbulence, too high and too fast, and lineup with wrong parallel runway."

The author emphasizes that "only those pull-outs from final approach accomplished in vmc conditions were tallied as go-arounds in this study. Missed approaches resulting from 'no visual contact' at decision height (DH) or at minimum descent altitude (MDA) displayed considerably different operational and human factors than go-arounds; they were eliminated from this analysis." Reporting pilots and controllers "were exceedingly loose in the description terminology they applied to the maneuver; for example, 'pullout,' 'go-around,' 'abandoned approach,' 'wave-off,' 'overshoot,' appeared indiscriminately."

It is hypothesized that in visual weather conditions ATC controllers expect an aircarrier approach to culminate in a completed landing. In the report narratives reviewed, "unexpected go-arounds sometimes resulted in hasty, unplanned, or incompleted coordination reactions."

> I watched on radar as an air carrier on a go-around merged with another aircraft that was departing off Runway 04. Apparently no separation was being exercised. Then they dumped them both on to my frequency; both pilots were somewhat mad, to say the least.

> We were advised we were overtaking traffic and told to climb out to 3000 feet. At 1800 we broke out of some rain showers and found ourselves head-on with another aircraft at our twelve o'clock position. I feel no provision was made for a go-around in the controller traffic picture.

Causes for the intrusion of one aircraft into the flight path of another on final approach were identified as: "1. Human behavioral failures, by airmen or ATC controllers, usually stated objectively in the reports as errors, omissions, or coordination breakdowns; 2. The coincidental presence of operational situations or flight activities involving adjoining parallel runways, airspeed performance mix, training aircraft on opposite direction practice instrument approaches, pilot use of back-course ILS localizer approach, nearby peripheral airports, and other secondary environmental conditions." Analysis of human factors involved in go-around conflict events revealed evidence of "distractions,

worry, workload, aggression, schedule pressure, anger, inexperience, even the pressing requirement for restroom facilities.
These forces sometimes could be defined as the root causes of
behavioral failures."

> I kept making mistakes all day. I couldn't keep my mind on the
> traffic. I asked the supervisor for relief but he said he couldn't
> spare me. It was a boy! 8 pounds 8 ounces!

The conflicts causing the majority of the go-arounds studied
were classified as "in-flight" or "on-the-ground" (almost equally
divided) and by airspace type. Again, the distribution was almost equal for incidents in TCA, TRSA, and non-Stage III airspace.
All parallel runway in-flight conflicts were caused by pilot mis-
perceptions or misunderstandings; conflict-caused go-arounds
in general were precipitated nearly equally by controller actions
and by pilot actions. A significant finding was "the abrupt and
belated recognition by many airmen that the published missed-
approach procedures often could not be adhered to and were
sometimes potentially hazardous when a VMC go-around became
necessary."

> We had a minor control problem and advised the tower we were
> executing a missed approach. As we started to climb (I'd hate to
> call it panic) there was what I'll call severe concern on the part of
> the controller as he repeatedly called for a departing jet to abort
> his takeoff.

> If we followed the patterned procedure for the back course we
> would have been in a very dangerous situation, because it called
> for a straight-ahead path to the OM. The MAP obviously never had
> this situation in mind. As I realized the situation, I broke off to the
> left and advised Tower what I was doing. He seemed confused. He
> told me to make a right turn, which would have placed us head-on
> to opposite traffic.

In the concluding section of the "go-around" paper the author
states, "A VFR go-around with all engines operating may be a
'piece of cake' for the experienced transport pilot. When viewed
from the perspective of ASRS reports, however, pull-outs from
final approach may have more serious implications."

Obviously, CALLBACK's digest cannot cover this important
subject with the thoroughness of the formal research paper;
those interested in a more detailed discussion may request ASRS
Publication No. 22.

Information Transfer
between Air Traffic Control and Aircraft:
Communications Problems in Flight Operations

CALLBACK continues its series of Research Report condensations with this digest of one of a group of papers (No. 15 on the ASRS publication list) dealing with information transfer problems in the aviation system. The study was performed by a senior NASA scientist who has made major contributions to the ASRS project and an ASRS staff member, now retired, with many years of ATC communication experience. "The purpose of this report is to discuss problems in oral communication between pilots and controllers. The investigation consisted of review and analysis of pertinent information in the ASRS data base."

Initial examination of the data "produced a finding considered significant to the central issue of this study: 70% of the reports to ASRS involve some type of oral communication problem related to the operation of an aircraft. The nature of the problems reported varied widely, ranging from failure to originate an appropriate message to failure of the intended receiver to comprehend and confirm the message accurately."

These communications problems were subdivided into 10 generic types. . . . Before taking up these assessments, however, two aspects of communications difficulties require consideration: the expectation factor and the problem of conveying traffic avoidance information effectively.

ASRS reports indicate that many instances of misunderstandings can be attributed to the expectation factor; that is, the recipient (or listener) perceives that he heard what he expected to hear in the message transmitted. Pilots and controllers alike tend to hear what they expect to hear. Deviations from routine are not noted and the read-back is heard as the transmitted message, whether correct or incorrect.

"Aircraft A was in a block altitude of 12,000–14,000 ft. The instructor pilot and the student both thought the controller told them to turn left to a heading of 010 degrees and descend to and maintain 10,000 ft. At 10,700 ft. the controller requested aircraft A's altitude. The crew responded 10,700 ft. The controller stated the aircraft had been cleared to 12,000, not 10,000. There are two contributing causes for this occurrence: 99% of all clearances from that area are to descend to and maintain 10,000 ft., and as the instructor I was conditioned to descend to 10,000 by many previous flights. The controller may have said 12,000 but I was programmed for 10,000."

The conveyance of traffic advisories and avoidance information was found to be "the least satisfactory aspect of air/ground information transfer. . . . The pervasive difficulty . . . is the seeming inconsistency with which information about traffic is made available." It is pointed out that traffic advisories are provided as "an 'additional service', which means that workload permitting, the controller will issue advisories on traffic that he observes when he is not occupied with higher priority duties."

The ten generic types of communications problems identified by the authors are: (1) misinterpretable—phonetic similarity, (2) inaccurate—transposition, (3) other inaccuracies in content, (4) incomplete content, (5) ambiguous phraseology, (6) untimely transmission, (7) garbled phraseology, (8) absent—not sent, (9) absent—equipment failure, (10) recipient not monitoring.

During the past 50 years, "technical advances have improved the quality of voice transmissions and mitigated atmospheric or induced electronic interference. Remaining technical problems include blocked transmissions, line-of-sight limitations, and hardware failures that remain undiscovered until the next occasion for a communication arises. However, the retrieved ASRS reports concerning problems in air/ground communications indicate convincingly that most of such communications problems involve human error."

Taking each of their categories in turn, the authors of the study have provided illustrative reports from the large retrieved ASRS data set. Of the subsets, no. 8, messages not transmitted, is by far the largest, with 37 percent of the occurrences. Inaccurate messages (no. 2 and no. 3) accounted for 16 percent of the total; messages transmitted too early or too late (no. 6) made up 13 percent.

> The captain spotted the traffic and pointed it out to the F/O who was flying and nosed the aircraft over into level flight to go under the other aircraft 50 to 100 feet and slightly behind him. . . . We feel that radar should have had the aircraft in radar contact at the time we took off and we should have been advised of the traffic at or before takeoff.

Ambiguous phraseology (category no. 5) appeared in 10 percent of the data set; another 10 percent dealt with recipient not monitoring (no. 10). The following is an example of ambiguity:

> Controller said . . . "Can you see the runway?" We responded yes. He said, "Okay, turn to 360 degrees." At this point we started our turn and (thinking we were cleared for a visual approach) began a

descent. . . . Then he said he had not yet cleared us below 4,000. . . . Shortly thereafter he cleared us for a visual.

None of the remaining categories were represented in the study with more than 2 percent of the incidents. The related matter of ATIS was represented by a small number of reports; in most cases these were complaints of too-rapid or otherwise unclear transmissions. In detailing the various problems, the researchers have segregated the data into "terminal operations," and "en route operations," and they have included a discussion of the "party line" concept. "A popular point of view among pilots is that there is substantial benefit in . . . monitoring a communication frequency [which] can provide useful information, for example, about traffic flow and locations of other traffic."

"It is concluded that ATC-aircraft communications problems are involved in a large fraction of the occurrences reported to the ASRS. Many or most of these communications problems involve human errors on the part of the sender or receiver of the message."

Information Transfer within the Cockpit: Problems in Intracockpit Communications

This *CALLBACK* capsule commentary is a digest of a paper in the ASRS series of Information Transfer Research Reports; it deals with communications between cockpit occupants and is No. 17 on the ASRS Publication List.

The introduction points out:

> Communication patterns among cockpit crew members probably play a more significant role today than ever before. With the large air carriers (many employing thousands of pilots) and their complicated bidding procedures for assigning flight duties, it is possible that pilots may fly together without having met before. . . . Thus, responsibilities that may be implicitly understood by crews that fly together frequently have to be explicitly assigned to members of a newly assembled crew. . . . It is the central thesis of this paper that the patterns of communication between cockpit crewmembers determine in a large degree the response patterns of the crewmembers.

The authors, two NASA human factors scientists who work closely with the ASRS staff, describe a NASA-sponsored full--mission-simulation project that enabled them to examine closely the role played by communications patterns in the management of cockpit resources and performance. The results of that project, combined with material in the ASRS database, provide the material for their discussion.

The principal finding in this study, emphasized with appropriate excerpts from incidents reported to ASRS, was that "within-cockpit patterns seem to be significantly related to performance. The lack of appropriate communications between cockpit crewmembers is an obvious problem, but it is also apparent that the style of communications plays an important role." As an aside, it was also noted "that pilots are reluctant to report instances of interpersonal conflicts in the cockpit."

> Nonetheless, many pilots did report communication problems with other crewmembers as causal factors. Of these reported within-cockpit communications difficulties, 35% involved problems with crew coordination . . . poor understanding and division of responsibilities. Often the lack of appropriate acknowledgments and cross checking was a factor:
> "I said '075, the heading, right?' The First Officer looked at me quizzically and said . . . 'Yeah, OK.' We continued to climb and were told to contact departure . . . they told us to turn immediately to 110 . . . then asked, 'What heading were you cleared to?' I said, 'Tell them 075; that's what we read back, wasn't it?' The copilot did not answer me, so I looked at him and he again had that odd look. . . . At no time were we aware of the serious problem with the other aircraft that unbeknownst to us had taken off on Runway 8. . . . I believe it was solely due to poor cockpit communication. . . . I thought 075 degrees was the correct departure heading, and to confirm it, I asked the copilot. But my question came at a time when we were very busy . . . he thought I was asking his evaluation of a direction. Coincidentally, that, to him, was a good direction and he answered in the affirmative. I took his answer as a concurrence of my question of proper takeoff heading."

The study also notes that

> lack of appropriate acknowledgments and cross-checking is a frequently occurring problem. . . . A total lack of communication between cockpit crewmembers was cited as a factor in 12% of the [ASRS] reports. The following typifies the potential severity . . . :
> "I was pilot in command. . . . I lined up for takeoff. As throttles were advanced the takeoff warning horn sounded. Following checks . . . the warning horn sounded two more times and then stopped. My hand was in the process of transitioning back to the thrust levers with the intent of aborting the takeoff. . . . I was at 60–70 knots when the horn stopped. I elected to continue the takeoff since in my judgement all the parameters for a safe takeoff were accomplished. *What I did not know, however, was that the*

warning horn circuit breaker was pulled by the engineer without his advising me of such action. . . . He preempted my actions by pulling the circuit breaker, an action I never intended to make . . . not advising the crew . . . resulted in a false impression of a safe configuration for flight."

Examination of the data revealed many examples of crew members "not communicating regarding errors even when they had access to correct information. Misunderstood clearances (examples of ground-to-air communication problems) posed frequent problems; . . . these often evolved into within-cockpit communication difficulties. . . . Over 15% of the reports dealt with information which was believed by one or more crewmembers to have been transferred, but for one reason or another (e.g., interference or inadequacy of the message) was not."

In a number (10%) of instances, communications between cockpit crewmembers were deficient as a result of overconfidence and complacency—assumptions that everybody understood what was taking place, when in reality they did not. In about 5% of the reports a lack of confidence in subordinate crewmembers caused Captains to become overloaded by trying to do too much. This . . . is a frequent contributor to the hesitancy of subordinate crewmembers to question the actions of Captains.

Sixteen percent of the reports cited "interference with pertinent cockpit communications by extraneous conversation between crewmembers or between crewmembers and flight attendants. This often reflected a cockpit atmosphere that had become too relaxed." An example describes a flight during which the Captain returned to the cockpit after a brief visit to the cabin: "We were about 70 miles off course. . . . *The copilot was telling war stories (he had been a fighter pilot . . .) and wasn't paying any attention to his job.*"

A number of reports described "role and personality conflicts creating a state of affairs on the flight deck such that communications between crewmembers have completely deteriorated: . . . I repeated, 'Approach said slow to 180',' and his reply was . . . 'I'll do what I want.'"

In summary, "Cockpit communications are related to flight-crew performance. It would be a mistake, however, to infer . . . that more communication among flightcrew members necessarily translates into better performance. The type and quality of communications are the important factors—not the absolute frequency."

Distraction: A Human Factor
in Air Carrier Hazard Events

This *CALLBACK* capsule commentary is a condensation of a research paper published early in the life of the Aviation Safety
Reporting System. The study was based on reports submitted to
ASRS and was performed by a retired international airline captain, now an ASRS staff member. It is No. 8 on the ASRS
publication list. In the introduction, the author states: "One of
the frequently occurring causes of hazardous events in air carrier operations is the human susceptibility to distractions. This
report describes the study of this topic, carried out as one element in the series of air carrier human factors investigations
being conducted by the ASRS research group." He notes that "distraction appeared more frequently than any other human factor
in the ASRS database." Causes for the distraction events studied
fell into two distinct categories:

   1. Nonflight operations activities consisting of company-
required tasks, such as public address announcements, on/off
blocks messages, logbook paperwork, and flight-service/pas-
senger problems. Untimely cockpit conversations that interfered
with airman duties were also classified in this category.
   "We were climbing out of XYZ airport. The First Officer was
flying. I acknowledged a 7,000 ft restriction, then went back to
my paperwork. I didn't see the F/O set 17,000 in the alititude select
window. As we passed 12,000, Center called, wanted to know
where we were going."
   2. Flight operations tasks, internal to crew functioning, with
the cause of distraction often noted in ASRS reports as "workload"
or "excessive workload." These workloads consisted entirely of
routine duties normal to every flight: running checklists, looking
for traffic, communicating with ATC, handling minor malfunctions, avoiding buildups, and monitoring radar. An overlap of any
combination of these tasks in a short time frequently triggered a
distraction event.
   "We were cleared to descend to 5,000. I was doing the approach
checklist. Suddenly I saw the altimeter going through 4,200. Before I could do anything, a light airplane came over the top of us.
We missed him by maybe 200 ft."

A footnote to this section states that "Air carrier airmen, especially senior Captains, may have some difficulty in accepting
'distraction' as a cause of any pilot's failure to accomplish simul-
taneous routine flight tasks. . . . 'Doing two things at once is
what we're paid for.'" While acknowledging the validity of this

point, the author feels that "to accept a summary judgement of competent/incompetent, good/no good for a single mistake due to workload . . ." invokes the old "pilot error" attribution, averting the "need for further investigation as to why the failure occurred."

An examination of the data established that "both categories of distractions compromised safe flight operations in two separate ways: 1. An essential task was not accomplished. For example, failure to watch for traffic resulted in several near-miss incidents. 2. Crew coordination or . . . management was . . . interrupted. . . . This loss of . . . teamwork frequently led to crew inattention to flying the airplane with resultant deviation from a desired flightpath."

As in other ASRS research studies, statistical tables are presented. Both "operational" and "nonoperational" distraction types are discussed in detail, with narrative examples of typical distraction-induced incidents included.

The nonoperational category accounted for about one-third of the incidents making up the material for the study; of these, 50 percent involved distractions blamed on use of company radio or public address system; the balance were related to nonessential cockpit conversation or paperwork, or to interruptions by flight attendants. In the operational group it was found that half the incidents were laid to checklist performance, attention to malfunctions, or traffic watch. Seven additional operational types of distraction were identified, of which radar monitoring and chart study were predominant, with fatigue and ATC communications cited frequently. "Distraction is as likely to happen during ground operation as in flight. Schedule pressure combined with taxi checklists, wing-tip clearances and ATC transmissions can result in unauthorized and potentially dangerous crossings and entries into active runways."

In summary, the author concludes that "though distraction, as a human factor, cannot be eliminated from the cockpit, the identification and type-classification of distraction incidents suggest possible improved means and techniques for minimizing causes of distraction and also for assisting in maintenance of basic concepts in cockpit management and crew coordination. . . . Causes for nonoperational distractions may be minimized through continued emphasis on cockpit priorities during climb and descent."

It is a matter of satisfaction to the ASRS staff that this study and other program data were cited among the sources leading to

FAA's "Sterile Cockpit Rule." FAR Parts 121.542 and 135.100 define critical phases of flight as "all ground operations involving taxi, takeoff and landing, and all other flight operations conducted below 10,000 feet, except cruise flight," and prohibit the performance of any duties during these critical phases of flight "except those duties required for the safe operation of the aircraft."

One large air carrier lists these specific prohibitions: "1. Radio calls for such nonsafety related purposes as ordering galley supplies and confirming passenger connections; 2. Announcements to passengers promoting the company or pointing out sights of interest; 3. Paperwork unrelated to the safe operation of the flight; 4. Eating meals and drinking beverages; 5. Engaging in nonessential conversation within the cockpit and nonessential communications between cabin and cockpit crews; 6. Reading publications not related to the proper conduct of the flight; and 7. No flight crew member may engage in, nor may any pilot in command permit, any activity during a critical phase of flight which could distract any flight crew member from the performance of his or her duties or which could interfere in any way with the conduct of those duties."

Observance of these caveats, in spirit as well as letter, will eliminate many incidents of distraction in the cockpit.

A Study of ASRS Reports Involving General Aviation and Weather Encounters

This is a condensation of a research study (ASRS Publication No. 23) performed by three professors in the Aviation Department at a major university; subject to stock on hand, the full report is available on request. As stated in the formal abstract, the paper

describes a study of material in the ASRS data base dealing with weather-related incidents in GA. Factors leading to such incidents are discussed and analyzed. The report considers the nature and characteristics of problems involving dissemination of weather information, use of this information by pilots, its adequacy for the purpose intended, the ability of the air traffic control system to cope with weather-related incidents, and the various aspects of pilot behavior, aircraft equipment, and NAVAIDS affecting flights in which weather figures. It is concluded from the study that skill and training deficiencies of GA pilots are not major factors in weather-related occurrences, nor is lack of aircraft equipment. Major problem causes are associated with timely and easily interpreted weather information, pilots' judgement and attitude, and ATC system functions.

The study was stimulated by NTSB tabulations of general aviation accidents, which "indicated that weather-related accidents led all other types of causes." It cites the question "often posed about the ability of GA pilots to cope with weather problems. What is not known is the extent to which such problems are due to inadequate weather information systems, inadequate aircraft capability, insufficient training for GA pilots, or lack of responsiveness by the air traffic control system." The usual discussion of objectives, approach, and methodology is presented, with graphs and tables presenting statistical data.

The report data set used for the study was classified into six categories:

1. Single aircraft under IFR flight, 15 percent.
2. Single VFR aircraft in adverse weather, 29 percent.
3. Less than standard separation (LTSS) or potential conflicts between two aircraft on IFR flight plans (IFR/IFR), 19 percent.
4. LTSS or potential conflicts between two aircraft, one of which was presumed to be VFR and one of which was usually on an IFR flight plan (mixed flight rule operation), 24 percent.
5. and 6. These two categories consisted of reports not involving specific in-flight events but were included in the study because of complaints about the weather information system or the inadequacies of the FSS and ATC systems (8 percent); and balloon reports (5 percent).

The four major categories were found to differ significantly "in terms of the involvement of small GA aircraft (less than 5000 lb) which was one of the main interests in this analysis. In the IFR/IFR cases, small GA aircraft were virtually non-existent. Yet, for the single VFR aircraft incidents, 90% were small GA aircraft." In categories 1 and 4 (single IFR and mixed flight rule, respectively) the small aircraft figured in about half of the incidents. Another finding was that IMC conditions existed in 75 percent of the single IFR incidents, but in only 45 percent of the single VFR incidents.

Each major category is treated in detail. For example, in the single IFR group, 75 percent of the reported incidents took place in the daytime; 55 percent occurred under 1,000 feet above the ground and were involved with approach, landing, or takeoff phases of flight. "Unlike other categories of incident reports of GA aircraft in weather, which were over-represented in the summer months, the winter months were over-represented in single IFR incidents. . . . Note that except for four or five incidents, the weather should not have been a significant factor. IFR flight systems are designed to permit safe and efficient air transport in poor weather. . . . thus it might be argued that, in single aircraft IFR operations, weather should not pose a serious problem."

Summing up the single aircraft IFR data, the

> weather-related incidents could almost be considered substandard performance in the IFR system. Severe weather abnormalities were involved infrequently. Most incidents involved normal IMC. The incidents were less involved with GA small aircraft than with larger GA transports, suggesting that pilot experience and aircraft equipment were probably not key factors. . . . If weather, experience, and aircraft capability were not key causes, what were the bases of the incidents? Four major causes appear from the data: Violations of instrument flight rules; communications breakdowns between FSS specialists or air traffic controllers and pilots; poor preflight planning; weather interpretations, i.e., the recognition of when conditions have gone from VMC to IMC.

The incidents involving VFR pilots who encountered adverse weather conditions made up the largest group studied. Almost all of the incidents were reported by the pilots of small aircraft. "Typical . . . : The pilot checked the weather with flight service and the forecast was for VFR. He took off and either encountered low visibility conditions or a cloud deck closing in beneath him. He continued in IMC or marginal IMC before electing to execute a return to VMC. He then landed at an enroute airport or received an assist from ATC for vectors to his destination airport or an alternate." The authors deduce a need for more timely weather information (more PIREPS, better coordination between ATC and FSS) and for better indoctrination of pilots in the sources of information regarding weather, as well as communication facilities and frequencies.

Most reports involving multiple aircraft address potential conflicts. A combination of factors generated nearly every event in the two groups: weather diversions by one or more aircraft; difficulties in coordinating handoffs between controllers; violations of ATC clearances by flight crews—these appear in the IFR/IFR situations. In mixed flight rule cases the factors are entering control zone without clearance when the weather is below VFR minimums; VFR flight in (reported) IMC; and aircraft popping through holes in clouds, maneuvering around broken clouds, or cruising near cloud decks being penetrated by IFR aircraft.

This study suggests "that the reduction of GA weather-related incidents does not require more experience for the GA pilot, nor better equipment; but, rather, improvements in attitude and willingness to utilize experience . . . a need for better utilization of the current resources."

Information Transfer during Contingency Operations: Emergency Air–Ground Communications

Although radio communication is always crucial to the safe and efficient operation of the nation's aviation system, the necessity for the effective transfer of information is never more clearly obvious than when an aircraft is in distress.

The reports in the data base of the Aviation Safety Reporting System (ASRS) provide a unique resource for identifying deficiencies that have occurred in communications in actual emergencies, and for a pragmatic evaluation of the causes and consequences of information transfer dysfunctions.

This report presents the results of a study of safety-related problems in emergency situations. All information was obtained from a review of pertinent reports contained in the ASRS data base.

So goes the introduction to research paper No. 18 on the ASRS publication list, which deals with communications associated with in-flight emergencies and condensed in this *CALLBACK* capsule commentary. "The objectives of this study task," performed by a principal research scientist for Battelle Columbus Laboratories, NASA's ASRS Contractor, "were: (1) to describe the safety-related problems occurring as a consequence of information transfer deficiencies that arise when air/ground communications are (or should be) used as a resource in in-flight emergency situations [contingency operations], and (2) to define the system factors, the human errors, and the associated causes of these problems."

As usual in these studies, there is a discussion of scope, approach, and methodology, accompanied by appropriate tables and graphs. Emergency situations were segregated into those involving power plant and other aircraft system problems (37 percent); VFR pilot/weather (20 percent); low fuel (15 percent); severe weather avoidance, and lost (about 5 percent each); with the remainder made up of miscellaneous or unspecified events. Included in this category typically were off-airport landings by light aircraft operating VFR, usually caused by sudden engine stoppage. Nearly all "the emergency situation reports contained an explicit or implied reference to radio communications. Regarding [those] that did not, it cannot be concluded that radio was not used because the nature of the problem was such that the immediate value of such communication would have been limited, and reference may have been omitted by the reporter." In about one-third of the emergency cases studied subsequent communications problems occurred. The study presents a breakdown within the various categories between air carrier, military, and general aviation involvement.

The "information transfer" problems encountered in the study were assigned in a ratio of about two to ATC for one to Aircrew, with a small fraction related to radio/radar limitations or equipment failure. Listed under ATC were the lack of coordination, controller inattention/distraction, the lack of perception of emergency, faulty technique, frequency congestion, and auditory interference. Aircrew difficulties included language barrier, reluctance to declare emergency, failure to use all resources, and pilot communication errors. It is noted that, although only the primary problem is listed, more than one problem is sometimes evident. An example shows primarily a language problem, but the problem is complicated by a lack of ATC coordination:

> While on duty as an air traffic controller at the [XYZ] Tracon, an alarmed pilot began screaming. "Mayday," obviously wanting assistance on frequency 121.5. For approximately 10 minutes, between transmissions to other aircraft, I tried to radar-identify the aircraft. He had a very poor (self-admitted) understanding of the English language. His number was never found out until he landed. Due to the position of the aircraft, ORL Approach was able to assist aircraft, along with myself. Neither I nor ORL Approach knew of each others' intentions, which added to the confusion.

"Controller inattention" cases pertain to "a problem caused by the distraction of the controller by an emergency . . . a communication deficiency with one or more aircraft other than the one actually involved in the emergency." This incident was reported by the pilot of a four-engine air carrier aircraft: "Aircraft A was cleared to land . . . Runway 1L by Tower. After touchdown, we observed a light (white) aircraft B, in position for takeoff at about mid-runway. Prior to A's landing, B had been cleared into position and forgotten by tower controller due to a landing emergency situation on Runway 1R. . . . Aircraft was stopped without incident."

"The 'lack of perception of emergency' category appears in some cases as an attitudinal problem (as viewed by the reporter), or as a simple lack of understanding of the problem by the controller. . . . This study considers these cases as situations in which the flightcrew has apparently not been able to communicate the urgency of the situation to the controller." The author explains that his tabulations "may seem to place an imbalance of blame on the controllers. In this regard, it must be pointed out that not only were 65% of the emergency cases handled without incident, but a high proportion of reporters (pilots) explicitly praised the assistance received from the air traffic control system."

Traffic conflicts emerge as the most prevalent safety-related problem associated with emergency communications. Collision hazards, often not involving the aircraft which was the subject of the emergency, appear in nearly half of the incidents studied. "The next most frequent problem is a delay in the landing of the emergency aircraft. . . . The emergency was prolonged through a delay in rendering assistance" in a nearly equal number of cases, and in several "the subject aircraft landed without the alerting of emergency equipment."

Concluding his discussion of emergency communications, the author notes:

1. The most common safety-related problem is a traffic conflict NOT involving the emergency aircraft itself. . . .

2. The most common information transfer problem arising from an emergency is a lack of interfacility co-ordination within ATC. The second leading problem is controller inattention caused by distraction resulting from an emergency.

3. Emergency situations in which non-instrument-rated pilots are trapped in instrument meteorological conditions lead to subsequent communications problems much less frequently than other emergency situations. It may be inferred that controllers, for whatever reason, are particularly sensitive and adept with regard to these emergencies.

4. There is no evidence in these data that pilots, even with minimum experience levels, are not familiar with proper emergency radio procedures.

Information Transfer in the Surface Component of the System: Coordination Problems in Air Traffic Control

Do not allow an aircraft under your control to enter airspace delegated to another controller without first completing coordination.

Air Traffic Control Handbook 7110.65B

CALLBACK's series of condensed research papers continues with a discussion of coordination problems in the Air Traffic

Control system. Study No. 16 on the ASRS publication list was performed by an ASRS staff member retired from a career in ATC; it is available in its unabridged form on request.

In his introduction, the author explains,

> Coordination is a term used widely in the air traffic control (ATC) system to describe control activities that affect aircraft traversing jurisdictional boundaries of airspace. It is usually used in reference to the transfer of information between air traffic controllers who control separate segments of airspace through which controlled aircraft are or will be passing. This information transfer process is used by the controllers in developing and executing operational plans for controlling traffic through their respective airspace segments. . . .
>
> Coordination is the most pervasive, and perhaps the most complex, aspect of the U.S. ATC system. It is widely recognized as a controller function that is particularly vulnerable to human error. Furthermore, a coordination failure usually results in the loss of standard separation distance between aircraft.

This paper is based on a study of ASRS reports involving coordination failures. It contains the usual explanation of methodology and scope, with statistical graphs and tables.

> An ATC coordination transaction is a communication between controllers (not necessarily verbal), the purpose of which is to arrive at and execute a plan for handling aircraft as they pass from the jurisdiction of one controller to that of another . . . in effect a contractual agreement between two controllers arrived at by negotiation and binding them to perform in accordance with that agreement. . . . The process involves . . . :
>
> 1. A Communication by one controller to another of a request for coordination.
> 2. Responsive message of concurrence or nonconcurrence by the controller receiving the request; nonconcurrence will result in a discussion of alternative action.
> 3. Agreement on a plan of action and who is to execute it.
> 4. Execution of the plan.
>
> For the purposes of this study these four steps are referred to as initiation (step 1); agreement (steps 2 and 3); and execution (step 4).

The author explains that each step must "be taken with due consideration for time available to complete the entire process. Allowance must be made for communications with other controllers or flightcrews and their responses. Furthermore, each step must be completed in a timely manner with an appropriate time buffer for unforeseen contingencies such as delay in establishing radio contact. The best plans are to no avail if the enabling clearances cannot be implemented in sufficient time to preclude loss of separation."

Coordination information is transferred in various ways.

For example, most interfacility coordination is done by telephone. Also, large sectorized facilities (centers, large TRACONS) use the telephone for communications between different positions within the facility—intrafacility coordination. Among smaller facilities, and also within multisector facilities where the working positions are close together, less formal means often are employed—direct voice, informal or abbreviated messages, hand signals. . . .

Routine transfer of flight data is communicated almost entirely by automated equipment. Flight plans are entered into computers at the en route centers where they are stored until they become timely; flight-progress strips are then routed to terminal facilities and appropriate center sectors. Radar handoffs are automatically initiated by most en route center computer systems. . . . [These routine data transfers and handoffs] present few problems. However, if the originally planned flight must be changed in order to maintain standard separation as an aircraft passes from one sector to another, some type of specialized communication is necessary between the controllers involved. Most coordination failures reported to ASRS concern such complex operations.

Analysis of the study data set produced three principal coordination failure modes: (1) incomplete, (2) inaccurate, (3) absent. Reports describing the failures were examined with relation to the phase of coordination during which each occurred (initiation, agreement, or execution). Nearly 65 percent of the incidents reflected absence of required coordination, predominently in the initiation phase. "These data leave little doubt about where the main problem with ATC coordination lies. However, the data also indicate significant difficulty with the next most frequently cited failure mode—errors in executing agreed-upon coordination plans—and the third most common failure was in agreement (incomplete or inaccurate)."

The human factors observed in this study are tabulated and discussed in combination with the predisposing factors leading to coordination errors. "FAILURES OF PERCEPTION, the most frequently occurring errors, resulted in instances in which a controller based his plans or actions on inaccurate or incomplete information . . . controller may have failed to take into account pertinent traffic. . . . FAILURES OF TECHNIQUE, the next most frequently cited error, resulted from a controller's choice of procedural steps or applications that failed to establish or maintain standard separation. The individual actions . . . [were] inappropriate, untimely or ineffective." Example: Use of a "point-out" in lieu of full transfer of control. Other error types and predisposing factors are considered in detail, with examples from ASRS reports.

> Coordination failures occur throughout the air traffic control system. The most frequently reported . . . is failure to initiate action to establish coordination; the second . . . is failure to execute the agreed plan. . . . The remaining failure modes . . . consist of misunderstanding the transferred data or the plan agreed upon, or the data used to develop the plan are incorrect. Errors in coordination often result in hazardous incidents, and they continue to be reported to ASRS in substantial numbers.

Human Factors in Air Carrier Operations: Knowledge of the Limitations of the ATC System in Conflict-avoidance Capabilities

This installment of *CALLBACK*'s capsule commentaries is a much abridged version of an earlier research study produced by an ASRS staff member now retired from a flying career on an international airline. The full paper is No. 9 on the ASRS publication list; subject to stock on hand, it is available on request. The author's premise is as follows:

> No air carrier pilot could operate efficiently or successfully within U.S. airspace without anticipation of many and diverse ATC procedures, controller actions, and clearance communications. In fact, from a user's pragmatic viewpoint, the entire ATC system functions as a series of to-be-fulfilled expectancies as to what will occur next. It is when pilot expectations are not fulfilled, or when expectations are premised on erroneous or unrealistic concepts, that the first circumstantial links for a potential midair collision are formed in the typical accident chain alignment.
>
> The ATC system, which is operated and utilized by human beings, is always vulnerable to human error. Its capabilities can be limited by equipment malfunctions, saturation, overload, and miscoordination. Knowledge of the limitations of the system, and of when and where it is most likely to fail or to display deficiencies or inadequacies, can serve in the early recognition and avoidance of potential midair conflict situations. As ASRS statistics indicate, "Big Brother" is not always watching. Furthermore, he is not always listening.

This study developed the view of the situation summarized in these paragraphs:

In the anticipation that airplanes will not always function as designed, air carrier airmen spend considerable training time in the study of in-flight recognition and handling of aircraft system malfunctions and failures. Despite the fact that controllers also train to handle malfunctions and abnormalities in the ATC system, the majority of controller reports to the ASRS are, in a broad sense, "logbook" entries of malfunctions and failures of the system. The primary causes of the problems are usually human behavior factors, but the errors invariably result in temporary deficiencies or lapses in what might be called "normal" ATC operation in U.S. airspace.

The impetus for this study derived from the surprise reported by so many professional airmen in their individual encounters with "abnormal" ATC operation during conflict avoidance situations. Routine expectation of radar surveillance often apparently produced an exaggerated dependency on controller intervention; there was minimum consideration of possible service interruptions or of breakdowns within the monitoring service. The adequacy of the see-and-avoid responsibility in overcoming the deficiencies of the radar surveillance concept may be questionable and debatable ("more a hope than a method," states one airman) but the present ongoing realities of the operating limitations of the ATC system should be recognized and anticipated.

Drawing from the narrative contents of many hundreds of ASRS reports, this study attempts to highlight certain areas of air carrier operations during which ATC radar services may fail, may be withdrawn, or may be misled into passive target observation. During traffic converging situations, when controller intervention is anticipated but is not implemented, the pilots of the converging aircraft are thrust unknowingly and unexpectedly into the final evasive phase of the see-and-avoid response.

In discussing "Airman Assumptions and Expectations of the Capabilities of the ATC System," the paper quotes the Airmans Information Manual (AIM), noting that it is corroborated by a substantial number of ASRS reports, on the problem of the many primary returns from light aircraft not displayed, or painted only faintly, on the controllers' radar scopes: "It is very important to recognize the fact that there are limitations to radar service and that ATC controllers may not be able to issue traffic advisories concerning aircraft which are not under ATC control and cannot be seen on radar."

We had a near midair climbing out of XYZ airport. We were on a radar vector in the TCA, just turning to 090 degree heading and leaving 9500 ft. Just as I levelled the wings, the flight engineer called out, "traffic twelve o'clock!" I had to push the yoke forward to miss a small red and white aircraft. We passed underneath him by approximately 200 ft. When we advised the controller that we almost hit a small aircraft, he said, "Now I see him. Six o'clock and a mile." Why is it always six o'clock with the close ones?

"This typical ASRS narrative APPARENTLY indicates a controller's perceptual error. . . . No traffic advisories on a converging aircraft had been transmitted; therefore, the controller had failed to do his job properly. However, analysis . . . reveals other secondary causal factors." Pilot assumptions and expectations led the flightcrew "down the garden path" of wrongful anticipation.

The airliner had left the terminal airspace and

was penetrating the congested TCA boundary altitudes used frequently—and legally—by non-transponder-equipped light aircraft skirting the control area. . . . Studies of near midair collisions reported to ASRS . . . show that most air carrier encounters with VFR traffic that occur just outside TCA airspace boundaries are not pointed out. . . . The controller may be occupied with higher priority duties which prevent issuance of advisory messages concerning aircraft not normally participating in the air traffic control system. Furthermore, if the VFR aircraft are not equipped with altitude reporting transponders, the controller would be calling out numerous targets that might be at altitudes far removed from the air carrier's flight path.

The paper gives many ASRS report excerpts in illustrating various reasons for pilot misunderstood expectations of the ATC system. Some of these are: the "Ground-to-air link or 'Whaddesay?'; 'I heard what I expected to hear'; limitations associated with visual approaches; the air-to-ground link; ATC system errors [now called 'operational errors']."

To sum up, probably the most important link in midair conflicts is the inability (or difficulty) of the radar controller to sight and point out numerous light aircraft not equipped with transponders. The importance of clear and immediate two-way communication is emphasized. "Faulty cockpit management in the validation of ATC clearances or instructions" is cited. A report narrative dramatizes the problem vividly: "Climbing out of XYZ airport we were given traffic, twelve o'clock. We asked for vectors around the traffic. The controller said, 'Unable.' We asked, 'Why not?' The controller said, 'It's too late!'"

Nonairborne Conflicts: The Causes
and Effects of Runway Transgressions

This is a condensation of Research Study No. 32 on the ASRS publication list; subject to stock on hand, the paper is available on request. The study was performed by an ASRS research staff member in response to an FAA request, and is based on pilot and controller reports in the ASRS computerized data base. It includes the usual discussion of methodology as well as extensive detailed statistical tables and graphs. These compare the events studied by controlling facility, aircraft type, primary problem, day of week, time of day, weather, airport type, whether pilot- or controller-enabled, whether a conflict occurred (and if so, by degree of severity), and other defining characteristics. Obviously, the subject is exceedingly complex and, although it does not receive the general attention accorded other anomalous occurrence types, it is of considerable importance in the assessment of aviation hazards.

"We define runway transgression as any erroneous occupation of a runway at a controlled airport by an aircraft or other controlled vehicle. This omits occurrences at uncontrolled airports or airports where the tower is closed. . . . Certain runway conflicts are just as likely at either type of airport. . . . However, since operating practices at the two are innately dissimilar, this investigation is limited to examining problems in the controlled airport environment."

Many terms have been used in the ASRS analysis process to define more precisely the broad "runway transgression" category. "Among these are: 'runway incursion,' 'unauthorized landing,' 'wrong runway takeoff,' 'occupied runway takeoff,' 'uncoordinated runway crossing,' and 'uncoordinated landing.' . . . It was found that ground vehicle transgressions usually arose out of behaviors quite similar to those of aircraft transgressions."

The author defines the *"enabling actor"* in a transgression incident as "the participant who is adjudged as bearing the primary responsibility for the transgression . . . , the individual who had the last reasonable chance to prevent the occurrence," but points out that "apportioning responsibility for an incident was not always straightforward. There appeared several examples of reports where a participant, seeing the runway occupied while an aircraft was approaching, took no action to avert the situation . . . it may be plausible to assign some responsibility to that individual. Witness the following controller-submitted report":

> Small aircraft "A" called on frequency and was cleared to land. Small transport "B" called ready at 12L approach end and was told to taxi into position and hold with an aircraft on landing roll. During this time, Approach called on hot line for voice coordination about small aircraft "C" . . . for landing on runway 12R. . . . As I returned my attention to approach end of 12L, I observed aircraft "A" landing approximately 1000 feet down 12L, over small transport "B". . . .
>
> This incident, which occurred during daylight hours in visual meteorological conditions (VMC), was obviously precipitated by the local controller's error. His attention was diverted from the runway and he failed to clear the small transport for takeoff in a timely manner. Aircraft "A," however, was in excellent position to see that the runway was occupied, yet failed to question the situation or execute a go-around. Instead, the pilot chose to land over the top of the transport, putting it behind him and blinding him to its movements. Had the pilot of "A" gone around, as would be consistent with good operating practice. this runway conflict would not have occurred . . . *both* the pilot and the controller were coded as Enabling Actors.

This research effort revealed that 60 percent of the relevant reports were submitted by pilots, with the remainder coming from controllers; pilot errors, however, appeared $2\frac{1}{2}$ times as frequently as errors by controllers. Unavoidably oversimplified in this brief digest, the incidents studied may be divided into six main types of events: pilot-enabled arrival, departure, and taxi; and controller-enabled arrival, departure, and taxi. Unauthorized (that is, lacking clearance) landings constituted the largest segment of the incidents studied—about 30 percent—with unauthorized runway crossings in second place with 25 percent. Unauthorized runway entry followed with about 15 percent; the remainder of the data set was made up of incidents of unauthorized takeoff and various types of improper clearance. Within the pilot error group, "transgressions during arrival and taxi dominate over those occurring during departure. Reports of controller-enabled incidents show that errors during taxi are relatively high. However, instead of being eclipsed by arrival events, as are pilot errors, incidents during the departure phase are predominant."

Although pilot taxi and arrival transgressions dominate the total occurrence comparisons, in considering only those incidents involving hazardous or critical conflicts "controller-enabled departure incidents now take the lead." The author notes that "overall the large number of pilot-enabled arrival transgressions do not result in safety-threatening situations. . . . This notwithstanding . . . , in IFR conditions the consequence of this type of error can be very severe." Narratives from both flightcrews involved in one such incident are included in the study. Here are dramatic highlights of the two reports; the second flightcrew had not changed to tower from approach frequency:

> "After rolling approximately 200 feet we were told to . . . cancel takeoff clearance due to [another aircraft] still on the approach . . . Tower advised [the other aircraft] to go around because we were still sitting on the runway. . . . Next thing we knew he came right over the top of us, missing us by—it seemed like—inches. His thrust rocked our aircraft as he initiated a go-around. His aircraft came within five feet of touching down."

> "As decision height . . . and threshold sighting occurred, [an aircraft] was also sighted (fortunately) in takeoff position. . . . Immediate go-around was initiated. . . . Later I discovered that Tower had been advising us to go around. . . . It never occurred to them that perhaps I wasn't receiving their transmission."

The abstract of the paper summarizes:

> In general, runway transgressions attributable to both pilot and controller errors arise from three problem errors: Information transfer, awareness, and spatial judgement. Enhanced awareness by controllers will probably reduce controller-enabled incidents. Increased awareness within the cockpit, as well as a mitigation of information transfer errors, are the two most pertinent focuses for minimizing transgressions that are pilot enabled.

Addressee Errors in ATC Communications: The Callsign Problem

The typical reaction of any airman or controller to the subject of ATC radio communications probably parallels the typical reaction of a housewife to the subject of the kitchen sink. Both items represent important job functions—must-do activities—but the tasks involved are too commonplace, mundane, and repetitive to be intellectually challenging or capable of arousing emotional enthusiasm. Yet, the routine of controller-cockpit-controller message exchange is one of the most—if not the most—important factors in navigating an aircraft safely through the airspace and the ATC structure. Furthermore, as the Airman's Information Manual states, "The link (between airman and controller) can be broken with surprising speed and with disastrous results."

Thus begins the introduction to Research Study No. 29 on the ASRS publication list. Two thousand ASRS reports, typical of many others, describing potentially serious aviation incidents involving faulty pilot-ATC communications provided the material for the study. The author is a retired international air carrier captain, now a member of the ASRS research staff, who has contributed several of the studies previously summarized in *CALLBACK*. As with others in this series, the full paper is available on request—subject to stock on hand.

The introduction notes that in the study of misunderstood messages,

> Problems with aircraft call signs appeared as major factors. Abbreviated aircraft identifiers, smeared or partially blocked call signs, transposed trip numbers, human factors such as hearing "what you expect to hear" conditioning, misunderstood call ups and a tangled confusion of similar sounding aircraft callsigns—these front-end deficiencies in radio message transmissions contributed significant numbers of hazardous occurrences in airline, corporate, air taxi, military, and General Aviation operations. They were reported causal agents for unauthorized climbs/descents, simultaneous takeoffs from intersecting runways, aborts, go-arounds, wrong-way headings, runway incursions, missed crossing restrictions and near collisions, both on the ground and in flight.
>
> Analysis . . . revealed three characteristic event sequences in the flawed call up/acknowledgement exchanges: controller transmission of a wrong call sign in the call up message, airman acknowledgement and compliance with a clearance issued for another aircraft, and call up message failures in which an airman neither heard nor acknowledged ATC instructions. Two of the three event sequences represented double failures in controller/cockpit/controller dialogues. Airmen's acknowledgements for clearances intended for other aircraft and airmen failures to hear/acknowledge ATC instructions developed into reportable incidents only when controllers failed to notice the pilots' errors or omissions. . . .
>
> The causal factors pertinent to all of these call sign communication problems consisted primarily of human performance inadequacies and limitations. However, these behavioral patterns never operated independently from system constraints and complexities; heavy congestion on the frequency, controller workload in traffic management, and operational priorities in the cockpit produced very demanding conditions and distracting influences that predisposed the errors in the communications exchanges.

Analysis identified five categories of errors associated with callsigns; these are covered in detail in the discussion section of the paper.

"Faulty Radio Techniques; or, 'Mumble, Mumble—On Down Wind" This category includes both mechanical misuse of microphone or speakers and incorrect or inappropriate phraseology; the overabbreviated callsign figures prominently in this group, as illustrated in this controller report: "Both biz-jets were using only the last two digits of their call signs when acknowledging various altitude assignments. As a result, '12SK' and '13AK' caused great confusion and required many additional instructions to keep them apart."

"Call Sign Errors Related to Frequency Congestion; or, 'Was That for Us?'" Three separate error types are identified in this group: "dilemmas of uncertainty and expectation; clearance amendment problems; nonstop ATC transmissions." Here are some examples:

> My Captain understood the message to be for us. I was not so sure.
>
> I wanted to confirm the clearance but could not get through.
>
> After crossing, the tower asked if we had heard his "Hold short" clearance. We replied we had not.

"Addressee Problems with Similar Sounding Aircraft Call Signs" The author writes, "Similarities—of sounds, of names, of letters and of numbers—tricked the ears, the tongues, and the minds of both airmen and controllers." From a frustrated controller's report: "Air carrier ABC123 and ABC124 both arrive at this airport at the same time and on the same frequency. They should try to remember their trip numbers!"

"Airman Acknowledgement/Readback Errors; or, 'Is Anyone Listening Up There?'" A typical report states: "Center advised, 'We would appreciate your listening more to your clearance.' We rogered and apologized."

"Error Involving Controller Confirmations of Acknowledgements/Readbacks; or, 'Is Anyone Listening Down There?'" The study notes: "The most obvious, the most repetitive, and perhaps the most significant deficiency identified in the reported call sign incidents was the failure of a controller to listen to a pilot's acknowledgement or readback of an ATC clearance message. . . . What is the value of readbacks if no one on the other end is listening?"

In summary, "Perhaps the most significant of the study find-

ings concerned the double error sequences in the last of these
five categories: the incidents in which an airman acknowledged
and complied with instructions intended for another aircraft,
followed by controller failure or delay in detecting the misper-
ception." According to the author, "The inability to comprehend
immediately what was happening—or why it was happening—
epitomized the hazardous nature of call sign errors in ATC/cock-
pit communications. If not immediately caught and corrected,
call sign mismatches often plunged the airman into confusion
and the aircraft into hazard."